Japanese Fashion Designers

CW01081947

QUEENSLAND COLLEGE OF ART, GRIFFITH UNIVERSITY, BRISBANE, AUSTRALIA

The Research and Postgraduate Studies department has generously supported the production of this publication. The heritage-listed Queensland College of Art (QCA) is a specialist arts and design college located in South Bank, Brisbane, and Southport, Gold Coast, Queensland, Australia. It was founded in 1881 and is the oldest arts institution in Australia. The College offers courses including Fine Arts, Design Animation, Digital Media, Film and Screen Media, Multimedia Photography, Contemporary Indigenous Australian Art and Visual Art and Design History. The College amalgamated with Griffith University in 1992.

Japanese Fashion Designers

The Work and Influence of Issey Miyake, Yohji Yamamoto and Rei Kawakubo

Bonnie English

Oxford · New York

English edition
First published in 2011 by
Berg
Editorial offices:
50 Bedford Square, London WC1B 3DP, UK
175 Fifth Avenue, New York, NY 10010, USA

Paperback edition reprinted 2011

Berg is the imprint of Bloomsbury Publishing Plc.

Library of Congress Cataloging-in-Publication Data

English, Bonnie.
  Japanese fashion designers: the work and influence of Issey Miyake,
Yohji Yamamoto and Rei Kawakubo/Bonnie English.
      p. cm.
  Includes bibliographical references and index.
  ISBN 978-1-84788-310-0 (pbk.)—ISBN 978-1-84788-311-7 (cloth)—
ISBN 978-0-85785-054-6 (individual e-book) 1. Miyake, Issei,
1938– 2. Yamamoto, Yohji, 1943– 3. Kawakubo, Rei, 1942– I. Title.
  TT504.6.J3E54 2011
  746.9'20922–dc22   2011015573

British Library Cataloguing-in-Publication Data

A catalogue record for this book is available from the British Library.

ISBN	978 1 84788 311 7 (Cloth)
	978 1 84788 310 0 (Paper)
e-ISBN	978 0 85785 054 6 (Individual)

Typeset by Apex Publishing, LLC, Madison, WI, USA.
Printed in the UK by the MPG Books Group

www.bergpublishers.com

Dedicated to my beloved grandson, Lachlan

This book also pays tribute to the courageous Japanese
people who have faced the March 11, 2011 tragedy
with great strength, character and honour.

Contents

List of Illustrations

FIGURES

PLATES

Acknowledgements

This book is the culmination of years of research, not only in terms of collecting written material, but of experiencing a different culture, different traditions and customs. More importantly, Japanese design has taught me to appreciate how a very sophisticated aesthetic can become an inherent part of daily living. I would like to thank the Queensland branch of the Australia-Japanese Association for providing a travel scholarship for me to visit Japan for the first time in 1997. It was the beginning of a long journey that resulted in the curatorship of a fashion exhibition of Japanese and Australian garments at the Brisbane City Hall Gallery in 1999 entitled *Tokyo Vogue*, the first major fashion exhibition ever held in Queensland and the first major exhibition of the leading Japanese designers in Australia. My friend and colleague, Dr Craig Douglas, and I worked hard for two years for this significant event to occur, an exhibition which later inspired Louise Mitchell to curate *The Cutting Edge* Japanese Fashion exhibition at the Powerhouse Museum in Sydney in 2005. Over a number of years, I presented papers on this topic in Brisbane, Sydney, Melbourne and Perth. In terms of gathering background material, I gained invaluable help, initially from Akiko Fukai, and later Rei Nii, of the Kyoto Costume Institute, Kyoto, and spent numerous hours with Laurence Delamare of the Yohji Yamamoto organization, after the October collection showing in Paris in 2005.

I respectfully acknowledge and thank the Director of the Queensland College of Art, Griffith University, Professor Paul Cleveland, and the Deputy Director for Research, Professor Ross Woodrow, for their continued support and financial assistance to allow me to continue my research focus in fashion design studies. I am grateful for the magnificent organizational help and research assistance of Ben Byrne, QCA Postgraduate Administrator and friend, in the process of sourcing, selecting and documenting the images that are included in this publication. Ben and I share a mutual love of fashion, and over the past year this project has become very much a joint venture.

I have appreciated the wonderful encouragement and enthusiasm of my Berg fashion editor, Anna Wright, and the guidance that she provided to me throughout the publication process. I also thank Tristan Palmer, senior editor at Berg, for his direction over the years. I am overwhelmed with the generosity and goodwill of designers, and photographers, amongst others, who have willingly supplied beautiful images to be used in the book; in particular, Ann Demeulemeester, Dries Van Noten, Reiko Sudo of the Nuno Corporation, Sylvain Deleu, Gene Sherman and Caroline Evans.

As always, without the buttressing of colleagues, friends and family, completing this task would be very difficult. To my children, Katie and Sarah, and husband Justin, my very close friends Rhoda who read through the first draft of the book for me, Lynda, my off-shore researcher, David, Liliana and Doris, I give my love and thanks.

Introduction

Since 1970, the work of the Japanese fashion designers has had an unequivocal impact on Western dress. Initiated by Issey Miyake, and followed ten years later by Yohji Yamamoto and Rei Kawakubo of Comme des Garçons, they offered a new and unique expression of creativity, challenging the established notions of status, display and sexuality in contemporary fashion. Miyake celebrated forty years in the fashion business in 2010 and Kawakubo and Yamamoto followed suit in 2011 marking thirty years since their first show in Paris. In London, in the spring of 2011, the Victoria and Albert Museum unveiled a retrospective of Yamamoto's work, commemorating his contribution to the world of fashion. In the *Financial Times Weekend*, of 11 October 2009, journalist/photographer Mark O'Flaherty wrote:

> The middle-ageing of the triumvirate of revolutionary Japanese design is as shocking as any of their more confrontational collections; to many of their modernist followers they still seem like box-fresh radical upstarts, while for the high street they have only recently come into existence through diffusion projects with the likes of H&M and Adidas. So, four decades on, have they really revolutionised the world of fashion?

Japanese Fashion Designers: The Work and Influence of Issey Miyake, Yohji Yamamoto and Rei Kawakubo is a book which will provide you with the knowledge that you will need to answer this question. It is not only a study of the aesthetics of fashion but it is a study of cultural aesthetics, and the differences, in this respect, between East and West. There are countless examples in the history of art which evidence how the West has been informed by the East but none quite as dramatic as in the history of contemporary fashion design. This book will provide an understanding of how Japanese thought, tradition and advanced textile technology became an intrinsic part of fashion design practice in the late twentieth century. It will show how the Japanese designers influenced a whole generation of young, emerging Belgian designers, amongst others, and how this inter-cultural and inter-generational influence has infiltrated the soul of the international fashion industry.

LOOKING BACK—A CULTURAL HERITAGE

The legacy of an understated elegance has become an intrinsic characteristic of modern Japanese design, clearly evident in the work of Issey Miyake, Yohji Yamamoto and

Rei Kawakubo of Comme des Garçons. But, in reality, it is historically underpinned by its samurai origins, an intrinsic part of Japanese culture. While this may seem surprising, to say the least, the historian Ikegami explains:

> In terms of dress, when the role of the samurai changed by the late 17th century, and their military duties were replaced by bureaucratic duties, their lavish and luxurious custom-made kimonos, made from expensive fabric and worn especially for ceremonial purposes (which had been seen earlier as appropriate to their rank in society), were replaced by a more sober style of everyday clothing. Instead, the wearing of darker clothing, especially black which symbolised self-discipline, became accepted as more sophisticated urban attire and a sign that good taste was expressed by subtle stylistic differences and intelligence in design. (2005: 275)

Also, other subtle practices such as wearing cotton kimonos lined with silk or using silk in undergarments became common. In other words, certain luxuries were not abandoned but simply hidden to all except the wearer. The historical precedent of placing restrictions on excessively sumptuous dress (common across all cultures) ultimately encouraged restraint and refinement.[1] It is this adage that has been adopted by Japanese contemporary designers. Yet, still allowing the past to resonate in the present, Rei Kawakubo, in her typically masked way, asks 'What is in front and what is behind?'

For the Japanese, elegance and refinement do not concur with glamour, or with status or class. In this context, one can understand why Yohji Yamamoto and Rei Kawakubo did not want to be associated with haute couture and would only show their designs in the prêt-à-porter collection showings. Throughout history, a love of restraint, a special type of subtle beauty, incomplete perfection, a cult of refinement based on simplicity and austerity have always been elements of Japanese aesthetics.

THE TEA CEREMONY

The same sensibility is applied to everyday life as to art, so that even ceremonies directly bound up with everyday living are extremely highly developed. Hasegawa, in his *The Japanese Character: A Cultural Profile* (1988), argues that this approach is part of the Japanese character and can be applied to the art of packaging, garden design and food preparation, as well as dress. Westerners find it interesting that ritualization in the traditional Japanese tea ceremony is a social construction which underscores the nature of Japanese culture. Seen as a social sacrament, its rites were codified and conventionalized and the ceremony, still prominent today, is a means of consolidating the links with tradition and the past. Kakuzo Okakura, in *The Book of Tea* (1964), originally written in 1906, points out that in the late nineteenth century many of the old traditions were cast aside, as Japan embraced the Western world.

This ritual, which was meant to arouse feelings which were associated with a sense of beauty, was often relegated, almost as an apology, to the more conservative facets of Japanese society.

For Keene, in his *Appreciations of Japanese Culture* (1981), the symbolic reference inherent in the tea ceremony reflects the importance of simplicity and perishability in the Japanese aesthetic. He believes that 'it is possible to say of certain aesthetic ideals that they are characteristically and distinctly Japanese' (1981: 11). In terms of simplicity, Keene argues that 'the tea ceremony developed as an art concealing art, an extravagance masked in the garb of noble poverty' and that perishability 'came to be a necessary condition of beauty' (1981: 22, 30). When Yamamoto and Kawakubo first paraded their 'shrouds' on the catwalks of Paris they were greeted with howls of disapproval and their 'look' was dubbed the 'aesthetics of poverty'. The notion of beauty being found in objects which were aged with time and use, such as the old, irregular and worn drinking vessels often used for the tea ceremony, was difficult for Western audiences to appreciate. In Japan, however, it reflected individuality and appealed to the humanistic spirit. Perishability, it would seem, is closely allied with suggestion, another component of Japanese aesthetic ideals. That which is omitted, whether in literary writing or in the visual arts, creates an ambiguity that, in turn, becomes a 'suggestion of meaning' that is the source of its beauty. For instance, in Haiku poetry in particular, it is the absence of certain words that creates an ambiguity (Keene 1981: 14), and when negative space dominates positive space, it creates an ambiguous spatial element in Japanese watercolour painting. These characteristics of simplicity, irregularity, perishability and suggestion of meaning have been instilled in the history of Japanese writing and painting for thousands of years. In aesthetic terms, this sensitivity and subtleness are still considered important cultural components and remain a dominant force in contemporary Japanese art and design.

Interestingly, while the element of perishability was underscored in the early work of Yamamoto and Kawakubo in the form of deconstructive practices including ragged edges, tears, knots and uneven hemlines, it was addressed much more literally in the work of some of the Belgian designers, and in the work of Martin Margiela in particular. He experimented widely to show how garments decompose when exposed to the elements and how used clothing could be given a second life. In Japan, fashion designers are closely aligned to the textiles that inspire their work, collaborating closely with textile designers to create new fabrics which develop from technological processes that subtly imitate the essence of individualized handcrafted surfaces. The Japanese have a heightened respect for materials, whether natural or synthetic, partly based on Japan's indigenous Shinto religion, which centres on the worship of, and communion with, the spirits of nature. This book has dedicated a chapter to the distinguished textile designers who have helped to establish the textile culture in contemporary Japan.

THE IMPORTANCE OF THE KIMONO

One of the most visible indicators of the image of Japan as a culture which connects its people to its past is the continued wearing, even today, of the kimono for formal occasions. Ancestral techniques have not been replaced but adapted and expanded so that the kimono, for example, has remained a symbolic unit of measure for cloth, like the *tatami* for Japanese architecture (McQuaid 1998). It is an example of a beautifully simplistic construction technique. Eight rectangular pieces of fabric are sewn together, using straight not curved seams, and the sizes of the pieces are standardized. It could be argued that this garment, worn for centuries by the Japanese, became the foundation of a sensitive and subtle aesthetic which is still considered an important cultural component in their arts. It is a garment, very much like the Roman toga, that confers a dignity upon the wearer and that symbolically connected people from all parts of Japan throughout its history (Figure 0.1). To a certain extent, as it was worn by members of all social classes, it had the ability to bestow pride and to spread nationalistic spirit across all stratifications of Japanese society.[2]

Miyake, Yamamoto and Kawakubo have all commented during their lengthy careers that the kimono is the basis of their fashion design. It is the foundation upon which they build their garments and conceptualize their ideas regarding space, balance and the relationship of the shape of the garment to the underlying body. Miyake's work, for example, comments on the re-contextualization of the kimono to create a different aesthetic milieu. Miyake rejected the traditional forms of Paris collection clothing. Through the inventive use of fabric and successive layering, he developed a concept of fashion based on the use of cloth, or rather the 'essence' of clothing—the wrapping of the body in cloth. He has created anti-structural, organic clothing, which takes on a sculptural quality which suggests a natural freedom, expressed through the simplicity of its cut, the abundance of new fabrics, the space between the garment and the body, and a general flexibility. Miyake stated, 'I learned about space between the body and the fabric from the traditional kimono . . . not the style, but the space' (Knafo 1988: 108).

The kimono (or 'dressing in *wafuku*') also affords a fashion system which is based on convention for both the designer and the wearer. It is the perfect vehicle for semantic analysis as outlined by Roland Barthes in his 1968 publication, *The Fashion System*, as it is a form of dress that has changed little throughout the course of history. While in Japan today the kimono is surrounded on all sides by Western clothing, it is seen as a unique art form that symbolizes many dimensions of social life, distinguishing the gender of the wearer, identifying the season, defining age distinctions and signifying taste. The very subtle degree of skin revealed at the nape of the neck, the set of the *obi* (the wide sash fastened in the back with a large, flat bow), the depth and placement of hem designs and the shape of the sleeves are all matters which identify the taste of the wearer. Liza Dalby, in *Kimono: Fashioning Culture* (1993: 12), compares the kimono to

Figure 0.1 Japanese multi-layered and multi-coloured kimono, kimono parade, Nishijin Textile Centre, Kyoto. Photograph: author.

poetry: 'Like poetry, dress was a vehicle for the expression of artistic sensibilities.' In recalling history, she alludes to the 'coherent system of meanings, metaphors and nuances' linked to the kimono and how nature's imagery, plants, insects and other animals, colour, weather and especially the seasons, played out in both poetry and dress, became part of the visual language of the garment. These sensibilities emphasize the complexity of meaning which underlines the fashion culture in Japan and which must be considered seriously in any study of Japanese contemporary fashion.

THE KEY DESIGNERS

This book will attempt to show how these cultural traits are embedded in the design work of Miyake, Yamamoto and Kawakubo, providing a cultural richness and meaning that defies and deconstructs the notion of a globalized fashion industry. It will identify how these designers have tailored art to everyday life and have embodied features such as asymmetry, imperfection and incomplete beauty, rejecting the idealized, the majestic, the imposing, the superficial and the minutely detailed—all facets of a continental civilization.

Japan's willingness to embrace the avant-garde is evident in its fine art, architecture and fashion design and, for this reason, Japanese design had an unprecedented impact on Western design during the twentieth century. The designers Miyake, Yamamoto and Kawakubo produce work that is imbued with the history of the past, yet looks dynamically towards the future through a poetic amalgam of ideas and functions. All three Japanese designers rejected 'change-for-change's sake', and instead chose to work on the refinement and evolution of previous collections. This evolution of an idea was the basis of Japanese fashion. The conceptual process of serialization, re-visited by many conceptual visual practitioners since the 1960s, is integral to the Japanese approach to design. They have become leaders in the international fashion industry. Miyake, Yamamoto and Kawakubo are often described as niche designers—designers who do not follow stylistic trends or directions. Unlike their European and American 'stylist' counterparts, they have not exclusively embraced the revivalist or popular cultural imaging that has inundated Paris catwalks for decades. Their clothing has created a visual language that strengthens the converging line that exists between fashion and art. Miyake is amused when his work is so often referred to as an art form. 'Why,' he frequently replies, 'clothes are more important than art.'

Ignoring stylistic trends, these Japanese designers work within a postmodernist visual arts framework, appropriating aspects of their traditional culture and embracing new technological developments and methodologies in textile design. Yet, at the same time, they infuse their work with meaning and memory. The subtleties inherent in their textiles and forms promulgate a new aesthetic in Western dress. Miyake, perhaps the most revered designer in Japan today, has consistently propagated new ideas, new materials and new design directions which accommodate the modern lifestyle of contemporary women. While the work of Yamamoto and Kawakubo was initially framed as another form of anti-aesthetic, their contribution to the evolution of twentieth-century fashion has been more profound. Their understated design underlines the notion that culture, conceptualization and experimentation can be integral to fashion, as it is to art. By the end of the century, they had helped to change the face of fashion irrevocably.

THEIR INFLUENCES

Perpetuity in design is ensured by the Japanese system of apprenticeship. In the fashion design studios, younger designers follow in the footsteps of their head designers and the leading fashion masters for up to eight years. These 'second-wave' designers will often continue their practice under the banner of their mentors and become internationally famous when they show their own collections in Paris. Dai Fujiwara and Naoki Takizawa of the Miyake Design Studio (MDS), Junya Watanabe and Tao Kurihara of Comme des Garçons and Limi Feu of Yohji Yamamoto are key examples of this system and are, possibly, the designers who will lead fashion forwards for the next thirty years. Innovation, experimentation and individuality are encouraged but their training builds on commitment, self-discipline and motivation.

Many international fashion designers have paid homage to Miyake, Yamamoto and Kawakubo and it is difficult to know which designer has ultimately had the greatest impact upon the industry. While their influence has been widespread, their revolutionary trends stimulated a pronounced response from the younger Belgian designers who graduated from the Antwerp Academy in the 1980s. The avant-garde Japanese designers inspired radical thinking, and their philosophy about designing persuaded their followers to challenge traditions, to re-think old ideas and to re-configure old forms. By example, they had introduced both men's and women's garments that became looser and more comfortable, with little attention to detail. Deconstruction of tailoring, with stitching revealed and seams sometimes incomplete, unhemmed edges, tears, rips, hanging threads and frayed sections, often tied in knots or left to decompose, became the prototype for cutting-edge design practice. Innovative fabric determined the design of their garments and conceptualization and meaning became more important than individual styling. Designers including Viktor & Rolf, Helmut Lang and Hussein Chalayan picked up the gauntlet and continued this legacy of intellectual design.

The notion of 'conceptual' aesthetics led to many changes in the established fashion system. The Japanese broke away from the historical paradigm of using conventional models and replaced glamour with uniqueness and individuality. This included substituting young models with more mature ones—for example, Miyake's *Beautiful Ladies* collection (1995) used six models aged between sixty-two and ninety-two. Miyake set the precedent for displaying fashion exhibitions in major museums and art galleries around the world, consolidating the idea that fashion could be an art form in its own right. Encouraged by this lateral thinking, the younger Belgian designers, including Margiela, Van Noten and Von Beirendonck, and the British designers John Galliano and Alexander McQueen, among others, subsequently adopted the practice of holding their fashion collection showings anywhere and everywhere, a trend that became universal. By the turn of the twenty-first century, fashion students around the world became engrossed in the avant-garde fashion world of the Japanese, the Belgians and the neo-conceptualist designers. *Japanese Fashion Designers: The Work and Influence of Issey Miyake, Yohji Yamamoto and Rei Kawakubo* celebrates their significant achievements, not only for what they have attained in the past but for what they will contribute to the evolution of twenty-first-century fashion in the future.

Issey Miyake

Figure 1.1 Japanese fashion designer Issey Miyake smiles after receiving the gold medal of the Premium Imperiale at the awarding ceremony in Tokyo, 18 October 2005. Photograph: Yoshikazu Tsuno/AFP/Getty Images.

Clothes . . . speak many languages . . . and have to be seen on the outside . . . as well as felt on the inside.

Miyake

Issey Miyake does not want to be called an artist (Figure 1.1). Nor does he want to be labelled a 'Japanese' fashion designer. However, from a Western point of view, he is both. He argues that stereotypical boundaries limit the possible concepts of design and yet his history has revealed that nothing has prevented Miyake from melding the past, the present and the future in his life's work. By challenging convention as an aesthetic stance, he states, 'I believe in questioning.' For over forty years, Miyake has reinvented form, redefined the boundaries of clothing in both functional and aesthetic contexts, and rejuvenated new modern methods of clothing production. He has promoted an integral liaison between the fine arts, photography, the applied arts and fashion and shown the world the true meaning of collaborative effort. He has fostered new talent and he has 'given back' or 'passed forward' that which he has learned from his predecessors, his colleagues, his years of experimentation and his time-honoured experience in the fashion industry. Undoubtedly, he is considered one of the most creative forces in the world today.

Miyake has been dubbed 'The Picasso of Fashion', presumably in relation to the diversity of his work, his propensity for discovering new artistic methodologies and his challenging of traditional concepts of design. One might argue that what constitutes the greatest challenge of his work is his ability to force the viewer to confront their own assumptions about what comprises clothing or 'dress'. Miyake draws on both artisan production and new technologies and explores all expected and unexpected possibilities in the process. In both his *Pleats, Please* and *A-POC* collections, he has embraced the new postmodern woman of the late twentieth and early twenty-first centuries. He has shown her that, through the beauty of simplicity, clothing can be unaffected by the shifting tides of taste. His work suggests that meaning, either symbolic or inferred, can allow the imagination to expand well beyond the literal needs of clothing. Yet Miyake also sees clothing as something to use, and more recently something to renew or reuse. He has devised new ways of minimizing waste in clothing fabrication and sees the customer as his greatest collaborator.

PLEATS, PLEASE

I feel I have found a new way to give individuality to today's mass-produced clothing.

Miyake

Arguably, Miyake's renewed or re-designed concept—the 1993 *Pleats, Please* range—owes much to Fortuny, a Spanish couturier, who was the master of the 'poetic pleat'. As an early twentieth-century designer, Fortuny used ancient methods to revive a Grecian pleating system. He perfected this in his *Delphos* garments, created in the first decade of the twentieth century, which subsequently inspired numerous designers of the 1920s and 1930s. Taking the process one step further, Miyake combined this technique with new-technology synthetic fabrics as an innovative approach to pleating, and the result inspired his *Pleats, Please* collection, shown for decades around the world. Miyake's garments are cut two-and-a-half to three times larger than the finished garment and sewn together first, then they are sandwiched between layers of paper and individual pieces are hand-fed through a heat press, where they are pleated. According to Miyake, 'Even when I work with computers, with high technology, I always try to put in the touch of the hand . . . two or three people twist them . . . and put it all into the machine to cook it' (Simon 1999). The fabric's memory holds the pleats and when they are released from their paper coating, they are ready to wear. This industrial process allows both texture and form to be created at the same time. Vertical, horizontal and zig-zag pleating is used to create varying effects and architectural shapes (Figure 1.2). *Interview* magazine quotes Miyake as saying: 'Pleats give birth to texture and shape all at the same time. I feel I have found a new way to give individuality to today's mass-produced clothing' (Saiki 1992: 34).

When Miyake designed dance costumes[1] for William Forsythe's Frankfurt Ballet in 1990, he used ultra feather-light polyester jersey, permanently pleated. He

Figure 1.2   Issey Miyake, 'Minaret' pleated dress with seven hoops, 1995. Photograph: author.

realized that this new method of making clothes was a marvellous thing for dancers—a type of second skin—as it held its shape so well. He wanted to work with
the body in motion and wanted the clothes to move as the body moved. He spoke
to many dancers and studied how they wore their clothes. In the following year
(1991), he sent 200 to 300 garments for the dancers to choose what they wanted
to wear in each performance of *The Last Detail*, so that each day the performance
was different. Ultimately, this led to the development of the *Pleats, Please* range.
It would seem that 'nobody was able to capture the flexibility and lightness of
contemporary pleats better than Issey Miyake' (Kiss 2004). Subsequently, this inspired him to use dancers, rather than models, to display his work on the catwalk.
For his 1991 *Fête* collection, which celebrated life and technology, Miyake's fabrics
were cut into complex patterns by using ultrasonic waves that emitted heat vibra-
tions. Arguably, he created the most intricate and sophisticated pleats to date,
clearly evident in his *Colombe* dress. This garment, made with snap fasteners that
transformed a single flat panel of cloth into a softly draped dress, proved that there
was no need for sewing as fasteners could be used both functionally and deco-
ratively. This seminal garment was later exhibited in an installation at the Benaki
Museum in Athens in 2004 called *Ptychoseis: Folds & Pleats: Drapery from Ancient
Greek Dress to 21st Century Fashion*.

The *Pleats, Please* series attests to Miyake's desire to produce adaptable clothing
that is both functional and reflective of modern simplicity in an egalitarian society.
Suzy Menkes, fashion writer for the *International Herald Tribune*, pointed out that 'Polyester was embraced by the Japanese when Paris Couture was embalmed in a cocoon
of silk' (Menkes 2006b), thereby marking the significance of this new diversion away
from European high fashion. Pleats and polyester jersey, part of standardized clothing conventions, were used in a new and challenging way by Miyake, which forced the
viewer to reassess their role in modern society. But are pleats really modern? Issey
Miyake would cry 'yes' as they were lightweight for travelling,[2] offered freedom of
movement (the elasticity of the polyester allowed enough stretch to pull it on and off
comfortably without the need for fasteners) and did not change with the seasons. In
1993, he became involved in the production side of the fabric, because the prices
were too high for the majority of people to buy. Affordability has always been a main
concern for Miyake.

Miyake placed great emphasis on the actual methods of construction of his garments, informing the buyer that there was something more to his clothing than just the
superficial 'skin' (Plate 1). This becomes evident when one views his award-winning
website, www.pleatsplease.com, which details the research and development of his
products and alludes to the nuances of production techniques by providing an illustrated storyboard which outlines the step-by-step process involved in the making of his
Pleats, Please range. It is a didactic approach to marketing which appeals intellectually

to an older clientele, and yet he combines this ploy with the paradoxical imagery of vibrant, colourful and very active dancing figures which swirl around focus points, invigorating and energizing the computer screen.

Pleats, Please and the Guest Artist Series

Miyake's collection ranges until 1996 consisted of neutral-coloured trousers, skirts and tops. After this he introduced high fashion colours and they often incorporated printed designs by different guest artists: Yasuma Morimura the contemporary Japanese fine artist, the photographer Nobuyoshi Araki, and artist Tim Hawkinson. Known as the *Guest Artist* series (1997), Miyake invited artists to use his modular pleated garments as a medium for their own work. He chose collaborators who used the body as an erotic or conceptual entity. Morimura is an artist who uses his body as a tool of expression. When Miyake invited him to incorporate a number of his printed images into the *Pleats, Please* series, Morimura chose the top half of the French neo-classicist nineteenth-century painter Ingres' famous *Le Source* painting of 1856, where an image of a young woman about to pour water from a jug was used. An inverted photograph of the artist himself covered with scarlet netting was featured on the bottom half (Figure 1.3). In another garment, the photographer Nobuyoshi Araki used optical illusions as images on the pleated fabric which move with the body. Araki, one of Japan's most controversial photographers, also uses his craft as an autobiographical tool. His optical images either 'appear', if they are printed on the clothing before it is pleated, or 'disappear', if they are printed after the fabric has been pleated. Thus the photo images come in and out of focus, so to speak, as the clothing follows the wearer's movements. Hawkinson uses a variety of experimental techniques to fragment the image of the body into sections or 'visual patches'.

MAKING THINGS: A RETROSPECTIVE EXHIBITION

Miyake's trademark designs were celebrated at the *Issey Miyake: Making Things* exhibition held at the Cartier Foundation for Contemporary Art in Paris in 1998, where ten years of his work was on view. The museum, designed by Jean Nouvel, opens into a three-storey, glazed ground floor space where dozens of Miyake's *Pleats, Please* garments were suspended from cables coming from the ceiling. The multi-coloured array of moving pleated tops, trousers and dresses resembled party lanterns, sorceresses or exotic birds flapping their wings and could be seen by passers-by as well. This section of the exhibition explored the notion of body movement and showed how Miyake could transform a flat two-dimensional shape into a billowing three-dimensional polychrome dress. According to Herbert Muschamp of *The New York Times*,

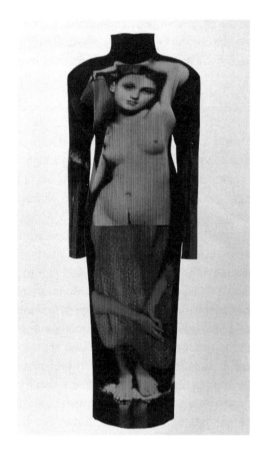

Figure 1.3 Issey Miyake/Yasumasa Morimura, *Guest Artist* series No. 1, screen-printed polyester *Pleats, Please* collection dress, autumn/winter 1966–7. Collection: Sherman Contemporary Art Foundation. Courtesy of Dr Gene Sherman.

> As you walk past, your movement activates a mechanism that reels the dresses swiftly up to the ceiling and lets them float down like gaily colored parachutes. The room is constantly in motion, animated by what looks like a parody of that old fashion game of rising and falling hemlines . . . Miyake intends the Cartier Foundation show to be seen as a collaboration, too. He has conceived the installation as an exchange between his clothes and the Nouvel's building. (Muschamp 1999)

This exploration of the formal potential of new materials and methods is revealed both in the architecture and the clothing.

Another section of the exhibition was themed 'The Laboratory', where gigantic rolls or knitted tubes of fabric were partially unfurled to display several laser-cut dresses. A row of headless mannequins were arranged here, all wearing black garments that were connected to one another and, at the end, to one of the same large rolls of fabric. Simultaneously, this became both a display of fashion and a display of process. Miyake explained his new concept of *A Piece of Cloth* (*A-POC*):

> One of my assistants found this old German (knitting) machine. It was originally used to make underwear. Like Chanel, who started with the underwear fabric—jerseys—we used the

machine (later guided by a computer program) . . . to make something else. It's called 'Just Before'. The fabric is like a long tube dress—it's over 130 feet long. You can cut it as you like; it can be a long dress, or you can make it shorter, or baggy. If you cut it one way, it makes a long dress with sleeves. If you cut it another, it's a short dress without sleeves. It permits that kind of choosing. (In Simon 1999)

A-POC

People are waiting for something that is fun which they feel that we can create together.

Miyake (in Menkes 2000b)

The concept quoted above (in Simon 1999) was to become the foundation of all of Miyake's later work—particularly his second major series, the *A-POC* (*A Piece of Cloth*) range.[3] Like the kimono, the main principle was not to cut into the woven cloth, but to respect the integrity of the material and to use its shape to house the body. This series evolved from a conceptual basis that challenged existing conventions—it became another form of renewed clothing production. Lee, in her *Fashioning the Future: Tomorrow's Wardrobe*, argues that 'APOC proposes a radical rethink of fashion manufacture for the twenty-first century' (2005: 30).

A-POC started in 1998 as revolutionary garments cut either by heat-punch or, better, by extreme cold-punch methods, from tubes of Raschel-knit material (a warp-knitted fabric that resembles hand-crocheted and lace fabrics and nettings) and has now evolved to include jeans and furniture coverings. At the 2006 Milan Furniture Fair, a collaborative *A-POC* project between Miyake and designer Ron Arad displayed upholstery that can switch from covering Arad's *Ripple Chair* to clothing a human. Called *Gemini*, it is used to cover a body-cushioning seat pillow, blurring the edges between designer chairs and designer clothing. This new concept becomes part of the 'performance' that is also an inherent part of the *A-POC* process. It would seem that the interactive part that the consumer plays, not only in the process of making, but also in the wearing of individual garments, is paramount to its appeal. The garments can become customized for individual purchasers and Miyake contends that 'People are waiting for something that is fun which they feel that we can create together' (Menkes 2000b). *A-POC* was initially revealed to the fashion world at the Ecole des Beaux Arts in Paris in the autumn of 1999 and shortly afterwards in Tokyo. In his Omotesando shop,

Rolls of fabric in bright red, green, black, navy and white are stacked upon a display case . . . If [the customers] want to try on something, there is a selection of items ready-cut. These can be bought individually but the idea is that one size fits all, and there is no right or wrong way of wearing it. Miyake says 'You can wear it as you like—they're your clothes'. This idea of making clothes from a single piece of cloth—like the Indian Sari or the Roman toga—has always been central to his work. 'The basis for clothing design lies in a piece of cloth, which no fashion or trend can alter', he argues. (Blanchard 1999)

The tube of stretch jersey fabric, which starts with a single thread, so each garment is woven complete with welts and seams, metamorphoses into a variety of different forms when cut. The tube of fabric is initially pressed flat so that the shapes of the garments can be woven into them. A ribbed outline demarcates the shapes, which can then be cut out with a pair of scissors. Menkes (2000b) refers to this process as a 'Miyake Slice-Your-Own', suggesting that it is a type of 'deli self-serve' construct. In the high-tech twenty-first century, consumers have been programmed to cope with DIY fashions, self-serve department stores, ATM machines and petrol stations. Theoretically, one might suppose that the A-POC concept is not much different.

While seen by some as a marketing gimmick and by others as a utopian vision to fetishize technological progress, this new approach to fashion was successful in Tokyo, but when his Paris store opened, in September 2000, it was slower to catch on. He argues that it usually takes eight years for a revolutionary trend to take hold, but it seems it is taking longer for the concept of A-POC to find its footing. But is this really what the postmodernist consumer wants? Miyake argues that

> We are looking to people, not the fashion (community) and we are fascinated by technology. People have become consumers; they forgot the ways they can participate in their clothing. A-POC does that. It is important people participate in making their own clothing. (Graham 2007)

Conceived as a unique, futuristic interactive fashion system, A-POC tube designs, made from high-tech fibres and woven by a computer-instructed machine with the clothing pattern etched on, allow the buyers to become their own pattern-cutters and designers. According to Miyake, this process provides a framework for 'design and fit' and subsequently could be seen as clothing that becomes universal (Plate 2). The fact that the A-POC garments could be produced without machine-sewn seams is revolutionary in itself and stimulates interesting possibilities that could totally revolutionize the ready-to-wear fashion industry. Significantly, while the concept is primarily about uniformity and the streamlined body, it also minimizes waste in clothing fabrication. This has become a major issue in terms of ecological sustainability over the past decade. Miyake suggests that 'we make a single pattern and we send it to many places—Africa, the Middle East—and people can make it their own . . . To me, it's the future of clothing, the 21st century way of making clothes to use frameworks and technology to use cloth efficiently and beautifully' (Graham 2007). Arguably, in both his *Pleats, Please* and A-POC ranges, Miyake has attempted to redefine the role of design in daily life.

Miyake's vision, setting the standards for a universal fashion production system, may not be fully realized for decades, but it has offered the world a new insight into 'what might be'. Conceptually, it might be too difficult for today's Western fashion buyers to grasp. Anna Wintour, long-standing editor-in-chief of American *Vogue* complained that the Japanese designers' clothes were 'too difficult to wear' to be a commercial success (Warady 2001). Miyake admits that 80 per cent of his clothes are sold in Japan, while he has retail outlets in New York, Paris and London, among other cities. Today, Miyake insists that *A-POC* intrigues the Chinese, whom he says are his best customers as they are learning quickly to wear lighter, unusual clothes and they understand the advances technology promises. 'The great thing about Japanese designers', argues Miyake, 'is that we have our own companies. We don't do licensing. We are not controlled by someone else. We are our own' (Simon 1999). Franka Sozzani, editor-in-chief of *Italian Vogue*, applauds the Japanese designers' independence and suggests frequently that they are considered icons in the fashion world.

EAST MEETS WEST

I realized these two wonderful advantages I enjoy, and that was when I started to experiment creating a new genre of clothing, neither Western nor Japanese but beyond nationality.

Miyake

In the fine arts, the interface which existed between Eastern and Western culture has been well documented. In terms of fashion, Jun I Kanai (Fukai 1996: 195), curator-at-large of the Kyoto Costume Institute, argues that there are many Western clothes that are 'strongly reminiscent of the decorations, patterns, constructions or overall sensibilities of the Japanese kimono'. She asserts that the fascination with Japan and an acknowledgement of its influence upon Western art is the basis for 'Japonism', which produced a new visual direction, a modern style. The well-known American painter James McNeill Whistler frequently visited two Japanese shops in Paris in the 1960s—La Jonque Chinoise, an Oriental curio shop on the rue de Rivoli, and an antique shop, La Porte Chinoise, on rue Vivienne—to purchase kimonos, porcelains, screens and *ukiyoe* prints. Such items appeared in his paintings, including *Caprice in Purple and Gold: The Golden Screen* (1864) and *The Princess from the Land of Porcelain* (1863–4). In the early twentieth century, 'kimonomania' appeared in the work of Paul Poiret, the designer who freed women from the shackles of the corset and introduced loose-fitting, non-restrictive clothing. It also inspired the work of Poiret's contemporary, Madeleine Vionnet, heralded as the 'designer's designer' as she was considered one of the most influential couturiers of the twentieth century. She also advocated the wearing of comfortable, draped garments that liberated the body in the early 1900s, and she relied on simple, unfitted clothing characterized by geometric lines and flat construction in the 1920s. The stylized, geometric patterns of all Art Deco textile design reflected the impact of Japanese applied arts upon Europe while, at the same time, many examples of silks patterned with Japanese motifs were coming out of Lyon, the textile centre of France. These were used to create fashionable Parisian haute couture clothes.

In 1996, A key exhibition entitled *Japonisme in Fashion* was held in Tokyo at the Tokyo Fashion Hall, Ariake, and later in the year travelled to Paris to be held at the Musée de La Mode et du Costume, Palais Galliera. Organized by the Kyoto Costume Institute and curated by Akiko Fukai, its aim was to illustrate the historical development of Japanese cultural influence upon Western costume. The Kyoto Costume Institute has been collecting, studying and preserving Western costume, including undergarments and accessories, and related documents since its inception in 1978.

Writing a treatise on Japanese art, Yoshida (Yoshida *et al*. 1980: 17–18) outlined four key characteristics that epitomized the cultural differences between Eastern and Western art: symmetry, balance, perspective and affinity with nature. He points out that the Japanese developed their own particular form of symmetry, as they used a diagonal rather than a centrally placed horizontal or vertical line when dividing a rectangle. Secondly, they attempted to achieve a balance based on an inner meaning rather than shape or proportion. Thirdly, they placed a greater emphasis on negative space in their compositions, a technique adopted from the Chinese in the sixteenth century, to create a sense of depth. Finally, Japanese art reflects an intense sympathy with nature, evoking an emotional response inherent in the beauty of the natural world. Even Sir Rutherford Alcock,[4] previously the British Minister in Edo (Tokyo), also maintained, in *Art and Art Industries in Japan* (1878), that the power of expression, combined with simplicity of treatment, was characteristic of all Japanese art.

While Japan was attempting to protect its cultural boundaries, Western clothing infiltrated the higher circles of Japanese society in the late nineteenth century. European fashions were adopted by the Japanese Imperial Court and the leaders of the government and, by the 1890s, old sepia photographs reveal that bowler hats, high-collared shirts and leather shoes were worn with the kimono. By the 1930s, there was a growing trend for many businessmen to adopt the conventional Western-style suit to the office during the day but convert to the traditional *yukata*, a casual summer kimono usually made of cotton, when returning home. Katzumie (Yoshida *et al*. 1980: 7–8) attributes this to the dichotomy, present for the past 100 years in Japanese society, that lends itself to a 'perpetual oscillation between the opposed phenomena of tradition and progress, Japanese and Western'. He adds that 'this peculiarly Japanese brand of dualism has invaded every aspect of our life from clothes, food and houses to art and culture in general'.

One might argue that the secret of Japanese creativity is found in the past, embodied in the concept that change and diversification are used to bring together all the parts into a single landscape. The Japanese belief in the transience of all earthly things, embedded in their preoccupation with the ephemeral, is an important factor in a discussion of Japanese aesthetics and, in turn, recalls the dynamism of fashion. Another cultural strength lies in their 'pragmatism in converting necessity to opportunity' (Jansen 2000: 686). This is particularly relevant to twentieth-century history as, after the Second World War, Japan rose from being a previously poor Asian nation to one which became a world leader in industry, manufacturing and design. Issey Miyake has been described as one of the leaders who not only contributed to Japan's post-war recovery and cultural and creative growth, but was also one of the first Asian designers to infiltrate French fashion (Plate 3).

Dorinne Kondo, in a seminal essay entitled 'The Aesthetics and Politics of Japanese Identity in the Fashion Industry' discusses how the fashion industries

> define a critically important arena where global economical power and cultural authority are contested. Keen economic competition is paralleled by competition for cultural recognition, and here Japan is assuming a place at the forefront of design, the meeting point of high tech and aesthetic. (1992: 176–7)

Japan is one of the leading countries in the world for consumer spending in fashion. By 2000, it was estimated that 70 per cent of Japanese designer garments would be purchased in Japan and that 50 per cent of selected leading European high fashion collections would be purchased by Japanese consumers. By 2010, the younger Japanese consumers looked more towards European designed clothing as, according to Godoy (2007), they want to look like celebrities. Kondo discusses how 'nation' and 'culture' are problematic as fashion industries participate in a global fashion industry. She argues:

> How does one speak of 'Japanese' design when flows of creative talent and capital are truly transnational and when 'Japanese' designer garments are consumed not only in Japan but throughout the world? Indeed, what counts as Japanese clothing when Western clothing has been on the Japanese scene at least since the 1860s and when today's designers grew up with blue jeans more than with kimono? (1992: 177–9)

It could be effectively argued that postmodernity in fashion is inherently cross-cultural as more Japanese designers and firms infiltrate Paris's stranglehold on the international fashion industry. This hegemony is slowly giving way to a cosmopolitan identity in the fashion capital, where the House of Grès was purchased by Japanese textile and apparel company Yagi Tsusho in 1988, the head designer of the House of Cacherel became Atsuro Tayama and the Japanese firm, Onward Kashiyama, financed French designer Jean Paul Gaultier. Cultural ambivalences abound and contest notions of what constitutes mainstream fashion. This has been further clouded by multinational financing, licensing and the controlling role of major syndicates such as LVMH (Louis Vuitton Moët Hennessy) in determining and rotating the head designers of many of the leading couturier houses.

Would the East/West paradigm be dissolved if the Japanese philosophy was adopted? Fashion, they say, should transcend nationality (*mukokuseki*) and this is embedded in Miyake's words:

> Away from the home country, living and working in Paris, I looked at myself very hard and asked, 'What could I do as a Japanese fashion designer?' Then I realised that my very disadvantage, lack of Western heritage, would also be my advantage. I was free of Western tradition or convention. I thought, 'I can try anything new. I cannot go back to my past because there is no past in me as far as Western clothing is concerned. There was no other way for me but to go forward.' The lack of Western tradition was the very thing I needed to create contemporary and universal fashion. But as a Japanese (person) I come from a heritage rich in tradition . . . I realised these two wonderful advantages I enjoy, and that was when I started to experiment creating a new genre of clothing, neither Western nor Japanese but beyond nationality. I hoped to create a new universal clothing which is challenging to our time. (Miyake 1984)

WALKING BACKWARDS TOWARDS THE TWENTY-FIRST CENTURY

> I learned about space between the body and the fabric from the traditional kimono . . . not the style, but the space.
>
> Miyake

According to a contemporary Kyoto textile artist, among others, after the Second World War there was a growing influence of American popular culture on Japanese society. It seemed that the Japanese people were no longer selectively focused on their cultural heritage, instead desiring new and novel consumer items rather than cherishing traditional pieces. By the 1960s, this sentiment reversed and a 'fresh' embrace of their indigenous culture was read as a backlash against a previous celebration of 'outsider' popular culture. Through a detailed visual analysis, Miyake's early 1970s collections, in particular, seem to owe a great deal to his cultural heritage. It is generally contended that a common or shared trait among the three leading Japanese fashion designers—Miyake, Yamamoto and Kawakubo—is that they all based their designs on the concept of the kimono and the traditional Japanese way of packaging in which everything is somehow folded, wrapped, revealed and shaped. Bénaim referred to this cultural phenomena as walking 'backwards towards the twenty-first century, and [it] offers suggestions for the future' (1997: 7).

The Kimono

For Miyake, these traditional kimono techniques of draping, pleating and overlay are evident throughout his designing career. The notion of wrapping the body is linked with the Japanese genius for enclosing space. Japanese clothing is seen as a form of packaging the body. Miyake stated, 'I like to work in the spirit of the kimono. Between the body and the fabric there exists only an approximate contact.' It is this central concept of space between the body and the cloth, called *ma* in Japanese, which creates a natural freedom, and general flexibility in the garment. 'Clothes', Miyake explains, 'have to be seen on the outside as well as felt on the inside' (Cocks 1986: 44). He sees clothes as tools for living that should be relaxing, convenient and useful.

The kimono has always played a significant role in the culture of Japan. The great value attached to kimonos and textile design is evident in the involvement of some of Japan's most famous artists in the design of the garments, such as the nineteenth-century printmaker Utamaro. Kimonos are handed down from generation to generation, and they have defined the Japanese tradition of beauty. Dating back to the Heian Period (eighth to twelfth centuries), the kimono was primarily a garment of the leisured class and the way that the colours overlapped, changed and harmonized according to the season was of great aesthetic concern. The choice of the kimono's colours, designs and materials became governed by a precise code of social appropriateness. While the kimonos worn by wealthier people were made from exquisite silk fabrics, the farmer wore kimonos made from cotton. Cotton was first cultivated in the fifteenth century and before that various natural fibres were used for clothing—most common was 'ASA' a hemp-like fabric favoured for summer garments. 'Kozo' fibre, from the bark of the mulberry tree, long used to make exquisite handmade papers, was a mainstay for clothing worn by commoners. In northern Japan, in particular, paper was used as a lining for warmth and this inspired Miyake to produce a collection of paper dresses. When paper first arrived from China, it was seen as a precious commodity. A proverb explains, 'Draw on silk and it will last 500 years; draw on paper, it will last 1000 years.'

Miyake's work comments on the recontextualization of the kimono to create a different aesthetic milieu. Miyake rejected the traditional forms of Paris collection clothing. Through the inventive use of fabric and successive layering, he developed a concept of fashion based on the use of cloth—or rather, the 'essence' of clothing: the wrapping of the body in cloth. He has created anti-structural, organic clothing which takes on a sculptural quality that suggests a natural freedom, expressed through the simplicity of its cut, the abundance of new fabrics, the space between the garment and the body, and its general flexibility. Interestingly, the basic measures of the kimono, such as its reliance on uncut lengths of fabrics, crossed bodices and loosely cut sleeves, had been copied by European designers[5] at the turn of the century for tea gowns and opera coats, at a time when Eastern design had great influence upon Art Nouveau styling.

CULTURAL APPROPRIATIONS: TECHNIQUES AND MATERIALS

Miyake uses the traditional techniques of dyeing, draping, pleating, wrapping and over-lay consistently in his work. This reinstates the ancient art forms of *shibori*, or tie-dye, and origami, or paper-folding, into contemporary dress. Folded paper has a religious significance in Japan, often tied to straw ropes and hung before a sacred place.[6] The concept of folded or pleated material is critical to Miyake's practice. He began experimenting with pleating using a variety of different materials including linen crêpe, woven cotton, polyester and tricot jersey. For him, pleating represented the ultimate functionality, coupled with a superb surface texture.

Early in his career, Miyake produced garments that featured the same type of checked cloth and *sashiko* technique (a Japanese form of cotton quilting) used in coats traditionally worn by Japanese peasant farmers as an alternative to denim (Figure 1.4). He also used a fabric called *tabi-ura*, formerly reserved for the bottoms of the fitted Japanese sock. Miyake references his cultural heritage via textiles in many different ways. *Aburi-gami*, an oiled handmade paper often used for making parasols and lanterns,[7] is often woven in traditional *ikat* designs and printed with woodblocks. It would seem that Miyake's *Cicada Pleats* garment, of 1989, shares the nature of this semi-transparent paper, where light is diffused and softened. Miyake continuously investigated the concept of clothing as a 'second skin' and *Cicada Pleats* refers to similar phenomena in the insect world. The underlying reference to metamorphosis, alluding to an insect shedding its outer skin, is suggested and his use of transparent textiles heightens the magical effect:

> The model glows through this golden paper skin, like an insect set in amber . . . One of Miyake's most innovative images is found in the bark of a tree. The body can move inside a tube of fabric as if in a caterpillar skin. Miyake asked: 'Did you know there's a tree in Africa where the bark comes off completely? It's round, just like a tube of jersey. I wanted to make something woven, that was warped like African bark.' (Penn 1988: 15)

In Miyake's work, the process of simplification dictated the use of a single piece of fabric that flowed over the body. His sculptural creations symbolize a purist approach to design, as his garments seem to become art forms in themselves. His Japanese affinity with nature inspires shapes in his clothing which are reminiscent of shells, stones

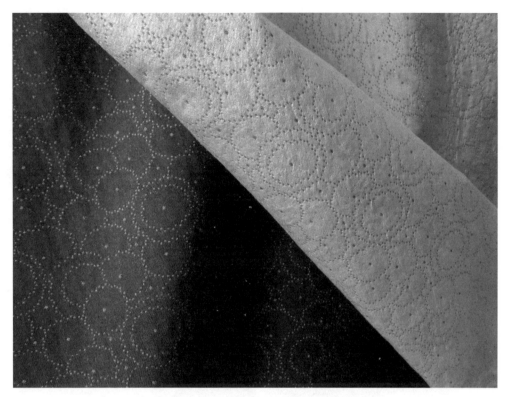

Figure 1.4   Sayuri Shimoda/Nuno Corporation, textile—*Sashiko Flower*, 1986. Collection: The Minneapolis Institute of Art, USA. Photograph: Peter Page. Courtesy of Reiko Sudo & Nuno Corporation.

and seaweed and are often made from natural materials such as paper, silk, linen, cotton, leather, furs and bamboo. The famous *Shell Coat* (1985), for example, appeared when Miyake's designs were becoming increasingly biomorphic. The textures of this coat enhance the simplicity of the design and simulate the surface of a seashell.

Ancient Japanese historical reference is evident in many of his collections and this, combined with a fascination with surface texture and a search for innovative form, inspired his experimental use of shiny silicone in primary colours, which he forms into moulded bustiers. These forms became metaphors of the armour of the Samurai warriors. In Japanese history, the Samurai warriors were fierce and highly skilled warriors. They were highly respected members of society and samurai descendents treasured their fine swords as family heirlooms. Their armour encased the upper torso and the colour black became symbolic of their strength and courage. *Red Plastic Bustier* (1980) is a moulded bustier which investigates the relationship between the body and clothing and, in a paradoxical manner, replicates the body as clothing (Figure 1.5). It was made in collaboration with Nanasai, a mannequin manufacturer. The bustier is often shown with long pants or skirts in order to juxtapose hard and soft materials, thereby emphasizing the corset-like appearance which underlines the underwear–outerwear paradigm. The modulated form highlights the sculptural nature of the piece. These pieces were central to Miyake's *Bodyworks* exhibitions held in Tokyo, LA, San Francisco and London between 1983 and 1985.

Miyake's design also has strong parallels with architecture. His *Rattan Bustier* of 1982 was woven by Shochikudo Kosuge, a bamboo and rattan craftsman. Again, this cage-like form mimics ancient samurai warfare clothing, but also becomes a rigid house for the body. These constructions exemplify ideas of the body moving within a space beneath an outer space (Holborn 1988: 120). It would be difficult to find another designer who has been more experimental in his use of materials than Miyake. He sees that the possibilities are limitless—iron, paper, cane, bamboo and stones.

Fabric technology has become part of the ritual of Japanese textile development. Numerous companies, particularly in Kyoto (the ancient centre for textile development

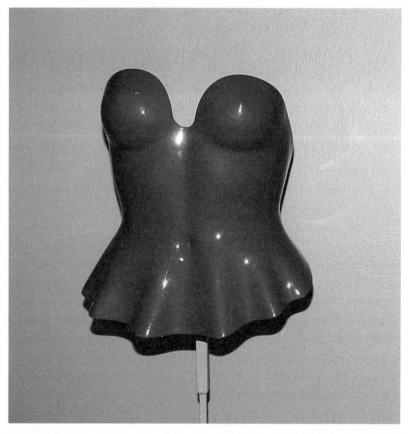

Figure 1.5 Issey Miyake, red silicone bustier, 1980 at FIT (Fashion Institute of Technology), NY, 2006 exhibition *Love and War: The Weaponized Woman*. Photograph: Robyn Beck/AFP/Getty Images.

for thousands of years) and Tokyo now lead the world. Also, individual design work-shops, including the Miyake Design Studio (MDS), have established a reputation for their exciting textile experimentation and exploration.

HIGH-TECH FIBRES

Make me a fabric that looks like poison.

Miyake (in Handley 2008)

Miyake's contribution to the invention of new synthetic fibres cannot be under-estimated. In 'Miyake Modern', Simon remarks that one of the most remarkable aspects of his work is determined by 'an understanding of textile fibres, both natural and synthetic, and of fabrics, both hand-woven and traditionally dyed, as well as high-tech textiles that are not woven at all' (1999). Louise Mitchell, then curator of fashion in the International Decorative Arts department of the Powerhouse Museum in Sydney, suggested that Miyake's work aims 'to rediscover the traditional beauty of a Japan which is disappearing; to emphasise the importance of industrially produced clothes by using synthetic materials' (Mitchell 1999: 44). This symbiotic relationship between the past and the present inspired Benaim to comment that Miyake's work offers fashion a focus as it walks backwards towards the twenty-first century, and offers suggestions for the future (Bénaim 1997: 7).

Undoubtedly, Miyake will leave a legacy of avant-garde experimentation that the next generation of Japanese designers will find hard to match, not only in fashion styling but in the development of new fabrics. An understanding of textile fibres, both natural and synthetic, and of fabrics, both handwoven and traditionally dyed, as well as high-tech textiles that are not woven at all, is one of the most remarkable aspects of Miyake's work. Multi-directional pleating, garments encased in metallic skins, multi-coloured, felt-like clothing 'collaged' together from irregularly shaped pieces of cloth, and dresses with large sections that are selectively shrunk (*kibira*) represent some of the textile-conscious directions that Miyake has taken in recent years. As early as 1985, he coated polyester jersey with polyurethane, which was made into inflatable trousers that proved very comfortable to wear. Yet, at the same time, he pioneered the use of ethnographic materials such as the Asian *ikats* and, as mentioned earlier, he used paper for clothing, knowing that in ancient times Japanese farmers lined their garments with decorated paper to keep out the cold. He held a fascination for fabrics that had a rough, handmade look—textures that were produced by the rural people. Miyake insists that fibre is the theme of the twenty-first century. For over thirty-five years, he has worked with Makiko Minagawa, a textile 'artist-engineer' to explore new possibilities in fabrics and to make a fabric-based design, shifting the emphasis from the cut onto the cloth itself. This is evident in his 2008 men's collection where colour fading and surface texture is directly related to experimentation with the age-old *shibori* technique (Figure 1.6). Susannah Handley, in her book *Nylon: The Story of a Fashion Revolution* (2000), discusses Miyake's poetic approach to technology, which, she argues, underlines the Japanese aesthetic. Reportedly, Miyake once asked Minagawa, 'Make me a fabric that looks like poison' (Handley 2008).

Arguably, Japan has become a leader in producing high-tech fibres and finishes, and fashion designers like Miyake consult at length with textile designers and fabric houses to produce 'state-of-the-art' materials that ultimately make the difference between high street and haute couture fashion. These secrets are as carefully guarded as the next season's collection designs. Japan's textile manufacturers are willing to make very short runs of experimental fibres. While very costly, they serve the purpose of providing exceptional products for the international luxury market. For example, Honshu Island's Amaike textile company created a 'super organza'—the lightest and thinnest fabric in the world, made of 100 per cent polyester. Like the diaphanous wings of a butterfly, it is an invisible floating film that drapes the silhouette.[8] Miyake's later collections showcased high-tech thermoplastic synthetic fabrics which he twisted, creased, folded and crushed, securing their shapes by heat-setting. His transparent *Hoc Jacket*

Figure 1.6   Issey Miyake, men's jackets with snow hats; Issey Miyake, Omantesando window display, Tokyo 2008. Photograph: author.

and Trousers (1996) were made from monofilament polyamide with a holographic finish which shimmered against the skin, creating a visual delight. Using inflatable plastics consolidated a link with childhood experiences as well as a sci-fi tactility. Miyake will often provide his customers with a description of the fabric in order to explain the techniques used. He feels that it is important to interact and communicate the actual process of design to his customers.

INFLUENCES ON MIYAKE

> I felt, through the images I saw in the magazines, that fashion could be like beautiful architecture for the body . . .

> Miyake (in Sischy 2001)

It is difficult to pinpoint specific ways in which Miyake's childhood, education and apprentice-based early work impacted upon his later work as an accomplished designer. It seems that he was a man who always preferred to look towards the future rather than the past. As a child, he wanted to become a dancer and perhaps for this reason his clothes today celebrate the vitality of the human body. He liked to draw and this would have directed his thinking towards a career in graphic design, which he studied at Tama University, Tokyo, but his interest in fashion design was fuelled by studying his sister's fashion magazines—especially those from America. He said that:

> They were much more inspiring than most of them are now. I felt, through the images I saw in the magazines, that fashion could be like beautiful architecture for the body . . . I was amazed at how architecture and other design fields completely ignored fashion design. (Sischy 2001)

According to one of the fashion teaching staff at Bunka, he must have been intrigued by the fashion competitions that were held at the Bunka Fashion College, Tokyo,[9] as he entered designs into a number of them but he did not win a competition as he did not have the pattern-making or sewing skills that were required (English 1997b). When he graduated from university in 1965, he went to Paris, where he enrolled in the Chambre syndicale de la couture parisienne school.[10] He spent his time visiting museums and while he indicated that he was influenced by many sculptors, including Brancusi and Giacometti, in the fashion world it was Balenciaga, and especially Vionnet, who provided the greatest inspiration for him. According to Miyake, Vionnet really understood the kimono as she used the geometric idea to construct her clothes, and this brought much freedom into European clothing in the 1920s and 1930s. From the First World War onwards,

She abandoned the traditional practice of tailoring body-fitted fashions from numerous, complex pattern pieces, and minimised the cutting of the fabric. A 'minimalist' with strict aesthetic principles who rarely employed patterned fabrics or embroidery, Vionnet instead created surface ornamentation through manipulation of the fabric itself . . . The wavy parallel folds of a pin-tucked crepe dress evoked the abstract image of a raked Zen rock garden, itself a Japanese metaphor for the waves of the sea. (Mears 2008: 105)

While in Paris, Miyake was apprenticed to Guy Laroche as an assistant designer and with Hubert de Givenchy, for whom he drew 50 to 100 sketches every day. Some were coloured and sent to celebrities like the Duchess of Windsor and Audrey Hepburn. He admired and respected the techniques that Givenchy used to fit the clothes on the models, and commented that Givenchy had a beautiful way of working in a very traditional way. But, for Miyake, it was the kind of world and society that he didn't want to belong to; the rigidity of haute couture didn't appeal to him. Julie Dam (1999) notes that Givenchy commented in retrospect, 'I don't think that I influenced him in any way.'

For Miyake, Paris was a stepping stone to New York. According to Ingrid Sischy (2001), he said, 'I wasn't sure that I wanted to be a dress designer, but I knew that I wanted to come to New York and do something new, something that only I could do . . . I felt that to survive in the artistic field, New York was the only place to be.' He travelled to New York in 1969 and stayed five or six months, getting to know great artists like Christo and Robert Rauschenberg, who 'showed me another way to see, they lent me a lot of eyes. I'm covered with their eyes' (Sischy 2001). While he was enrolled in English classes at Columbia University and Hunter College in the evenings, during the day he worked on Seventh Avenue for designer Geoffrey Beene. Beene was renowned for his stark, simplistic styling. As Beene explained, 'The more you learn about clothes, the more you realise what has to be left out. Simplification becomes a very complicated procedure' (in Watson 2004). Not surprisingly, Beene was known as 'The Godfather' of modern American minimalism, and was one of the few who put art before commerce.

In 1970, Miyake returned to Tokyo, which was hosting the World Expo, and he was infused by the very positive excitement in the city. While Miyake had intended to return to New York, he made a decision, with the help of some friends, to set up the Miyake Design Studio in Tokyo in the same year. In *Interview* magazine, Sischy documents Miyake's recollections:

'I made my first collection for New York. I'll never forget it. I brought it to New York in January 1971—one of the pieces was polyester, but just one size and all hand-made. It was revolutionary at the time'. Bloomingdales immediately started working with Miyake and he was given a small corner of the store. 'I made a tattoo dress that was inspired by Jimi Hendrix and Janis Joplin. They had both died in the 70s so I wanted to do it because I think tattoo is like a homage. So I took these Japanese traditions and made them contemporary'. By the 80s, New York had fallen in love with his work. 'What I do involves all sorts of people, all genres, and I think people in the art community appreciate it as they see it's another form of expression, they see another point of view. I never wanted to make clothes just for fashion shows, I preferred to develop a relationship with the people who wear my clothes.' (Sischy 2001: n. pag.)

ARTISTIC COLLABORATIONS

I also started working with photographers, and artists and filmmakers and graphic designers—collaborating with them felt like a more natural way for me to work, and one I knew would ultimately lead to my work being seen by the world.

Miyake

Miyake's collaboration with other visual arts practitioners creates a culturally diverse interface of ideas and recontextualizes fashion within a conceptual arena. Miyake's work—a form of postmodernist artistic practice—has never fallen within the dictates of the fashion industry and, as a result, was not consumed by its self-imposed boundaries. Perhaps this is why his work has appealed to noted art photographers such as Irving Penn, and also Leni Riefenstahl, whose photographs underline the notion that fashion can step beyond its immediate frame of reference. For example, the publication entitled *Issey Miyake: Photographs by Irving Penn* was a collaborative effort between the Japanese designer and the Western photographer, printed by Nissha in Kyoto (Penn, 1988). Three tons of Miyake's designs were shipped to New York, where Penn made his own choices. Penn, like Miyake, 'employs an art of reduction—his fashion photographs are emptied to allow the geometry of his clothes to be the sole, uncluttered force. Penn's photographs are contextless, the subject without the surround' (Holborn 1988: 118). In a similar way, Japanese landscape and woodblock print artists also concentrated their images by juxtaposing them with bare, unadorned elements. Penn presents Miyake's clothing as flattened, near-abstracted images in a white nothingness. The clothes disclose nothing of the bodies underneath, and sexuality often becomes ambiguous. Penn places Miyake's clothes within a neutral space to underline the notion that fashion can be seen as a reconsidered form. Miyake contended that Penn's photographs 'could tell me if what I was doing was all right or not, and what I should do next' (Sischy 2001).

The tattooed body[11] became a recurring theme in Miyake's work and was especially prevalent after 1976, when his work was inspired directly by his interests in photographs taken by Leni Riefenstahl. Riefenstahl's photographs of the Nuba of the Sudan emphasized the textural beauty of the dark skin's surface when raised patterns created by scarification became a rendering similar to a second skin. He incorporated these body markings into a collection entitled *Twelve Black Girls* (1976), which reinforced the notion that his work extended beyond an exclusively Oriental style. Again in 1989/90, he created a series of tattoo-like body stocking garments that were worn close to the body by using a stretch fabric. According to Holborn, 'This sense of design provided a window on world culture with a modern look embracing ethnic beauty' (1995: 42). This globalisation of culture is inherent to postmodernist design where appropriation and synthesis of both Western and non-Western elements occur. For Miyake, his embrace of African culture has negated the 'Japanese' tag with which he had previously been labelled. The issue of transnationalism challenged the notion of cultural identity in clothing and underlined the growing trend in the 1980s and 90s towards multi-cultural stylistic appropriations playing a dominant role in the international market.

Collaborative project work has been an inherent part of the Miyake Design Studio over the past thirty-five years. A Japanese photographer called Yuriko Takagi, who had studied fashion design and graphics, collaborated with Miyake to connect clothes to people in a real life situation, a lifelong project upon which she had embarked several years before. She took several trunk-loads of his pleated wardrobe series to remote villages in India. There, she invited the local people to try the clothing on so she could take photos which undoubtedly recontextualized Miyake's collection. Her images created a remarkable paradox of beautiful materials juxtaposed against male bodies, toughened by manual labour, working in the fields and rowing boats, and against women suckling babies and making food. While Takagi's work might comment on the artifice of the design studio and the runway, at the same time it raises questions regarding the moral exploitation of using the poor to advertise highly priced designer garments.

In 1988, Miyake commissioned the Dutch artist, Maria Blaisse, to design a series of hats for his spring/summer collection after seeing her 'flexicaps' in New York City. In response to his linen dresses that season, she designed hats from pineapple fibre, as they were able to sway in relation to the body's movements. She is renowned for her investigative research based on the use of atypical materials. Her work, very similar in a way to Miyake's, deals with releasing energy from existing materials. 'Common materials, simple forms and a great dose of ingenuity have earned Blaisse a solid reputation in what is considered by many to be largely uncharted areas of design' (Hemmings, 'Playtime').

A series of brief collaborations began for the autumn/winter 1996–7 collection when Miyake embarked on his *Guest Artist* series, a collaboration with artists of different nationalities who produced images to be printed onto the *Pleats, Please* garments (as mentioned earlier). One of these collaborations featured Cai Guo-Qiang, a Chinese pyrotechnic performance artist whose art is based on 1,000-year-old religious, aesthetic and philosophical traditions and who uses explosive fireworks to remember historic past events and to commemorate the victims from such atrocities as the atomic bomb in Hiroshima, and other terrorist attacks including the bombings in London and Madrid. Guo-Qiang sprinkled gunpowder over clothing placed on the ground in the shape of a dragon and then set it alight. Miyake then incorporated the images of the burned patterns onto his garments. Perhaps, not surprisingly, his clothes appealed to both the arty, bohemian crowd as well as the more conservative, elitist-minded socialite. Perhaps the main reason for this was that the stying was distinctive—distinctively Miyake.

In another collaboration, Miyake and Hiroaki Ohya designed sneakers for 'Onitsuka Tiger', which preceded the Nike marketing strategy by ten years to become the official brand for the Japanese Olympic team for over twenty years.[12] This clever marketing strategy has been adopted by numerous other sports shoe manufacturers since this initial collaboration. More recently, the 'rediscovering Japan' theme has become a big part of the Onitsuka design scheme and the company has hired artisans in Kyoto to develop beautifully embroidered kimono fabrics with cherry blossom motifs.

EXHIBITING FASHION AS ART

Will fashion be able to afford to keep the same old methodology?

Miyake

From the beginning of the twentieth century, fashion was displayed on mannequins in major department stores, particularly in America, where the public did not have immediate access to the French haute couturiers' work. The formatting of such displays was traditionally formalized, without any flair or ingenuity. Miyake took this formatting one step further by being one of the first to display his work in a bone fide art gallery or museum. The Dada artist, Marcel Duchamp, had established, as early as the 1910s, that when objects were placed in a museum by an artist, they were immediately awarded the new status of being classified as an 'artwork'. (Figure 1.7) While Miyake refuted this classification of his work, his garments were very precisely positioned in the form of an 'art installation'. Also, he adopted the artistic legacy of documenting his work and process, as if each garment was a painting or sculpture, in a series of publications, including *Issey Miyake: East Meets West* (1978), an exhibition catalogue for *Bodyworks*, Tokyo (1983), and a monograph on Miyake's design concept of *Pleats, Please* (1990). He also started collaboration with Irving Penn, the photographer, resulting in a series of books and posters from 1986 to 2000. These included *Issey Miyake: Photographs by Irving Penn* (1988); *Issey Miyake by Irving Penn* (1989,

Figure 1.7 Issey Miyake, models with inflatable hats, spring/summer 1996, RTW, Paris. Photograph: Pierre Verdy/AFP/Getty Images.

1990, 1991–92); and *Irving Penn Regards the Work of Issey Miyake* (1999). According to Patricia Mears, by carefully documenting his collections, 'he was also one of the first to create a comprehensive archive of his work, housed in a warehouse custom-made for that purpose' (2008: 98).

Miyake's exhibitions explored the notion that fashion could be seen as flat, 2-D geometric forms and yet, at the same time, could be transformed into 3-D sculptural shapes. He suggested the interface that existed between the two stages. His exhibitions also underline the evolution of the creation of the garments—the stages of development from conception to final product. His work featured as part of a group exhibition of fashion design called *Intimate Architecture* in 1982 at MIT in Chicago, an institution considered the hub of American cutting edge design. After this, Ingrid Sischy, then editor of *Artforum*, featured his work on the cover of this prestigious American art magazine. His first solo fashion exhibition, entitled *Bodyworks*, where he suspended the garments on dress forms over pools of black dye, was presented as an art installation rather than a traditional linear display of historical garments set in glass cases. It was held in Tokyo and then travelled to major museums in San Francisco, Los Angeles and London between 1983 and 1985, turning the idea of the display of material culture around. In 1988, he held another show, *Issey Miyake A-UN*, at the Decorative Arts Museum in Paris, when he began his experimentation with pleats and his shift towards simple, functional forms. In the 1990 *Energieen* (*Energies*) exhibition held at the Stedelijk Museum in Amsterdam, he further explored the inter-relationship between 2-D and 3-D forms. Garments, laid flat in recessed shapes cut into the false floor to emphasize their geometric nature, were juxtaposed with mannequins wearing the same garments, but as 3-D, non-objective shapes. Similarly, when unworn, his *Flying Saucer* dress becomes nothing more than a flat, abstract disc. This ongoing theme, which extended this concept of fashion as sculptural form, consolidates the link between fashion and art. In the same year, he held his *Ten Sen Men* commemorative exhibition at the Hiroshima City Museum of Contemporary Art (and was awarded the first-ever Hiroshima Art Prize). In 1990 he held the *Issey Miyake: Pleats, Please* exhibition at Touko Museum of Contemporary Art, Tokyo. This officially launched the range. This

Figure 1.8 Issey Miyake, man's pantsuit, spring/summer 2011. Photograph: Kristy Sparrow/Getty Images.

same year marked recognition of his outstanding achievement in the fashion industry when he was awarded an Honorary Doctorate from The Royal College of Art, London, was decorated as a Chevalier de l'Ordre National de la Légion d'Honneur by the French government, received The Medal with Purple Ribbon (*Shiju Hoshu*) for contributions to education and culture and was honoured as Person of Cultural Merit by the Japanese government.

Visiting museums had always been important to Miyake and it seemed a natural transition to move his clothes from the catwalk to both the museum and other urban spaces. While he has participated in numerous shows, there are three significant exhibitions worth mentioning: his 1996 *Il Tempo e la Mode*, held at the Venice Biennale, the leading international art exhibition, featured his clothing in city-wide art installations; his 1997 'Arizona' show in Japan (Genichiro-Inokuma Museum, Marugame), where garments were suspended on single wires to emphasize their sculptural abstraction, forcing the viewers to see the body in a different way; and *Addressing the Century—100 Years of Fashion & Art*, held in 1998 at the prestigious Hayward Gallery in London. By the time of this last exhibition, he had already handed the reins to his main designer, Naoki Takazawa, and he stepped quietly out of the spotlight to concentrate on other projects (Figure 1.8).

IDEAS FOR THE FUTURE

> There are no boundaries for what can be fabric, for what clothes can be made from. Anything can be clothing.
>
> Miyake (in Penn 1988)

Not only did Miyake transform the idea of fashion presentation into fashion installation in a gallery or museum, he turned a catwalk performance, with the emphasis on the clothing, into one where the performance becomes the process, as is the case with his *A-POC* range. Yet another new age process, still in its infancy, was developed in the late nineties to reuse old clothing to make new textiles. The 'Prism Collage Method' was first displayed at the *Making Things* exhibition at the Cartier Foundation, Paris in 1998 (mentioned earlier) and at the Ace Gallery in New York in 1999. Miyake devised a process by which old pieces of clothing—perhaps a hat, a sweater or blue jeans—are pressed or embedded into a white felt fabric by means of small needles. The needle holes, which are invisible, sandwich the fabrics together, making interesting patterns or stains across the surface, reminiscent of the post-painterly-Abstractionist paintings of the late 1960s period. Miyake sees this process as an idea for the future. While he argues that this is not recycling, it is a project which deals with reusing old clothes that people want to discard. This sustainable design concept was extended to a series called *Starburst* where, again, old clothes made of cotton, flannel, wool, felt or jersey are sandwiched between foil sheets of metallic paper made from silver, gold or bronze colours. They were heat-pressed and sealed between the thin membranes and when these items were worn, the pressure of the body caused the foil to crack and stretch, revealing parts of the old fabric underneath, streaked with bits of metallic foil. Also exhibited in the *Making Things* exhibition was another new technique of sewing garments together which included heat taping and cutting by ultrasound. Miyake reminds us, once again, that 'our society is poised to make dramatic changes based upon developments in science and technology. Will fashion be able to afford to keep the same old methodology?' (Miyake in Lee 2005: 59).

According to Quinn (2002: 150), the functionality of Miyake's designs reflects his philosophy that clothes should reflect the specific needs of a people and their culture and not just espouse the whims of the fashion elite. Quinn argues that this is why Miyake decided to show his clothes on women who were in their eighties in his autumn/winter 1995 *Octogenarian* collection. Such presentation seemed to communicate that his clothes were not only timeless but ageless as well. Perhaps this is another reason

Figure 1.9 Miyake's 21_21 Design Insight Gallery, Tokyo; architect: Tadao Ando. Photograph: Ben Byrne.

why many authors have described Miyake as the most optimistic and forward-looking designer of his generation. He does not see limitations, he sees instead challenges, followed by solutions, and dreams that become realities.

By 2000, Miyake had been awarded the Georg Jensen Prize by the Tuborg Foundation, Denmark, and was selected as one of 'the most influential Asians of the 20th century' in *Time* Magazine (23 August 1999, Asian issue). In 2007, Takizawa left the MDS to start up his own label and Dai Fujiwara was appointed the new creative director. In March of the same year, Miyake opened a Tokyo museum called 21_21 Design Insight (Figure 1.9), designed by Tadao Ando, which will be used as a design centre that goes beyond 20_20 vision to find ways of making clothing universal, connecting the world to new ideas of creativity. Duplicating the clothing design concept underlined in Miyake's *A Piece of Cloth* series, Ando devised a similar idea for the roof, using only one sheet of folded steel. In addition to the roof, the building incorporates Japan's world-leading technology, such as the longest sheet of double-glazed glass in Japan. The museum featured outstanding work by contemporary artists, designers and architects in their quest to redirect the viewers' eyes to everyday things and events, and expose them to the pleasures of design, often filled with surprises. The exhibitions provide the vision (sight) to search for, discover and make things indispensable to the times and to present design as culture that enlivens our daily lives. In this way, Miyake not only reinforces his lifelong philosophy but also endorses the work of the next generation of emerging design professionals.

Issey Miyake has made an indelible mark on the history of fashion through his remarkably positive view of the world. Having experienced and survived the Hiroshima atomic bomb blast in 1945, he wrote an article for *The New York Times* in 2009 endorsing US President Obama's pledge 'to seek peace and security in a world without nuclear weapons'.[13] For the first time, he spoke publically about the impact that the disaster has had on his personal life and it provides an insight into his philosophy towards design. In his own words, Miyake penned that he 'preferred to think of things that can be created, not destroyed, and that bring beauty and joy. I gravitated toward the field of clothing design, partly because it is a creative format that is modern and optimistic' (Miyake 2009).

–2–

Yohji Yamamoto

Figure 2.1 Yohji Yamamoto. Photograph: Chris Moore/
Catwalking/Getty Images.

> I happen to have been born in Japan. But I've never labelled myself in that way.
>
> Yamamoto

It seems impossible to discuss the early work of Yohji Yamamoto (Figure 2.1)[1] without referencing Rei Kawakubo, especially during their first decade of showing their collections. First in Tokyo in 1976 and then Paris in 1981, the designers seemed to share the same vision, the same heritage, the same ambitions and the same philosophy. In fact, it was difficult to tell their clothes apart.

Their work responded to the societal changes taking place in Japan in the post-war era. It is important to reiterate that, during and immediately after the Second World War, Japan suffered years of austerity and this impoverishment was imprinted on the minds of many. Interestingly, both Yamamoto and Kawakubo, who are now in their sixties, grew up in this period. After the war, especially among the young, an initial desire for the novel and the commercialized dominated. By the 1970s, this cultural attitude began to change and Japanese people started to respond to older, more familiar and perhaps even worn goods, as they made links with a more humanistic past.

THE JAPANESE TAKE PARIS BY STORM

Yamamoto and Kawakubo brought the beauty of poverty to the most glamorous stage of the world—the catwalks of Paris. In their 1981 joint collection, they paraded garments which symbolized neediness, destitution and hardship—clothing that appeared to have been picked up from rag-bags. They were entirely black in colour and irregular in shape, with oddly positioned pockets and fastenings. Their size appeared voluminous, as if the space between the external garment and the body had been exaggerated, emphasized by layering and wrapping. The clothing was characterized by torn, ripped and ragged fabric, uneven and unstitched hemlines; the designers had ruthlessly dissected the sartorial conventions of high fashion. Their clothes were heralded as not only anti-glamorous and anti-aesthetic, but asexual and anti-consumptive as well. While the designers asked the Western world to find elegance in their black shrouds, beauty in the unfinished, and strength in the enveloping folds of the fabric, the audience saw only garments that were distressed and in a state of disarray. A 'deconstruction' of style was the term later applied to these garments, a postmodernist term commonly used to describe the breaking down of elements, traditions and ideas in a fine art context. One might argue that the visual deprivation of the Japanese designers' garments could symbolize, in a more subtle and abstract way, their reaction to Japan's historical position in the post-war years. Within this context, the designers' early 1980s collection showings in Paris can be better understood.

Some argued that the scandalous garments of this 1981 joint collection were in keeping with the times as they responded to the global recession of the early eighties; however they were still dubbed a 'fashion revolution' by the international press. Yet others argued that they were criticized in political terms—not economic ones. Perhaps this explanation could explain the media reaction to these early collection showings,[2] when the derisory fashion headlines screamed 'Fashion's Pearl Harbour' and Kawakubo was described as a 'Rag Picker'. Dorinne Kondo suggests that an anti-Japanese sentiment still existed at this time and this was one of the main reasons that their work received such harsh treatment in the press. Yamamoto later explained, 'It's hard to appreciate that unless you were born in Tokyo in 1943 when the war had destroyed everything. I, and this applies to a whole generation of Japanese, have given up. I desire nothing, I want to be no one. Some people try and connect that to Buddhism, but that has nothing whatsoever to do with it' (Yamamoto 2002: n. pag.[3]). Yet, surprisingly, Yamamoto claims that he grew up free of anti-American feelings, even about the atomic bombings, and that instead he is of a generation that came of age harbouring ambivalent feelings about Japan (Foley 1997). Western fashion historian, Carnegy, sees this differently when he argues that 'the Japanese avant-garde designers produced clothes that appeared radical to Western eyes and could almost be seen as an homage to their country's past and a challenge to the increased western influence there' (1990: 20).[4]

Yamamoto and Kawakubo's models, dressed in black deconstructivist clothes, were described as looking 'cadaverous with either shaved heads or seemingly dirty unkempt hair', with pasty white faces that were 'devoid of make-up, apart from a disturbing bruised blue on their lower lips' (Mendes and de la Haye 1999: 234). Needless to say, the Parisian audience response was one of incredulity, with viewers stunned by the confrontational appearance of the models. For an elitist industry founded on visual sumptuosity, glamour and luxury, this avant-garde presentation of clothing was unexpected and threatening. Carla Sozzani, proprietor of 10 Corso Como in Milan, one of the most influential clothing stores in the world, remarked, 'For me it was an emotional shock when I first saw Yohji and Comme des Garçons . . . at that moment, everything was all Mugler and Montana, kind of big shoulders and a lot of makeup, but always incredibly feminine, always revealing a part of the body by leaving it uncovered—the shoulders, the back, the neck' (Trebay 2005). Fashion sociologist, Yuniya Kawamura (2004a: 128), had also commented that 'Although some of the responses to their first shows were mixed and critical, they were provocative enough to shake the French fashion world.' Yamamoto was amazed 'how journalists can excite and motivate designers through their criticisms and comments, but at the same time it was frightening' (Yuriko 1996: 591). They had learned their first lesson about the power of the fashion press, and had achieved their goal.

The onslaught continued in their successive shows. In Yamamoto's spring/summer 1983 collection,

Models marched down the great runway to the amplified thud of an electronic heartbeat, their faces blanked of colour by a film of whitened paint, their hair shorn or slicked back harshly. Not a smile broke those serried ranks who marched with grim, military precision . . . The clothes . . . there were armholes that bore no relation to the line of the shoulders, trousers that were neither trousers nor skirts but some new mutant jackets that seemed to be half finished with some major part completely missing. They defied convention as they defied the shape of the human body. (Brampton 1983)

When American *Vogue*, in April 1983, ran a feature article on Yamamoto and Kawakubo, acknowledging their impact as avant-garde designers, their reputation was established and their success was ensured. Harold Koda, fashion historian of the Metropolitan Museum of Art, referred to this new concept of dress, as seen in the work of Yamamoto and Kawakubo, as the 'aesthetics of poverty'—a phrase which seemed to aptly describe the new dress code. Historically, he compared the 1980s trend with the 1890s, a time which also 'saw decadence as an aesthetic ideal' (Martin and Coda 1993: 97).

In ideological terms, dress design has undoubtedly responded to social, political and economic instabilities throughout history: in the 1970s, 1980s and 1990s, global events such as high unemployment, youth revolutions, anti-war sentiment, global poverty and environmental catastrophes impacted greatly upon the conscience of society and became implicit to postmodernist visual arts practice. While cultural differences existed, both Punk fashion and the work of the Japanese designers, Yohji Yamamoto and Rei Kawakubo, reflected this practice. While Punk fashion in Britain is often compared to the Japanese 'glad rags', there is a distinct motivational factor that makes them quite different. Punk fashion must be discussed within the context of a generational protest, one which relied on provocation, visual obscenity and hard-core sexuality. For the Japanese, if the clothing symbolized a protest, it was realized in a more passive and discreet way, almost as a defeatist response to Japan's shackled political position in the post-war years.

However, the avant-garde designers themselves were adamant that they did not want to be categorized in this way and Yamamoto defiantly recalls that

> When I came to Paris, I remember the reaction to Comme des Garçons as so strong. Rei and I had to fight because she made a collection inspired by the Japanese kimono or something, and I hated it. Rei, I said, we are not souvenir designers. Japanese designers bringing Japanese ideas to Paris is not comfortable to me. I don't want to explain Japan to the world. (Yamamoto 2002: n. pag.)

Like Miyake, Yamamoto argued that 'I happen to have been born in Japan. But I've never labelled myself in that way' (in Baudot 1997: 13). Both designers shared the same qualities of the timelessness of Miyake's creations, the modesty and restraint of his mannequins, the same mystery and silence, the same quality of abstraction. There is an extraordinary tension that occurs in the East between the simple and the sophisticated, between natural materials and technological advance, between the empire of the senses and the tempered discretion of the feelings. These paradoxes are evident in Yamamoto's life and his work and he has made a significant contribution to transforming the appearance of men and women in the latter years of the century by expressing through his work their uncertainties, their fears and their contradictions.

NEW CANONS OF TASTE: ANTI-AESTHETICS

There is nothing so boring as a neat and tidy look.

Printed on the labels of Yamamoto's women's range in the 1980s.

For centuries, Western fashion has doggedly adhered to a structured and tailored fit, which extolled the virtues of sexuality, glamour and status—the mainstay of European haute couture design. Fashion historians have frequently used the well-worn phrase—'conspicuous consumption' (first coined by sociologist Veblen, in his text *The Theory of the Leisure Class*, written in 1899), as this term underlines the key motivational role that the display of wealth in dress has played throughout history. Visual sumptuosity reflected individuals' standing in society, their status in a hierarchal order and their position within a social class system. While Veblen questioned the need for this perceived pecuniary emulation, he argued that this material display of wealth reflected a 'status anxiety'. Arguably, this nineteenth-century notion of social class elitism gradually lost momentum as waves of middle class consumerism blurred the distinctions between the classes throughout the course of the twentieth century. As history has shown, this growing 'democratization' of fashion eventually led to a contradiction of modernist ideals and practices.

What had defined modernist haute couture fashion—the uniqueness of the design, fine finishing techniques, unblemished surfaces, exquisite tailoring and hand-sewing—gave way to the predominance of mass-produced 'prêt-à-porter' clothing. This new culture of dress actually appeared to mock the exclusivity of the earlier modernist fashions. Undoubtedly, the powerful clothes of Yamamoto and Kawakubo established the dominant aesthetic in the early 1980s. Fashion historian McDowell argued that the Japanese designers 'made few concessions to traditional western ideals of dress, chic or beauty' and their clothes were 'as much a statement of philosophy as they were of design' (McDowell 1987: 178). According to Koda (Martin and Koda 1993), a new form of anti-fashion had emerged.

By placing this 'revolution in fashion' within both an historical and postmodernist context, other interesting analogies can be drawn. One could argue that postmodernist fashion relies on visual paradox—underclothing becomes over-clothing, new is replaced by old, and propriety in dress is replaced by a total lack of respect for the display of status and value systems. In itself, this becomes an exercise of self-reflection—for the individual and society as a whole. What do we value in today's society? Arguably, highly priced slashed and torn garments symbolize an economic irrationality. Does this type of clothing become a form of social defiance, a parody about excessive commodification in contemporary society? Is this how it might have been perceived by Western eyes? Placed within a symbolic and philosophical concept, could the

Figure 2.2 Yohji Yamamoto, multi-fabric pantsuit with jacket, autumn/winter 2006–7. Photograph: Pierre Verdy/AFP/Getty Images.

actual deconstruction of fabric and finishing techniques also reflect the deconstruction of past values? Within this context, Koda's label, defining this new concept of dress as the 'aesthetics of poverty', seemed to aptly describe the new dress code (Figure 2.2).

It can be argued that this Japanese influence upon young international designers has been both direct and obtuse. Ms Akiko Fukai, curator of the Kyoto Costume Institute, which holds the largest fashion collection in Japan (10,000 garments), feels that the international trend, which began in the 1980s, for young women to wear 'long black street dresses', flat black boots, white ankle socks, no make-up and unevenly cut hair was a direct result of the impact of Yamamoto and Kawakubo. In fact, she argued that the introduction of this postmodernist version of 'the little black dress' was 'their most outstanding contribution to international design in the 80s' as it was adopted as a classic look by women around the world (English 1997c). In both direct and indirect ways, Yamamoto and Kawakubo encouraged typically 'anti-fashion' post-modernist trends in young designers by producing garments which defied all the codes of haute couture—no hems or finished edges to skirts or jackets except for the ragged edge of the scissor-cut, ill-fitting garments where seams wander as they please and, in Kawakubo's case, padded pouches inserted in the most unconventional places: between the bust and the shoulder, over the belly and on the shoulder blade at the back of the garment. Undoubtedly, these designers successfully deconstructed the image of the 1980s and 1990s woman, not only in stylistic terms but also in terms of challenging the glamorous image of the models that had dominated the catwalks for over eighty years. There were no compromises. At the same time, they produced a range of menswear that significantly changed directions in male attire. Like womenswear, menswear became unstructured. They challenged the look of the Western business suit, which had always been allied with commercial success and corporate image rather than an emphasis on the individual. They subverted all clothing conventions, both Japanese and European.

While the work of Yamamoto and Kawakubo was initially framed as yet *another* form of anti-aesthetic, their contribution to the evolution of twentieth-century fashion has been more profound. Their understated work underlines the notion that culture, conceptualization and experimentation can be integral to fashion, as it is to art. Exploring the history of clothing in all its most ascetic variations, the 'Y'—Yamamoto—style celebrates and, at the same time, incessantly questions the ambiguous marriage between the enduring and the ephemeral. His work bridges the gap between 'classic' and 'contemporary' forms, imbued with a wealth of historical references that secretly perpetuate themselves in new guises. Faced with the irreversible decline of the traditional values of elegance, Yamamoto transposes them to an aesthetic and technological milieu that is resolutely contemporary.

Significantly, *A New Wave in Fashion: Three Japanese Designers* became the cornerstone exhibition of the work of Yohji Yamamoto, Rei Kawakubo and Issey Miyake, held at the Arizona Costume Institute, Phoenix Art Museum in 1983 and curated by Jean C. Hildreth. It became the inspiration for many of the later exhibitions and 'situated Yamamoto as a Japanese designer in a narrative of revolutionary, atypical dress' along with Paul Poiret's hobble skirt (1911) and Christian Dior's New Look (1947) (Hildreth 1983: 40). According to Alexis Romano (2008), it also established the designers' reputation as belonging to the 'avant-garde' and as being quite separate from 'Western' fashion. Later American exhibitions held at the Cincinnati Art Museum in 2007 and the Textile Museum in Washington DC in 2009 sustained a similar discourse, allying these designers to radical Japanese design.

Collectively, these exhibitions underlined the notion that, as postmodernist fashion designers, they proposed radical clothing concepts, which challenged the conventional meaning of dress. Their work clearly indicated that the Western concept of structured and tailored garments, which emphasized the sexual nature of dress, was being questioned. They placed greater emphasis on the sculptural interrogation of form, the nature and tactility of fabric and the interactive space between the body and the cloth;

Figure 2.3 Yohji Yamamoto, long, black, hooded coat with red shoes, March 2009. Photograph: Chris Moore/Catwalking/Getty Images.

all traits which were very much in keeping with the traditional Japanese garment, the kimono. The garments were loose fitting, and untailored to reduce or eliminate any element of sexuality. By obliterating the traditions of haute couture, they also negated the notion of glamour, usually associated with decoration and detail, and thereby diminished the element of status, usually visibly evident by a display of wealth. By the end of the century, in terms of styling, presentation and concept, these designers had helped to change the face of fashion irrevocably (Figure 2.3).

THE COLOUR BLACK

Black is modest and arrogant at the same time.

Yamamoto (in Menkes 2000a)

The colour black completely dominated the early collections of both Yamamoto and Kawakubo. For them, it assumed the status of a non-colour—an absence rather than a presence. In the Western world, black has always played a dominant role both in formal and designer wear. In *Black in Fashion*, Mendes describes how Balenciaga 'found black the perfect vehicle for his unsurpassed work that straddled the boundary between fashion and the fine arts' and states that his garments 'resembled powerful abstract sculptures' (1999: 12). In October 1938, *Harper's Bazaar* described Balenciaga's work as 'Here the black is so black that it hits you like a blow' (Mendes 1999: 12). For the West, black has signified dignity and pathos, but for the Japanese it symbolized secrecy, stealth and cunning—a colour that became invisible in the dark. Yamamoto explained that

> it wasn't exactly black but an indigo blue dyed so many times that it is close to black. The samurai must be able to throw his body into nothingness, the colour and image of which is black. But the farmers like black or dark indigo, because the indigo plant was easy to grow, and the dye was good for the body and kept insects away. (Yamamoto in Koren 1984)

Black became the colour of streetwear as well as eveningwear from the early 1980s onwards, as it was seen as a new direction in fashion that was cerebral and sophisticated, and was described as attracting a clientele made up of serious, intellectual individuals. In 1981 to 82 black became the bestseller and Deyan Sudjic wrote in *The Sunday Times* (20 April 1986) that Kawakubo's clothes 'were behind a wave of monochrome minimalism that has turned every fashionable gathering in London, NY, Paris and Tokyo into a solid all-black wall'.

Interestingly, in the 1980s in particular, but noticeably throughout his entire designing career, the majority of Yamamoto's clothes were black—as he held that bright colours quickly bored him. He also contended that black was 'an intelligent contemporary colour'. He was dubbed the 'Poet of Black' by Suzy Menkes (2000a), who underlined that

> Yohji Yamamoto has built a career on proving that black—aggressive, rebellious, sombre, romantic or seductive—is beautiful. He, more than most designers, is the poet of black, the director of fashion's film noir.

Adopted as his signature colour since he graduated from the Bunka Fashion College in 1969, Yamamoto explained,

> Black is modest and arrogant at the same time. Black is lazy and easy—but mysterious. It means that many things go together, yet it takes different aspects in many fabrics. You need black to have a silhouette. It can swallow light, or make things look sharp. But above all black says . . . don't bother me! (in Menkes 2000a).

Yamamoto's range of black street dresses, which became a uniform for young women, would sometimes be juxtaposed with a red accent—a 'wink' of colour which would make the black look 'blacker than black'. His work has always appealed to earnest intellectuals—its sensuality, its rituals, its tongue-in-cheek whimsicality. It also became a type of default uniform for the art crowd, including the more conservative architects, an extension of the bohemian 1950s look. Yamamoto is often quoted as saying 'people wear my clothes to make a statement' and that there was a kind of 'democracy' about black clothing. Like Miyake, he aims for enduring fashion rather than fashion novelty.

Yamamoto has been described as a designer who is driven by an existentialist philosophy and whose work elicits an intellectualism that ties form with meaning and memory, and perhaps this is one of the reasons he chose to show his collections at the Sorbonne University. In his autobiography *Talking to Myself* (Yamamoto 2002: n. pag.), he asserts that 'dirty, stained, withered, broken things seem beautiful to me'. The Japanese term *hifu* refers to a form of anti-style, and is seen as an undeniable element of Yamamoto's dressmaking. According to Yamamoto, one can actually *feel* such *hifu* clothing—its confusion, shabbiness and disarray—as if it reflects a meagreness of spirit or sadness in the people wearing the clothes. In other words, the disarray of the fabric mimics the emotional fragility of the wearer. This merging of the emotional, intellectual and aesthetic encouraged many viewers to see his collection showings as a form of subdued performance art. Yamamoto is the master of distressed cloth—his work was a protest against elitism, an example of tortured intellectualism and ragbag thinking. It marked the perfect fusion of populist culture and radical design. Black was glamorous, sobriety was success, minimalism was an acclamation, 'I believe my clothes are non denominational, without nationality. They don't belong to any country, any religion or any culture. They are outsiders' (Yamamoto 2002: n. pag.).

A sense of darkness permeated Yamamoto's work throughout his designing career—whether through the use of the colour black, or simply through a sense of heaviness in his choice of materials, or in the way his clothing cocooned the figure, serving as a kind of psychological protection (Figure 2.4). This joyless, sombre appearance was exaggerated by fabric gathered in folds and layered over skirts or by featuring models with their heads covered, like widows, in shrouds. This wistfulness is echoed in his words, 'I have always said that men never hold a woman in their arms but only a woman of their imagination. Is love reality or image . . . or is it image and reality?' (Yamamoto 2002: n. pag.). His October 2003 show featured side-gathered rayon skirts with cotton patches of shirting stripes, and oversized shirts, one with the dramatic message 'Don't touch me'. Miyanaga explains,

> Among the older generation, Jean-Paul Sartre had been extremely popular [in the 1950s and 1960s]. A series of his works translated from the French was prominently displayed in every bookstore. His philosophy suggested to those Japanese who felt lost between tradition and westernization that continuity between the past and the future is an act of social creation,

Figure 2.4 Yohji Yamamoto, long, full-skirted, black garment with train and triangular shapes defining the back view, spring/summer 2006. Photograph: Pierre Verdy/AFP/Getty Images.

brought about by human efforts. Many intellectuals attempted to create a synthesis between the past and the future, based on interpretations of Sartre's thought. By the 1980s, however, the youth no longer recognised such a gap between tradition and Westernisation. They were not concerned with origins. Sartrean existential themes held no appeal; fashion thrived, capturing the synthesis between tradition and westernization in fragmented visual messages. (Miyanaga 1991: 10)

The sartorial colour black has a very long history. In Western society it was designated for formal evening wear from the early 1800s, during the fashion and artistic era known as the Biedermeier period (c.1820–40), and became popular in the 1920s as suitable after-5 wear with the introduction of Chanel's little black dresses. By the 1950s, it became associated with rebellion and the artistic, intellectual fringe but from the 1980s onwards, as a result of the influence of the Japanese designers, the colour black has moved into the realm of the everyday. Yamamoto, more so than any other designer, has realigned the role that black has played in society over the past thirty years.

MEMORY AND MEANING IN DRESS: THE AESTHETICS OF POVERTY

I like old clothes, clothes are like old friends.

Yamamoto (in Chenoune 1993)

Upon reflection, Yamamoto recalls that, in the 1980s, his 'impoverished' aesthetic was greatly inspired by the work of the German photographer, August Sander. Renowned for his ability to reveal the dignity of the poor, Sander photographed subjects from all walks of life and created a typological catalogue of more than six hundred photographs of German people. Sander's photographs of anonymous figures date from the inter-war years, and many were taken as he rode his bicycle through the countryside. Yamamoto drew inspiration from the images of farm workers ploughing the dusty fields in their faded and tattered work clothes and railway workers in their boilersuits, dungarees and overalls. They exuded an honourable solemnity that Yamamoto tried to emulate in his own collections. Yamamoto believes that their clothes sharply reflect their lives and that a garment becomes one with the person who wears it, and becomes so much a part of him that it is entirely subordinated to the force of his personality. He explains his views in Wim Wenders' 1989 film *Carnet de notes sur vêtements et villes* ('Notebook on Cities and Clothes'), 'Twenty years ago, when I was young, I used to wish I could draw time. I liked used clothes, things that are old and worn.' He describes his work as being 'contradictory' to the commercialism of Western fashion. He creates clothing that has a universal appeal, a timeless quality—clothes that are meant to last a lifetime. He compares an old coat that was needed for warmth (Figure 2.5) to an old friend or a member of the family, both indispensable:

> I like old clothes . . . clothes are like old friends . . . What makes a coat truly beautiful is that you're so cold you can't live without it. It's like a friend or member of the family. And I'm terribly envious of that. (In Chenoune 1993: 293, 305).

Some have proffered that his clothing possesses a medieval severity, a second-hand look, lived-in, as though it had acquired a patina over the passage of time, like those items in our wardrobe that have become special favourites. Yet others adamantly argue that his clothing simply reflects a disdain for that which is new.

In the visual arts, photography and found objects were used by artists trying to capture a similar moment in time, a trace of both the presence and the absence of human existence. 'Photographs are seen both as facts and as ghosts or shadows. They are the imperfect means by which we fill the voids of memory in the modern culture' (Lippard 1997: 56). Photographs can be used to reference the fragile and ephemeral

Figure 2.5 Yohji Yamamoto, man's knitted brown/grey sweater with grey trousers and coat, January 2009, Paris Fashion Week menswear. Photograph: Karl Prouse/ Catwalking/Getty Images.

nature of both life and memory. The artist Christian Boltanski has spent most of his life working with ethereal materials—photographs, light bulbs and candles—to examine and evoke memory, loss and death. Boltanski used actual lost property from railway stations to memorialize the unknown owners. These personal effects relate to the memories that have been buried. They are meant to remind us of the experience of remembering. Like Yamamoto, Boltanski is challenging the basic assumptions of what constitutes an artwork—using old clothing or seemingly mundane elements to address some of the most fundamental and disturbing contradictions of twentieth-century life.

Similarly, the 1960s Italian art movement, *Arte Povera*, attempted to engage with everyday life. Assemblages made from basic elements such as wood shavings, rags, mud or coal by Jannis Kolunellis, Mario Merz and Guilio Paolini, among others, made manifest their refusal to be seduced by superficially shiny, smooth and attractive surfaces in favour of humble substances. Using clothing as a means to evoke an emotive response in their work and to link art with the everyday became an integral part of the work of many post-feminist artists. Annette Messager placed worn-out dresses under glass in wooden display boxes and hung them on the wall like paintings. Her *Histoire des robes* ('History of Dresses') series of 1990 is an affirmation of the feminine and dramatically evokes a sense of melancholia and lost identity. Her potent work, like that of Yamamoto, is at once intimate and universal, using familiar objects in a manner that challenges us to look at our world with fresh eyes. François Baudot, a French fashion journalist, was the first to draw attention to this process in Yamamoto's work in his 1997 book on the designer.

Yet Yamamoto has his own views on the relationship of fashion to art:

> To create something good, an artist has to take the plunge; he's testing the outer limits beyond which everything falls apart. Art is always a shock because it is pushing up against the acceptable. That's the relationship between artists and ethics. But in my line of work, there is another factor to be considered: clothes are bought and worn by people everyday, so they can't really be considered as works of art. (Huckbody 2002)

When Donna Karan presented Yamamoto with the 'Night of the Stars' Award from the Fashion Group New York in 1998, she announced to the world that she was a designer, but he was an artist. Yamamoto replied,

> She says so, and it's a compliment but I'm thinking I'm a designer, a fashion designer. I'm not putting special meaning on artist. There is no difference between designer and artist. Maybe I can say designer is the new genre of artist, because sometimes, for me the vocabulary of so-called art sounds odd. (Huckbody 2002)

Despite this, museum curators continued to present Yamamoto's work as 'high art', overlooking their garment function. The formal qualities of his work have been highlighted instead, treating them as abstract works of sculpture. Evident in both of the exhibitions, *Form Follows Function* (Fashion Institute of Technology, NYC, 2003) and *Stylised Sculpture: Contemporary Japanese Fashion from the Kyoto Costume Institute* (Asian Art Museum, San Francisco), the garments were portrayed within 'the artist as genius' context. Similarly, Yamamoto was portrayed as the heroic artist in Wim Wenders' 1989 documentary *Notebook on Cities and Clothes.* In the 2006 Museum of Contemporary Art in Los Angeles exhibition entitled *Skin & Bones: Parallel Practices in Fashion & Architecture*, curator Brooke Hodge compared the work of architects, including Zaha Hadid and Frank Gehry, to the concepts of space and the human body inherent in the work of fashion designers. For this purpose, she used Yamamoto's autumn/winter 2006 cage corset in his black silk crêpe ensemble as a form of construction, mimicking a human ribcage, but made from horizontal strips of fabric.

Undoubtedly, Yohji Yamamoto imbued his clothing with a sense of humanity never seen before on the catwalks of Paris. But it was an Eastern, not a Western sense of humanity. Buddhist philosophy, for example, equates symmetry in design as a symbol of perfection, a state which is not recognized as being human. In much the same way as the tea ceremony celebrates the imperfect, the irregular and the asymmetrical, so does Yamamoto's clothing. To Western eyes, he 'disrupted the codes by which clothes made their appeal; by redefining the glamorous signals sent out by their external appearance; by redefining their relationship with the male or female body; and, ultimately, radically reinterpreting the respective contributions of beauty and ugliness, past and future, memory and modernity' (*i-D* 1999).

MENSWEAR AND A DUALITY OF IDENTITY

I think that my men's clothing looks as good on women as my women's clothing.

Yamamoto

Along with the Italian designer Armani, both Yamamoto and Kawakubo were attributed with making a significant contribution to the international 'new look' in menswear in the late 1980s. In 1984, Armani produced men's suits that were fluid and disciplined masterpieces of understatement—white shirts, jackets with narrow lapels, narrow shoulders, three buttons and trousers that were tight to the knee and resting on a well-polished black shoe.

Yamamoto and Kawakubo went one step further. Quite literally, they deconstructed the traditional Western business suit. They started with the elimination of the padded shoulders, which had been seen as the litmus test of the male physique. By changing proportions and volumes, their aim was to make suits and jackets lighter and more comfortable. They not only removed linings and shoulder padding, but rounded the shoulders, created larger armholes, lowered the buttons and lengthened the lapels. Their asymmetrical cut created a 'visual imbalance', with sleeves lengthened and trousers shortened, lopsided collars and hems and seams in contrasting colours running rampant over the garment. Garments had strange flaps and misplaced pockets, giving the appearance of being ill-fitted second-hand clothes. These 'redefined' male clothing forms were first revealed in his autumn/winter 1985–6 collection, featuring 'unstructured' men's clothes with baggy, pleated trousers—a draped look—that approximated Turkish harem pants. Loosely-fitting suit jackets had lost their tapered waists and their architectural shapes as, when linings and padding were removed and the sleeves were mounted in a different way, the male silhouette changed dramatically. The new-age suits featured distinctive deconstructivist characteristics: shirt collars were permanently creased and stitching revealed in contrasting colours, giving the appearance of a partly-finished garment.

From 1987 onwards, different textiles were used, such as soft, elastic fabrics made of viscose and crêpe yarns which softened the 'boxy' fullness that characterized the earlier unstructured garments. According to Chenoune (1993: 316), the early collections started with 'fancy white shirt collars sometimes trimmed with lacy guipure, then sharpened the profile in a refined but puritanical way, drawing out fitted, sombre lines to create a frock coat effect complemented by short, ankle-length pants'. While these redefined forms heralded the direction towards comfort and simplicity, perhaps more importantly, Yamamoto saw this unique aesthetic as a reflection of a new 'ideal of clothing'. He said, 'People don't "consume" these garments, they might spend their entire lives in them . . . that's what life is about. Real clothes, not fashion' (Chenoune 1993: 305). In the early 1990s, Yamamoto suggested that, while he was still working in fashion, men's clothing probably would not change fundamentally in that it would remain based on tailored jackets and 'pants shirts'. Only in the future, after his time, did he think that men might start wearing a one-piece, dress or skirt.

Yamamoto, always heralded as a master tailor throughout his career, continued to create a softer, more draped appearance in his men's clothing (Figure 2.6) and is responsible for popularizing the art world's savvy combination of a black suit worn over a white T-shirt. His basic forms are classical and 'his double-breasted suits are asymmetrically cut out. The cut in the back is not centred, one coat tail is longer than the other. In this way he displaces his clothing through slight divergences' (Vinken 2005: 109). According to one of his promotional staff, Laurence Delamare (English 2005a), his work consistently relies on humour, often mocking the fashion system through exaggeration of form, and on his unwavering philosophy towards designing, which celebrates the aesthetics of poverty. He uses washed, unpressed fabrics in dark colours. He often juxtaposes red pieces with the black, according to Yamamoto as it serves as a 'shout' and creates a high contrast and vibrancy.

Throughout his career, he has consistently referenced traces of the colour red in both his menswear and womenswear collections. Whether it appears as a sash or an under-hem, it serves the purpose of 'lifting the spirit' of the garment and creating a visual centre of interest.

Over the past four decades, men's jackets and trousers have ranged from being tight, with sleeves and trouser legs seemingly too short for the wearer, to unstructured, layered and baggy working clothes. In recent collections, despite Yamamoto's earlier comments, draped skirts have replaced trousers altogether. In his 2002 menswear collection, Yamamoto introduced long skirts into the business sphere and frayed threads pulled in the trouser legs. Undoubtedly, the last battalion of corporate male dress had been destroyed. His hybrid clothing cannot to be viewed as either Eastern or Western but as a duality of identities.

Even as early as 1983, Yamamoto commented on the arbitrariness of men's and women's clothing. This androgynous gender imagery has puzzled many Western observers:

Figure 2.6 Yohji Yamamoto, bird-and-feather embroidered, skirted trousers with laced-up legs, spring/summer 2008 menswear. Photograph: Pierre Verdy/AFP/Getty Images.

I think that my men's clothing looks as good on women as my women's clothing . . . and more and more women are buying men's clothes. It's happening everywhere, and not just my clothing . . . when I started designing, I wanted to make men's clothes for women. But there were no buyers for it. Now there are. I always wonder who decided that there should be a difference in the clothes of men and women. Perhaps men have decided this. (In Duka 1983: 63)

His work comments on the paradoxical nature of the struggles between the masculine versus the feminine sides of women. To add to this gender duality is the inherent contradiction that he is able to create garments for women that are so chaste or monastic, as they do not reveal any part of the underlying body, yet, at the same time, are provocatively erotic. Yamamoto (2002 n. pag.) recounts that he was inspired by old French war movies starring actresses in army uniforms. 'I found that so sexy. The body is protected. And covered. In a very hard way. And so you are forced to ask yourself "what's inside?" When you have no freedom, your sexuality becomes stronger.' Again, this subtlety of observation and the implicit nuances regarding sexuality go against the Western notion, expressed by the designer, that 'Dolls . . . this is what many men want women to be . . . just dolls.'

This duality of vision, inherent in Yamamoto's work, extends to both his choice of fabric and the construction methods used. Like both Miyake and Kawakubo, Yamamoto starts with the fabric, the actual fabric, the 'feel' of it. He then moves on to the form. The construction of all of Yamamoto's garments, whether male or female, starts from the two points just above the shoulder blades. From there the cloth hangs best, allowing the material to take on a life of its own. During the first ten years in Paris, both Yamamoto and Kawakubo refused to design for haute couture collection showings. Instead, they wanted to show that, with fine fabric and construction techniques, any prêt-à-porter garment could equal the expertise of the haute couture ranges and this, in turn, would negate the differentiation of status. This emphasis on democratic fashion underpins Yamamoto's entire philosophy of design.

Historically, ceremonial wear had been discrete from everyday wear; in everyday wear there were no distinct differences before 1820. Yamamoto (2002: n. pag.) suggests that he is turning back time by democratizing the nature of the garment, not conceiving it as either dress-up or casual wear:

From the beginning I have been wanting to prove that simple cotton pants and gorgeous silk evening gowns, as a currency, are the same . . . there is no difference in class. My ideal garment is something like a rag. I mean clothing cannot make people beautiful or charming . . .

After his initial interplay with black, he then opted, at least momentarily, for stark white and proceeded to create smooth, minimalist, futuristic white garments. Their moulded quality, and beautifully curved shapes, achieved by his superb tailoring, hinted at

Courrèges and Cardin's clothing of the 1960s. According to Yamamoto, white was the most contemporary colour of them all.

Yamamoto is renowned for presenting the viewer with different layers of contradictory meaning. While he is in the business of selling highly priced fashion garments, recurring themes, alluded to in his collection showings since 2000, reflect his concerns that young women are being seduced too much by very heavy-handed merchandising and marketing strategies. In his October collection showing of that year he featured flowing pantsuits which were worn with halter tops that look like giant change purses. They blatantly commented on the ways women define themselves by what they acquire.

HAUTE COUTURE REVISITED

You want haute couture? Here it is! It's not hard.

Yamamoto (in Irving 2001)

Tradition plays an important part in Yamamoto's work, ranging from the structured planes of the traditional kimono to his loyalty to fabric. He has a craftsman's sense of materials, starting every collection with the fabric and then letting the collection take its shape. Like Vionnet, he is renowned for his ability to twist, piece and drape fabric; to create garments that appear to be folded like paper origami shapes; and for his innovative use of technological textiles. His inventiveness extends to his use of unconventional materials: his paper cut-out dresses of spring/summer 1983, made in white cotton and resembling geometric squares; his wool felt dresses, reminiscent of the refinement of Balenciaga's shaped garments which, in themselves, evoked the appeal of the kimono with its sculptural back; and his vest and skirt ensemble made of hinged wood slats for his autumn/winter collection of 1991 (Plate 17), and used again in 1992 for a man's suit—a conceptual extension of Paco Rabaswnne's experimentation with his plastic link dresses of the 1960s. According to Vinken (2005: 116–7), the man's suit is a metaphor for armour and the mail shirt was made meticulously from more than twenty pieces of wood, very much in keeping with couturier practices:

> On both sides of the trousers, plywood pieces are attached by massive screws, marking the position of the ankle: these correspond to the calf and the thigh, and recall the ballet drawings of Oskar Schlemmer. The pure light wood which, in its fully unprocessed state, is more delicate than silk, invokes the atelier; the project-character of the piece.

On the other hand, Yamamoto explained that 'he wanted to make a-once-in-a-lifetime garment that derived a natural, accidental beauty from being worn and exposed to the sun and rain' (Fukai 1995: 146). It is based on the deconstructivist concept of tearing apart a garment, the antithesis of the deliberate construction methodologies of Paris couture.

Yamamoto praises fashion's greatest individuals—Azzedine Alaia, Jean Paul Gaultier, Martin Margiela and Rei Kawakubo. In terms of haute couture designers, he has great respect for Yves St Laurent as he recognizes the revolution he made when he was young. He lauds Galliano's eccentricity and says that KL (Karl Lagerfeld) 'is like a king'.[5] Professor Wendy Dagworthy of the Royal College of Art believes that there has been as strong a Japanese attraction to the West as there has been a Western attraction to the insider-cool of the Japanese: 'They have a clear love of western fashion and culture. One of my favourite Yamamoto collections was in the 80s and shown as an homage to 60s Cardin; very molded with lots of holes cut out of it—the shapes were very beautiful' (in O'Flaherty 2009).

Yamamoto, in true postmodernist form, referenced both Western and Eastern histories in his borrowings. The early 1990s was a time of ambivalence in terms of his designing career, and Yamamoto had fallen somewhat from his position of the avant-garde leader as he was being overtaken by Martin Margiela, the Belgian deconstructivist designer. According to Fukai, Yamamoto has referenced more European design than any other Japanese designer. His most famous silhouettes around this period mirrored the late Victorian bustle (1986–7) (see Plate 4 for a later version) and the draped 1910 Edwardian dresses (1993–4), periods which were renowned for their interest in Eastern apparel. In 1995, his Kimono collection revisited his own cultural heritage and, at the same time, paid homage to European designers of the 1950s and 1960s. His kimono-inspired trench coats and shirts were influenced by pure geometric forms. He used the *shibori* technique to create crunched circles of colour. For a long time he didn't want to 'do' Japanese as he saw it as a form of creating 'souvenirs', but he decided to face his fears and break his taboos. In 1997, he returned to prominence with a collection inspired by 1950s Parisian haute couture including Chanel-type suits and Dior-inspired coats. Between 1997 and 2001 he was playing with the idea of haute couture. 'You want haute couture? Here it is! It's not hard' (Irvine 2001). Here he was reinstating his romance with the glamour of Chanel, Dior and iconic Penn imagery—references that symbolized the very things that he stood against when he first arrived in Paris. Some journalists suggested that it might be a cheeky one-finger salute to the ongoing games of musical *maisons de couture*. Others had varying views. Designer Azzedine Alaia (*Women's Wear Daily* 1996) commented,

> This was haute couture, done for today, and it was stunningly beautiful. Yamamoto showed some of the best clothes imaginable in a collection that had it all: depth, imagination, craftsmanship. Everything, from the cut of the jackets, to the depth of a cuff, to the play of bold, sculptural silver jewellery against black, was delivered with a level of artistry that isn't often seen. And Yamamoto even laced it with a sense of humour.

Later in the year, his *Homage to Dior* (winter 1997) show consisted of deliberately badly-fitted garments with uneven hems, see-through skirts and scissor-cut edges (Figure 2.7). This 'tongue-in-cheek' collection paid a deconstructed homage to Dior at a time in which the House of Dior was looking for a new head designer. As Dior's garments were renowned for their technical expertise and fine finishing details, Yamamoto critiqued his famous methodologies. He deconstructed and recreated Dior's 1947 'New Look' by creating hourglass silhouettes with defined waists and tailored fittings. Instead of seeing this collection as an insult to the memory of the famous designer, the Paris audiences heroically gave Yamamoto a standing ovation. This event attracted great media coverage around the world. In retrospect, designers like Hussein Chalayan have remarked that they believed that the Japanese, at times, caricatured the West. Despite this interpretation, Yamamoto's 2003 collection did mark a tribute to Yves St Laurent and honoured the inventiveness of the French designer.

Like so many of the leading contemporary European designers who underpin their collection showings with theatricality, novelty and panache, Yohji also held bravura shows. Full polka-dot skirts begin to swirl, accompanied by the whirl of hidden mechanisms. Black garments, lightly laced up the back like loosened corsets, were accessorised with hot pink gloves, dark glasses and tennis shoes, a kind of Audrey Hepburn remix. At the Sorbonne, he unfurled a parachute which became a dress; he presented his sportswear collection in a vast arena, as models almost froze to death backstage in a street vendors market where coats were the centrepiece of the show. Yamamoto became fascinated with crinolines and the spatial volume that they created. One of the most elaborate was modelled by Jodie Kidd, in his autumn/winter 1998 collection,

Figure 2.7 Yohji Yamamoto, *Homage to Dior* mannequin group display in Isetan department store, Tokyo, January 1997. Photograph: author.

in which the dress was monstrous in size—12 metres in circumference—and the hat was just as large. Four attendants with poles were needed to support the infrastructure. Yamamoto intended this to be a satirical statement about the excessiveness of contemporary fashion. In spring/summer 1999, his bridal or wedding dress show (*Le Mariage*) was staged as a striptease at the Moulin Rouge in Paris. A Victorian crinolined wedding dress in mother-of-pearl silk, described by numerous fashion journalists as being overblown, complete with zip pockets, a battered picture and even a calico fabric bouquet in pride of place, was discarded by the model to reveal a slim-line dress and trousers underneath. *The Herald Sun* (1998) reported that the androgynous bride and groom figures further blurred the sexual divide by exchanging not vows but outer garments on the runway, and offered this opinion:

> Of course this elaborate game of dressing and undressing was a gimmick . . . but it emphasised the play of volume and shape which lay at the very heart of this exceptional collection . . . it conveyed a sense of utter joy . . . his idiosyncratic definition of beauty is captivating.

The collection received a standing ovation from the audience. It was this show that made Yamamoto reconsider the direction in which his work was heading. 'The wedding dress show was painful,' he said. 'I said to myself: you have become an entertainer. You have to come back to ready-to-wear. I felt very unsure after that. As a show, it looked successful, but for business it was hard' (in Menkes 2002b). Ironically, the show was dubbed 'the designer's greatest collection in 20 years' by Susannah Frankel of the *Independent* Magazine (2006), the consensus of many who attended, and was exhibited in London at the Victoria and Albert Museum's key exhibition, *Radical Fashion* in 2001, and at *Breaking the Mode: Contemporary Fashion from the Permanent Collection* at the LA County Museum in 2006.

NEW DIRECTIONS: SPORTSWEAR

> The sports shoe in particular is a perfect match—the very idea of high heels with Japanese fashion is ridiculous.
>
> Claire Wilcox (in O'Flaherty 2009)

An interest in sportswear has dominated Yamamoto's thinking since 2001—clothes that are comfortable and free. He incorporates contemporary sportswear constructions and finishing details to evoke a postmodernist chic, coupled with functions of protection and durability. Collaboration with Adidas—the athletic shoe giant—resulted when Yamamoto noticed that young kids all over the world were wearing 'ugly technological' sneakers. He became fascinated with the Adidas shoes, researched their archives and began by redesigning their uppers and letting his imagination run free. He produced thigh-high women's boots with a Velcro catch, men's velvet wing-tips and a canvas motocross boot in red, navy or military. In Yamamoto's version of the Adidas emblem, the three parallel stripes either protrude slightly from the top surface or run down to the side of the shoe. His hybrid models are more conservative—comfortable and hip. The first production run consisted of 100,000 pairs and they sold out completely. Other products included high-heeled sneaker pumps, sweatshirt tuxedo jackets and windbreaker suits. His *Y-3* collections (Figure 2.8) appeal not just to his contemporaries but to the young as well, with ideas that have more popular appeal. Yamamoto had become a sports brand—one that represents authenticity, resistance to orthodoxy and enigmatic cool. Yamamoto's signature on Adidas sportswear has become much more valuable than that of a sports star (Irving 2001). At first, the combination of sportswear and high street fashion seemed an unlikely 'fit', but considering that different generations of consumers are looking for different products, 'it

Figure 2.8 Yohji Yamamoto, *Y-3* sports windcheater with three white stripes, *Y-3* and Adidas collection, Olympus Fashion Week, NY, February 2006. Photograph: Jennifer S. Altman/Bloomberg/Getty Images.

makes perfect sense. The sports shoe in particular is a perfect match—the very idea of high heels with Japanese fashion is ridiculous' (Wilcox in O'Flaherty 2009).

Yamamoto has introduced a new generation to his austere notions of clothes in relation to body and lifestyle. His *Y-3* flagship store opened in Roppongi Hills, Tokyo in 2003, and the first freestanding monobrand *Y-3* store opened in Miami in 2007, the same year that *Y-3* participated in the international contemporary art exhibition, *Art Basel*. A monobrand *Y-3* store opened in New York in February 2008. For the spring/summer collection that year, he staged a surprise catwalk show in New York to highlight his colourful line of windbreakers, cropped pants and buttoned-up dresses. It was held beneath disused railway tracks beside West Side gallery streets where *Y-3* producer, Etienne Russo, organized a thirty-minute simulated cloudburst, complete with thunder and the sound of heavy rain on rooftops. He is also collaborating with Dr. Martens, Mandarina Duck and on a new Stormy Weather pearl line with luxury jewellery brand Mikimoto. In September 2009, *Y-3* brought out elegant, high-shine sneakers in vivid colours and used mesh in both mens and womenswear. Items included see-through shirts, scarves and tube dresses made from laser-cut netting, high-concept trainers and very low-slung harem pants, and Yamamoto also featured the colours of the teams due to play in the soccer World Cup in South Africa in 2010.

IN RETROSPECT: *TALKING TO MYSELF*

A retrospective, to me, is just proof of all your mistakes.

Yamamoto (in Trebay 2005)

Yamamoto marked his twentieth anniversary in business by publishing his fashion memoirs, entitled *Talking to Myself* (2002), in which the book binding exposes the stitching of the spine and threads of the binding are tangled in an untidy array. The book itself will undoubtedly become a collector's item as it was produced in a limited print run and the binding has been constructed to deconstruct along the unbound spine. Provocatively, pieces of string and frayed edges create a textural surface not unlike a number of his men's suits. According to Menkes (2002b), the purpose of the book is to explain to the Japanese, whom he feels still regard fashion as 'lower class art or expression' what fashion is and his philosophy (towards it).

After twenty years of journalistic articles by fashion editors, magazine and newspaper journalists and critics—some who got it right, while others got it wrong—Yamamoto decided, with this book, to leave behind his own take on his thoughts, his work, his life and his legacy. In textual terms it is brutally honest; in visual terms, it provides an insight into how different fashion photographers define and interpret his garments. Paolo Reversi uses a monochromatic cinematic approach to show Yohji working in his atelier, contrasted with David Sims' edgy photos of model Stella Tennant, Sarah Moon's soft, atmospheric shots and Nick Knight's colour-saturated commercial images from the mid-1980s. Yamamoto had worked with the photographer Nick Knight, stylist Marc Ascoli and graphic artist Peter Saville to produce biannual catalogues documenting his work over a two-year period. Of particular note were Knight's images of black garments (autumn/winter 1986) embellished with red tulle manipulated to mimic a nineteenth-century bustle-back crinoline. The graphic nature of the silhouette of a model wearing a long, linear black dress, standing vertically with the peaked cap on her bowed head, looking downwards, was visually stunning. Coupled with the explosive bustle at the back, emphasizing form and texture, this image has become one of the classic fashion photographs of all time. Like Miyake and Penn, this collaboration presented Yamamoto's work in a specifically artists' milieu, in which the object of the photograph simplified and abstracted the form, creating a sense of heightened monumentality.

Yamamoto finds retrospective exhibitions of his work disturbing. In 2005, his work was displayed at three venues—Florence, Paris and Antwerp. At the Pitti Palace in Florence, *Correspondences* saw his work placed, unprotected by glass cases, alongside the historical collection of the Galleria d'Arte Moderna, emphasizing the relationship between fashion design and fine art. One hundred garments were scattered in thirty rooms which held the nineteenth- and twentieth-century collections. Guy Trebay (2005) reported that Yamamoto commented, 'A retrospective, to me, is just proof of all your mistakes.' Trebay continues: '"Seeing all these things from the past is hard," Yamamoto said, with the shrug that is one of his defining gestures. "It's like having the emotions of the time come back and climb onto my shoulders."' He was dissatisfied with the show as he felt that his garments looked heavy next to the works of art. In Paris, at the Musée de la Mode et du Textile, the exhibition was called *Juste des vêtements* and was spread over two floors of the museum, which is adjacent to the Louvre. It was a display of his work that focussed on the actual conception and production of the clothing. The ground floor recontextualized his working studio with a pile of bolts of fabric; a small office strewn with sketches and pieces of fabric. Wim Wenders' *Notebook* film played in the corner, providing a backdrop of his early work and inspiration. This was supplemented by antiques, books and historical garments and objects from the museum's archives. Upstairs, there was a large glass display containing a dozen of his finished garments dating from the 1990s and 2000s. Many of these garments paid tribute to European designers, including Vionnet, Grès, Chanel and Dior. A magnificent pot pourri of hats on individual hat stands of varying heights created a delightful spectacle and the intensity of the colours of the last garments on display were breathtaking. This exhibition was a collaborative effort between museum curator, Olivier Saillard, and Masao Nihei, Yamamoto's fashion show assistant. The final venue was the ModeMuseum in Antwerp, where Yamamoto's exhibition was called *The Dream Shop*, the museum's first exhibition dedicated to one designer. Significantly, it was also ground-breaking as the viewers were able to try on a number of garments on display:

> Here, visitors revelled in the materiality of Yamamoto's clothes: out of eighty silhouettes from the late 1980s to the time of the exhibition, they could try on about twenty in a white, dream-like space with neon-lit changing cubicles. This interactive experience challenged basic museum and conservation etiquette . . . In Dream Shop, the viewers perceived the clothes as consumable items, transforming the museum experience into a commercial one. (Romano 2008: 6–7)

By engaging the museum spectator as an interactive consumer, the exhibition symbolized a major break from traditional museological practice, a feat applauded by the designer himself.

Many fashion writers, especially women, comment on the understated beauty of Yamamoto's collections, which it seems are edged in melancholy. Menkes states 'the dark sweetness of his collection is still full of grace' (2007); Cathy Horyn of *The New York Times* comments of one show that 'there was an amazing tenderness to YY's show—a feeling of homecoming, with models dressed in dark masculine layers of beautiful white shirts, some with wide lace cuffs' (2006b) and of another which 'reminds us of the immense lure of romance' (2007a). Yet, despite the sobriety and heaviness of spirit which underlines so many of his shows, along with the fleeting moments of self-indulgence, his most recent work relies heavily on references to street style. His elegant clothes are counter-balanced to look serenely off-hand. This sense of nonchalance, so effortlessly enacted by the French, is, in essence, an innate aspect of elegance and taste.

Yamamoto has gained a reputation for being a design purist and an intellectual recluse. Guy Trebay, fashion writer for *The New York Times*, described Yamamoto as 'veiled and distant and dour . . . the cockeyed pessimist of fashion . . . the enigmatic outsider' (2005). Yet he is a designer who has consistently found beauty in a garment which drapes and wraps the body in an asymmetrical way, and in the textured weave of materials rather than applied decoration, and he became renowned for the long, loose shapes, the antithesis of the Western concept of the female shape. Again in his 2005 collections, his archetypal Japanese look still relies on layering, additional flaps, straps, knots and pockets in illogical arrangements, asymmetrical detailing, misplaced sleeves and adjustable waists. In subtle ways, he explores new ways of dressing by creating an anti-establishment or anti-commercial fashion statement.

For Yamamoto, growing up in Tokyo where mass culture, novelty and cosmopolitan urbanism was a way of life, he felt that he lived in a transcultural space that was neither Japanese nor European. His early clothes were seen as a rebellion against an age of gluttony. His attitude towards designing has changed over time. In 1984 he acknowledged that 'My way of working is an independent, egoistic way. Such people like to work against the existing way. I design *against*. I struggle *against*. If I lose this feeling, if my work is to be accepted, perhaps, I will lose my energy and my meaning of designing clothes' (Koren 1984: 98). In 1999, he admitted, 'I have changed a little since I was young . . . When I first came to Paris I was simply saying against, against, against, to tradition, to common sense, to conservative beauty, but it's different now' (in Foxe 1999). By 2002, he was quoted as saying, 'I think clothes should be made from the back, not the front . . . I want to achieve anti-fashion through fashion . . . That's why I'm always heading in my own direction, in parallel to fashion. Because if you're not waking up what is asleep, you might as well stay on the beaten path' (Yamamoto 2002: n. pag.).

Retrospectively, Akiko Fukai described his work as 'a distinctive tailored style, wielding brilliant couture techniques, but Japanese aesthetics, like asymmetry, have always supported his designs'. She also stated that Yamamoto rarely steps outside of the Western concept. Perhaps this alludes to the fact that his later collection showings have been influenced more directly by European designers than either Miyake's or Kawakubo's (Plate 5).

RECENT COLLECTIONS

People wear my clothes to make a statement.

Yamamoto

By 2009, Yamamoto's empire encompassed seven lines: Y's, Yohji Yamamoto, Noir, Y Yohji Yamamoto, Y's Mandarina, Coming Soon, and *Y-3* with Adidas. In addition to his designer collections he offers more affordable lines, accessories and a fragrance. His youth-oriented collection was taken over by his daughter Limi Feu.

In February 2009, Yamamoto's collection was formulated on the similarities between Eros (love) and death (Shackleton 2009). He said that 'sadness can be sexy' and that 'showing shade is to show light at the same time' (ibid.). This wistful, melancholic sentiment dominated the showing, in which the models were real people whose 'pains and struggles are carved on their bodies, as they continuously try to express themselves' (ibid.). In each of his shows, it is a character, usually an older gentleman, who communicates a message. Yamamoto is proud of the fact that his work shows 'a long obedience in the same direction'—words that he has adopted from Nietzsche's words (*Beyond Good and Evil*, 1886). An Existentialist sentiment echoes in Yamamoto's words, 'I wake up in despair and go to bed in resignation' (ibid.).

They say that timing is everything in fashion. Yamamoto has established a reputa-tion for not showing his collections during the official Paris prêt-à-porter fashion week. Always full of surprises, he has 'jumped the gun' and presented his show on the eve of the opening of the other Chambre syndicale de la couture parisienne showings. His spring 2003 line was presented at the Paris Opera three months ahead of the usual timetable, and ahead of the haute couture line-up as well. While he is not an haute couturier, his masterful garments suggest that he could be anything he wants to be. According to Cathy Horyn,

> The French . . . came out last night in a beautiful ready-to-wear collection for spring . . . [he] paid tribute to that certain *je ne sais quoi* that makes Paris a well of mystery and inspiration . . . A tuxedo with trousers and a jacket smartly peaked at the shoulders seemed a nod to St. Lau-rent, but a filmy black blouse tied at the neck was the definitive gesture . . . he also had subtle references to Elsa Schiaparelli in veiled cadet caps, which conjured up the make-shift refine-ment of World War II, and to Christian Dior and the small shoulders and full skirts that signalled fashion's return after V-E Day. (2002)

By the mid 2000s, socio-political unrest impacted upon Parisian fashion as well as so-ciety at large. Terrorist attacks, wars and riots had dominated international headlines and global affairs since 11 September 2001. In October 2005, several fashion editors and the buyers from Bergdorf Goodman, arriving in Paris from Milan, found that they were held up at Charles de Gaulle airport due to a bomb scare. Consequently, they missed the opening hours of the collection showings. Yamamoto's fashion show that October sent shivers down the spines of many in the audience when he presented a parade of innocent children's Halloween costumes, toy soldiers, devils, dinosaurs, and sad little clowns. This introductory mélange of bizarre caricatures created an uneasi-ness that was followed by tuxedo coats, worn over black jeans, with fishtails so long that they dragged on the floor, camouflage evening dresses with exaggerated ruffles and both black and white dresses bound with thick whips of long, bundled threads of silk which wrapped around the models' heads and bodies dozens of times (Plate 6). Over the next few years, the anxiety caused by political turmoil became painfully evident in a number of collection showings. In the October 2006 shows, Viktor & Rolf covered their models' faces with masks, obliterating their identity; Takahashi wrapped the models' heads entirely in eyeless cloth hoods with little metal Punk chains draped between the nose and ear; and Yamamoto's models wore hats so large that they swal-lowed up their necks.

Around this time, in the mid-2000s, Karl Lagerfeld made the comment, 'If you read the daily papers, you are not in the mood for pink and green. We have to deal now with the whole world connected.' Lagerfeld's very long, dark, layered clothes, ominous in black, set the mood for other collections. Both Yohji Yamamoto and Marc Jacobs also featured a heavy, layered look, with sturdy fabrics and thick leg coverings concealing the body entirely. Colours varied from pebble to charcoal, with shades of grey dominating the majority of collections (English 2007: 151).

Again in September 2008, when the Dow Jones dropped 777 points—the worst drop on record for the New York Stock Exchange, heralding a global economic depression, Yamamoto became the man of the day. His sombre collection, which rarely diverges from sweeping black coats and suits—this time made from gauzy rags sewn together with white stitching—was described as 'looking as if it were made for a Wall Street funeral procession' (Wilson 2008). Be that as it may, for over thirty years Yamamoto's works have evoked poetic memories underpinned by familiarity and a sense of the monumental. He attempts to make clothing that the wearer related to, clothing that evoked an intimacy, or reflected an understanding of what the wearer wanted to communicate. His clothes speak to artists, to intellectuals, and to professional people. Some writers argue that he has made a greater impact on menswear than on womenswear, perhaps more so than any other fashion designer of his time. With an underlying sense of humour, he admits, as he reflects on his long career, 'All I ever wanted to do in life, was to spend each day quietly in the studio making clothes' (in Trebay 2005).

–3–

Rei Kawakubo and Comme des Garçons

Figure 3.1   Rei Kawakubo, 1995. Photograph: Maria Chandoha Valentino, MCV Photos.

What is in front, and what is behind?

Kawakubo

Rei Kawakubo[1] has become one of the most influential designers of the past three decades, with almost every major fashion designer citing her as an inspiration (Figure 3.1). According to fashion journalist Claudia Croft (2008: n. pag.), Marc Jacobs of Louis Vuitton argues that 'everyone is influenced by Comme des Garçons'. Croft asserts that Kawakubo 'stands very much apart. She is truly a designer's designer', and cites a comment by Cathy Horyn of *The New York Times* that she 'works more in the spirit of an artist than any other designer working today' (ibid.). Designers including Alexander McQueen, John Galliano, Helmut Lang, Martin Margiela, Ann Demeulemeester, Jil Sander, Miucca Prada and Donna Karan have all acknowledged her influence.

Rei Kawakubo established her label in 1969 and formally established her Comme des Garçons company in Minami-Aoyama, Tokyo in 1973. She entered the world of international Parisian fashion in 1980 when she opened her boutique in Paris and showed her first collection, alongside Yohji Yamamoto, in 1981. Both designers were products of post-war Japan and grew up in a country that was responding to the economic woes of the 1930s and 40s, a time when Japan suffered the effects of economic depression. During their early childhood, Japan was one of the poorest countries in Asia and these decades were commonly referred to as *kuraitani*— the Valley of Darkness. The Japanese were tenuously picking up their social and cultural pieces, as well as attempting to reconstruct their homes and cities after the catastrophes of war.

FEMINISM IN JAPAN IN THE POST-1945 PERIOD

. . . women [in Japan] were condemned to be 'mothers' or 'whores'.

Vera Mackie (2003: 144)

In the post-1945 period, social and political monitoring was put into place by the occupying American forces which aimed, among other things, to democratize the voting system and allow Japanese women voting rights for the first time in history. Changing social mores and attitudes in Japan evolved slowly over the next few decades and the status of women, in this primarily patriarchal and conservative society, began to respond gradually to these changes. It is important to acknowledge that Japanese women shared a commonality in their struggle for emancipation and equality with many other societies. For this reason, initially, Japanese feminist research dealing with the issues confronting women relied heavily on translations of scholarly literature that emerged from France, America and Britain, among other countries, in the early 1970s. According to Vera Mackie (2003: 144), one exception was Tanaka Mitsu's article 'Liberation from the Toilet', of September 1970, which became part of the manifesto for the group *Tatakau Onna* (Fighting Women). This article provides 'an impassioned condemnation of the conventions of sexual behaviour whereby women [in Japan] were condemned to be "mothers" or "whores"'. Mackie argues that this polarized attitude was hinged on the premise of sexual domination and subordination, and subsequently intensified the oppression of women (145).

While certain aspects of Japanese society and culture, including traditions, values and social structures, have placed nationalistic impediments in the way of possible developments towards emancipation, other factors, including international economic, political and wide-ranging media communication, helped to facilitate progressive change. According to Kazuko Tanaka (1995: 348), 'the Japanese feminist movement changed its character from one that was targeted at bringing about changes in women's consciousness of themselves as women to one seeking visible changes in social institutions'. The early Japanese feminists, by the mid-1970s, tended to be older, and were more likely to be professionals and activists within the established political parties. By the 1980s, issue—oriented activities became the main focus for debate, including gender and education, sexism in the mass media, equal opportunity in employment and the importance of the advancement of women's studies through major nationwide and regional women's associations and study groups.

Kawakubo, the daughter of a professor, studied literature and philosophy at Keio University, Tokyo, in the 1960s and would have been familiar with intellectual debates relating to women's status and positioning within society. It could be argued that this is a factor that has been instrumental in her mission to question stereotypical images and perceptions of women through fashion. The meaning communicated through Kawakubo's work has often reflected an underlying feminist ideology. In an attempt to break away from social constraints and conventions, her clothing comments on the stereotypical Western image of the body, and the idealistic concept of sartorial beauty and glamour, versus the way that female role-playing can instead embrace the notion of dignity and perseverance through dress. Both Kawakubo and Yamamoto reacted against the unashamed American popular culture that was culturally endemic to the younger Japanese generation in the post-1945 era and, through their work, tried to re-instil a respect for traditional cultural traits.

Kawakubo and Yamamoto's first joint Paris collection, in 1981, startled the fashion world with its blatant disregard of accepted Western practices based on sexual difference, sexual commodification and sexual exploitation.[2] While there are distinct similarities in their work, especially in the early years, with time critics began to appreciate that the work is mutually discrete. As a Japanese woman who was not following the accepted family role, Kawakubo's own career choice would have been viewed with suspicion. According to Nanako Kurihara in the 1993 documentary *Ripples of Change*, Japanese women who choose a career are considered to be selfish and shirking their matriarchal role within the family unit. In a rare interview with critic Takeji Hirakawa, Kawakubo explained,

> When I was young, it was unusual for a female university graduate to do the same job as a man. And of course women didn't earn the same. I rebelled against that . . . I never lose my ability to rebel, I get angry and that anger becomes my energy . . . (1990: 21)

Both Yamamoto and Kawakubo indicated that they designed for independent women who work and do not rely on body shape to attract the opposite sex. They broke away from the conventional use of beautiful young women as models towards females who were unconventional, mature and 'ordinary'. According to Wilcox, their work 'consistently explored issues surrounding body shape, sensuality and the sartorial gender binary' and were 'often interpreted as feminist expression' (2001: 31). Yamamoto, in particular, whose father was killed in the Second World War, was raised by his mother, a dressmaker who worked long hours to support her son. As a result, 'he has made it his mission to serve working women' (Shoji 2005). When he was studying fashion at Bunka in the mid-1960s, the young women outnumbered the men by one hundred to one. Shoji argues that 'It was the years at Bunka that inspired Yamamoto to bring beauty and functionality to women's clothing.' Yamamoto confided, 'I don't know any woman who doesn't work. Between my mother and Bunka, this completely formulated my outlook on women' (ibid.). The hardship of Yamamoto's early years seemed to cloud his thinking for a very long time: 'I may be making fashion in the sense of craftsmanship, but I hate the world of fashion. Fashion is more about helping women to suffer less, to attain more freedom and independence' (Riedel 2004).

While Yohji Yamamoto (Yamamoto 2002: n. pag.) learned much about dressmaking from his mother, he also learned about the great hardships that many women had to endure. He resented her clients, who epitomized the wealthy, status-driven females within society who, like the prostitutes, wore high-heeled shoes and tight-fitting clothing. Very early in life, he observed that 'society was controlled by men, and women lived in a low situation.' It was this early epiphany that cemented his desire to build a career by celebrating women: 'I knew working women were independent, not only financially but spiritually.' It is for these reasons that the word 'status' does not fit well within the rhetoric of both of these Japanese designers, precluding them from ever wanting to be classified as elite haute couture designers.

Arguably, both designers, products of their own personal, social and cultural environments, were not willing to compromise their ideals for commercial success. For them, their work represented dignity, power and the beauty found in ugliness. Making a courageous stand, they addressed the notions of both poverty and gender stereotyping, issues which played a major role in their early collections.

CUTTING-EDGE DESIGN

I am looking for things that don't exist. It is like working on a Zen koan [riddle].

Kawakubo

At the infamous 1981 Paris catwalk show, 'Kawakubo showed trousers with sweater cuffs around the ankles, tunics that transformed into shawls, oversized overcoats and shapeless boiled knitwear constructed with holes' (Quinn 2002: 145). The Japanese 'black' fashions were characterized by torn, ripped and ragged fabric and uneven and unstitched hemlines—but this sense of random disorder was very carefully calculated to give the impression of spontaneity. Large, loose-fitting garments such as jackets or coats of oversized proportions were constructed in an atypical manner with a minimum of buttons or details. Street dresses had long sleeves and straight, simple lines and sometimes were tied together with knots of fabric. Significantly, due to their unprecedented influence, a new form of anti-fashion emerged as the dominant aesthetic in the early 1980s:

> In March 1983, Kawakubo presents a collection which included coat dresses, cut big and square with no recognizable line, form or silhouette. Many had misplaced lapels, buttons and sleeves, and mismatched fabrics. More calculated disarray was created by knotting, tearing and slashing fabrics, which were crinkled, creased and woven in unusual textures. Footwear consisted of paddy slippers or square-toed rubber shoes. (Kawamura 2004a: 138)

Historically, a precedent had been established for this type of dress—in other words, dressing down in order to 'dress up'. A similar phenomenon occurred in eighteenth-century England when the landed gentry quite deliberately imitated the more casual dress of their servants. However, in the twentieth century this constituted a different social paradigm and a new visual ethic. For some, the literal deconstruction of fabric, finishing techniques, draping and so on symbolically reflected the deconstruction of past values (Figure 3.2). For others, this new culture of dress presented by the two Japanese designers deliberately mocked the exclusivity of the earlier modernist European fashions. It could also have been seen as a form of blatant protest against the excesses of modern society. If we perceive the clothing as simply a means to an end, then it is the message rather than the final outcome, (in this case, the garments) that is of greatest significance. This type of thinking heralds the emergence of conceptualism in fashion.

Kawakubo's history of challenging traditional fashion tropes and questioning the status quo in terms of styling, construction, manufacture, presentation, marketing and distribution will be traced in this chapter by discussing major concepts that underpin her thinking and her design philosophy. They will include her cutting-edge notions of gender neutrality and the male/female discourse; deconstruction and reconstruction; the recontextualization of style, material and ideas; her strategies for success; her drive for 'newness for newness's' sake, which incorporates architectural spaces; and the rise of her perfume empire.

Figure 3.2 Comme des Garçons, deconstructed pleated skirt, 1999. Photograph: author. Courtesy of the late Paul Jellard, Fiveway Fusions, Sydney.

GENDER NEUTRALITY

Many designers cater to the idea of what they think men would like to see women as . . . I think it takes courage to do something [different] . . .

Kawakubo

Like Miyake, both Yamamoto and Kawakubo insist that the underlying influence of the kimono in their work is profound. They agree that it is the space between the fabric and the body that is most important. This negates the blatant sexuality of fitted Western clothes and introduces the possibility of layered or voluminous clothing that becomes a sculptural form of its own. Kawakubo comments on the 'gender neutral' design of her kimono-inspired constructions, 'Fashion design is not about revealing or accentuating the shape of a woman's body, its purpose is to allow a person to be what they are' (Jones 1992). This is abundantly clear in her spring/summer 1997 'dress becomes body' creations, commonly referred to as the '*Bump*' collection (Figure 3.3), and again in her 2010 collection, where padded sections are added to the clothes to distort the contours of the body including the shoulders, back and hips, allowing the actual clothing to critique the notion of the perfect female shape. It seems that Kawakubo sees these distortions as exemplifying the 'actual' rather than the 'natural'. 'The body becomes dress becomes body,' Kawakubo explained. This is very much in keeping with postmodernist practice, where self-critique and self-reflection challenge accepted norms of life and society. Does sexuality always have to be determined by body shape? Kate Betts argues in *Time* magazine that Kawakubo invites an open interpretation of her work but also suggests that the 1997 *Bump* collection calls for some level of self-awareness (Betts 2004). Not surprisingly, Kawakubo commented in 1983 that she saw the New York bag lady as the 'ideal woman' to dress, and, in 1984, that a woman who 'earns her own way' is her typical client. Another often-quoted statement of the 1990s refers to how she designed clothes for 'strong women who attract men with their minds rather than their bodies'. This inherent feminist critique, obvious in both her words and her work, was echoed in many different forms of art and design practice in the 1980s and 1990s, as well as in literature, media advertising, film and theatre.[3]

Over the past thirty years, clothing has surpassed the primary function of status and sexuality and some designers, like the Japanese, have embraced the idea that fashion can assimilate meaning and conjure up memories of place, time, people and

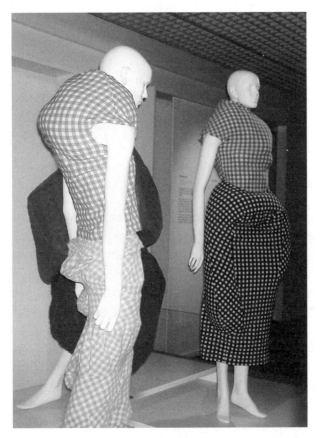

Figure 3.3 Comme des Garçons, 'body meets dress—dress meets body' collection, nylon with goosedown and feather filling, spring/summer 1997. Photograph: author.

feelings, as well as provide a psychological portrait of one's sense of being within to-day's society.

CONCEPTUALISM, DECONSTRUCTION AND RECONSTRUCTION

> With all collections, I start abstractly . . . I try to find two to three disparate themes, and think about techniques to express them not in a straight way. This is always the longest part of the process.
>
> Kawakubo

Kawakubo of Comme des Garçons fame finds beauty in the unfinished, the irregular, the monochromatic and the ambiguous. Placed within the context of Zen Buddhist philosophy, this translates as an appreciation of poverty, simplicity and imperfection (Leong 2003). What had defined modernist haute couture fashion—the uniqueness of the design, fine finishing techniques, unblemished surfaces, exquisite tailoring and hand sewing—gave way to the predominance of mass-produced 'prêt-à-porter' clothing. Kawakubo's work is the epitome of postmodernist visual arts practice in that it relies on challenging artistic conventions, including the notion of perfection or the ideal, sustainability, or planned progression. Instead, it became characterized as embodying notions of anti-fashion, often asymmetrical in appearance, using folds and pleats, exposed stitching and contrasting textures and fabrics, as well as incorporating 'found' objects. Kawakubo asserts that she does not have a set definition of beauty:

> I find beauty in the unfinished and the random . . . I want to see things differently to search for beauty. I want to find something nobody has ever found . . . it is meaningless to create something predictable. (Kawamura 2004b)

Kawakubo's conceptualization is inherent to her philosophy towards design as she always attempts to project forwards to the future, pushing boundaries, so to speak. 'It's not good to do what others do. If you keep doing the same things without taking risks, there will be no progress,' she has said (*Undressed* 2001). Kawakubo relies on spontaneity in her work. As Kawakubo was not formally trained in fashion, initially she had no preconceptions about the design or fabrication process. 'I could say that my work is about looking for accidents. Accidents are quite important for me. Something is new because it is an accident,' she adds (*Undressed* 2001).

Like the other Japanese designers, fabric was central to the design concept of the garment for Kawakubo. The design process always began with collaboration with the textile designers and the experimental formulation of the textiles. She worked with Hiroshi Matsushita to produce loom-distressed weaves in their textiles, by reformulating the actual fabric in the loom. By 1982, sweaters were intentionally produced with holes or dropped stitches in the knitting so they would appear as rips and tears. Tampering with the computer-controlled looms allowed her to create a variety of random 'flaws' in order to escape the uniformity of mass-produced textiles, and sophisticated computer programs allowed for self-generating patterns with interesting surface textures. This methodology reinforced her anti-commercialization of a fashion which relied on the conventional, the precise and uniformity in design. According to Sudjic (1990: 80), Kawakubo explained, 'I like it when something is not perfect. Hand-weaving is the best way to achieve this, but since this isn't always possible, we loosen a screw on the machines here and there so they can't do exactly as they are supposed to.'

While her work is uncompromising in its anti-fashion directions, like Yamamoto, it is still very personal and self-reflective: 'When I am designing, what's important to me is to express what's happening in my own life, to express my personal feelings through my designs' (*Undressed* 2001). Perhaps it is this notion regarding freedom of self-expression that prohibits Kawakubo from imposing her ideas onto her apprentices and production staff. Watanabe often remarked that he received very little feedback from her regarding his creative methodologies and Tao Kurihara, in turn, made similar remarks about Watanabe when she was his apprentice. According to Sudjic (1990: 30–4), Kawakubo would give a sketch to her pattern-makers without many details; sometimes no sketch at all; sometimes a crumpled piece of paper which she would ask her pattern-makers to interpret. At other times, she would give them verbal instructions or show them a photograph of a building. Clearly, her pattern-makers play a major role in the aesthetic and creative formatting of the design process. This collaborative, conceptual approach is quite unique in the world of high fashion. Sudjic retells (1990: 28–9) what Kawakubo's textile manufacturer, who has been working with her for some time, explained:

> Between four to six months before a collection, she will call to talk to me about what she has in mind . . . Usually it's a pretty sketchy conversation; sometimes it's just a single word. It's a particular mood that she is after, and that can come from anywhere.

He relies on his intuition to understand Kawakubo's abstract theme and comes up with some sample swatches. Their conversations go back and forth until they reach the exact fabric that Kawakubo has in mind. Garments made from different fabrics are often combined together to make a unique, but atypical, ensemble (Plate 7).

In terms of garment construction, first Kawakubo deconstructs, then reconstructs. Quinn, in *Techno Fashion*, provides some specific examples:

> Often she deconstructs clothing by disregarding its function—once she made a dress that had no openings, making it impossible to put on. But it can be worn, she insisted, and decreed that it could be used as an apron. She focussed on taking the lapel apart—she used

jacket lapels to design halter neck jackets and make scarves. Her menswear suits combined cropped trousers with double-breasted sports jackets, featured shawl collars and juxtaposed blown up and 'bleached' classic checked fabrics. Many of her designs are multipurpose, designed to be worn in a variety of unconventional ways, encouraging the boundaries between occasion-specific wear and everyday wear to collapse. (2002: 145)

Kawakubo also reconstructs proportions. She explores space and volume. Similar to her *Bump* collection, she re-thinks the relationship of the shoulder to the waist and the waistline to the hem without taking any notice of the underlying body. Her garment patterns rarely correspond to natural body proportions and fabrics are often draped or wrapped around the body with sleeves, collars, pockets and fastenings in unusual positions. As her garment designs defied common sense and standard dressmaking techniques of construction, her seamstresses had to be taught how to sew the pieces together. When her two-dimensional pattern pieces were formulated and laid flat, it became apparent that they would be impossible to copy as the shapes were unconventional and extremely complex. Not only did this eliminate much fashion piracy of her work, but it also gained her the admiration of her fellow designers. Similarly, Madeleine Vionnet achieved a comparable status in the early twentieth century with her uncopiable designs, many of which relied on hand-manipulated fabrics, when she was dubbed the 'designer's designer' by members of the industry.

STRATEGIES FOR SUCCESS

It is true to say that I 'design' the company, not just clothes. Creation does not end with just the clothes. New interesting business ideas, revolutionary retail strategies, unexpected collaborations, nurturing of in-house talent, all are examples of Comme des Garçon's creation.

Kawakubo

From the beginning, Kawakubo knew that in order to gain international recognition in fashion you had to be in Paris and your label had to state 'Made in France'. Going to Paris was a long-term investment and shortfalls in the short term were to be expected. Establishing a social network in Paris usually takes time unless you have the backing of other influential designers or have been 'picked up' by the press. Kawakubo appreciated that her first shows had to project maximum visual impact. Both Kawakubo and Yamamoto realized that they were taking a great risk in challenging the existing fashion tropes and that, while there was room in Parisian circles for the avant-garde, there was no room for anyone who challenged the French fashion system. Fortunately, the press dubbed their collection a sartorial revolution rather than a declaration of war on [Fédération] institutional values. They had learned how to play the game.

For Kawakubo, deconstructivist ideas could be applied to the interior design of her boutiques as well as to the clothing. In the late 1990s, her 'space' within Isetan department store in Shinjuku, Tokyo reflected revolutionary retail strategies in that the furnishings were very sparse, akin to a bargain basement outlet with basic folding rectangular tables, cracked cement floors and refrigerator cabinets painted red, used as storage. The boutique, juxtaposed with other luxury designer labels, became immediately apparent due to its visual contradiction.

During the twenty-first century's first decade, 'Kawakubo's intellectualism and restless desire to tackle newness' have set 'her apart from Yamamoto' (Mears 2008: 115). While Yamamoto looked back to the past, more and more, and looked inwards for inspiration—perhaps reflecting on notions of the existentialist ideal, Kawakubo had her gaze set firmly on the horizon, pushing forwards and testing new ideas. She does not like to 'explain' her work but wants her work to speak for itself. Kawakubo, like Balenciaga, was elusive and she rarely granted interviews and did not appear on the catwalk for the finale of her collection showings. While she disliked exhibiting her work in museums, she did take advantage of one very important opportunity early in her career. The *Three Women* exhibition was held in 1984 at the Fashion Institute of Technology in New York and was meant to be a celebration of the work of three outstanding women fashion designers. The American Claire McCardell, France's Madeleine Vionnet and Japan's Rei Kawakubo were chosen. The curatorial premise endorsed that each of these women had made a significant contribution to the international fashion industry. For Kawakubo, to be chosen along with two historical legends at such an early stage in her career was a considerable honour in itself, and acknowledged the potential that she showed as a cutting-edge designer in the 1980s. The international press also recognized Kawakubo's impact upon Western fashion thinking, effecting new directions in the industry, and they subsequently named her 'designer-of-the-year' in 1988. And her label has expanded to include, among others, Comme des Garçons Hommes, Tricot (garments made of knitted fabrics) and Robe de Chambre (simple clothes for bedroom and bathroom). By the late 1990s, 'multi-brands' had taken over the fashion industry.

Like Miyake in particular, Kawakubo worked collaboratively with numerous designers, artists and photographers, among others. Interestingly, both Miyake and Kawakubo were determined to draw the line between what constituted 'art' as opposed to what constituted 'fashion design'. While others might have disagreed, they both insisted that fashion was not art. In fact, Kawakubo unequivocally stated, 'I've always said I'm not an artist. For me, fashion design is a business' (Sims 2004: 123). In Japan, aesthetics is an innate part of everyday living, evident in their surroundings, their food, their wrappings and their clothing and, for that reason, perhaps, the Japanese view art and artists differently to Westerners. According to Suzy Menkes, Kawakubo explained,

You sell art to one person. Fashion comes in a series and it is a more social phenomenon. It is also something more personal and individual, because you express your personality. It is an active participation; art is passive. (1998: 11)

Despite this viewpoint, one of Kawakubo's most publicized collaborations was with American postmodernist artist Cindy Sherman, in 1994. She sent Sherman garments from each of her collections to use as she wished. Sherman produced a series of unconventional photographs for the clothing company Comme des Garçons, which 'centred on disjointed mannequins and bizarre characters, forcing the clothing itself into the background' (Glasscock 2003). Sherman presented Kawakubo's clothing in masquerade settings, but the confrontational, theatrical images are not about clothes. They are about performance art. Sherman is renowned for her interpretations of mass media stereotypes of femininity. Her critique of 'fashionable' photography is in keeping with Kawakubo's approach to the business of fashion design, which is strongly inspired by the values of the contemporary art world. Kawakubo's collaborations extended to working with other fashion designers and design companies. This was not only in keeping with her sense of collegiality but was integral to building a solid financial base for her company. Kawakubo collaborated with many, including Levi's, Speedo, Nike, Moncler, Lacoste, Cutler & Gross, Chrome Hearts, Hammerthor (shirt collection), H&M and Louis Vuitton. In 1997, she collaborated with the colossus American dance choreographer, Merce Cunningham, in New York, to create *Scenario*, a performance with music by Kobayashi Takashi, with Kawakubo's set and costume designs. The dance, inspired by Kawakubo's garments from the *Bump* collection, did not discriminate between the male and female genders of the dancers, as this was no longer apparent.

Kawakubo's intellectualism dominated all of her collection showings. One must look beneath the surface for clues as to the underlying motivation for her creations. Reflecting Japanese philosophy and traditions about art and design, her work adopted recurring themes; a form of serial designing where one idea developed from the last, or was reinterpreted and extended—a practice that sometimes creates a sense of paradox in Kawakubo's work. On the one hand, a garment can evolve into something new or different through deconstruction and reconstruction, or on the other it can simply be reinterpreted in a different way. Kawakubo (Sims 2004: 122) explains,

If you take the example of the tailcoat, for example, that kind of tailoring, and the fact that it has been worn for centuries without ever changing is something that I feel very strong about. It has been worn over the ages, it's comfortable to wear, and then based on that historical shape you can make something that is totally new but which also has the authenticity of being old. What I find tasteful is something you can wear and wear over and over again, so often that it becomes your own and when it becomes your own, your sense of style is expressed. That's why I've always been interested in the concept of the uniform: because it's worn over and over. Then the way you wear it becomes your own statement.

KEY COLLECTIONS AND THEMES

It's always good to see a show that makes you smile.

Michael Roberts, *Vanity Fair*

Different interpretations of recurring themes become evident when a decade of collection showings is reviewed: Kawakubo blurred the boundaries between dress and body; provocatively skirted political commentary in her work; blended notions of female and male discourse; attempted to confront the issue of 'taste' in fashion through a deliberate mix of fabrics, found objects and atypical materials; explored the persona of 'what's in front and what's behind', suggesting that fashion is a means of constructing disguises that we can hide behind; and also revealed rhetorical issues, 'I want to suggest to people different aesthetics and values. I want to question their being' (Frankel 2001: 158).

These themes are highlighted below in specific shows, listed chronologically. Also, by defying convention, Kawakubo deliberately tried to break with the conformity of holding her collection showings at venues designated by the Paris fashion week officials, which she dubbed 'circus-like', and subsequently moved them to more sedate locations. For her spring/summer 1997 *Bump* collection, where padding was sewn into the stretch, gingham-look garments in unusual places to distort the female form altogether, she decided to hold it at the Musée national des Arts d'Afrique et d'Océanie without a catwalk or music. This way, the shocked audiences could concentrate solely on the 'new' silhouettes that were being presented. One of her more controversial shows dealt with the politics of terrorism. The Comme des Garçons spring 2002 collection show was taking place in Paris at almost exactly the time that the United States retaliated against the Taliban in Afghanistan (October 2001). Unbeknown to Rei Kawakubo, who made a last-minute decision to have her models wear 'their hair matted down and tucked under skin-tight caps that looked like early-aviation-era helmets and were made from newspaper with *Le Monde*'s headlines in full view, these outfits appeared to make a political statement. They suggested that the privileged classes were now inhibited by political forces beyond their control. After the show, Adrian Joffe, who is the managing director of Comme des Garçons and the reticent Ms Kawakubo's husband, stressed that 'there was no such idea at play' (Bellafante 2001). In 2003, she revisits the anti-war sentiment again but this time her collection was laced with humour. Some of the garments were in camouflage-patterned mode, suggesting the rumbling of war. Raw and powerful messages were written across the clothes which stated: 'The majority is always wrong', 'Conformity is the language of compromise', and 'Long last the 1 per cent'.

In March 2004, at the Paris Lido, Kawakubo challenged the male/female discourse by using feathers as decorations on the skirts, and bunched on the breasts, coupled with appliqués of bows and flowers, juxtaposed with tailored trousers dropping at the waist to reveal mannish underpants, and flat brogues worn with lacy mesh socks. The same year, a collection of clothes referenced as *Frilled Fantasy* were presented by models wearing George Washington wigs to the music of Tchaikovsky. Dubbed the 'ugly ducklings', the 'Swan Lake' models wore ballerina tutus and sculpted leather jackets lashed together with giant whipstitches and worn over bike shorts or netted pants with ruffles below. This juxtaposition of materials—the tough hides of the jackets and the softness of the ruffles—created a gender paradox for which Kawakubo is renowned.

In October 2005, the collection entitled *England's Lost Empire* mixed typical and atypical materials, and Kawakubo created the entire collection without using a single dress pattern piece. Dresses and jackets were made from single lengths of union jack tartan knits, camouflage and Polynesian flower-printed fabric draped around the body. Often several different fabrics were draped together and makeshift crowns were designed by the English milliner Stephen Jones out of old jewellery and auto parts. Another critique of the traditional clothing construction methodologies is implied, as well as a contradiction in terms of a rejection of the elitist fabrics common in high fashion. Her 2006 collection, which attacked complacency and conformism, was held in a room in the Sorbonne (Plate 8). Models wore extraordinary Venice carnival masks, disguising their identity. Each outfit was a splicing of a traditional formal gentleman's clothing coupled with romantic feminine puffs, ruffles and corsetry—the underlying theme was 'what we choose to show the world about ourselves and what lies within' (Mower 2006b).

Highlighting the rise of the soccer ball as an icon of international popular culture, in October 2008, Kawakubo flattened hexagonal-shaped balls made of leather and moulded them to be worn as shoulder pads, helmets and bodices. As soccer was originally played by peasants and became the game of the working classes, her incongruous combination of these references, coupled with aristocratic powdered wigs and tailcoats, did not go unnoticed. In the same year, Kawakubo espoused the biker culture and featured a deconstructed biker jacket in the Comme range, in which it appeared that the parts had exploded and then were Franken-stitched together again. For this range, she used the finest leather, produced by the British firm Lewis Leathers, which also featured in Watanabe's classic leather biker jackets and boots as well (Figure 3.4). According to the buyer for Brown's in London, leather clothing became their best-seller in 2009. On the brink of global economic crisis, this was a curious theme, adopted by many of the Parisian designers. Perhaps they were simply acknowledging the irony that the biker culture was embraced by the baby boomer generation as it no longer had the 1950s stigma of being defiant and anti-establishment. Another

Figure 3.4 Junya Watanabe, leather jacket and zippered trousers, Man collection autumn/winter 2007. Photograph: Chris Moore/Catwalking/Getty Images.

reason proposed was that it was the ultimate 'hard times' textile, the least expensive, tough-wearing material and perfect for a time in which 'dressing-down' or 'investment-dressing' seemed the best option.

In contrast, Kawakubo's March 2009 collection, entitled *Cacophanie,* was one of her most mystifying collections, with jumpsuits made out of pink rosettes, a frothy tutu attached to the front of a pair of cycling shorts and cute paper-dolly dresses made from foam and superimposed on the front of an outfit. It seemed that Kawakubo was thinking about disharmony and randomness by playing with unlikely mixes of fabrics, colours and patterns and working with shapes that were built on the flat, rectangular bag.

The messages emanating from some of these collections were often confusing and difficult to decipher, for both journalists and the audience. The rather disparate direction of the collections continued in October 2009 with models parading to a soundtrack that shifted from classical music to a cacophony of noise. While fashion writers thought it might be a comment on the modern frenzied lifestyle, their garments collaged the look of trends past and incorporated Kawakubo's signature fabrics—pinstriped wool and polyester tartan—perhaps a retrospective of her forty years in the fashion business.

In 2010, numerous journalists from New York to London to Paris were amazed when Kawakubo reintroduced her new version of the 1997 *Bump* collection. Interestingly, for the younger writers, the look was new and exciting, but left the older journalists somewhat miffed. The garments were described by journalists as having padding that coiled around the body, cloud-like dresses that were bursting at the seams with pillowy fluff, or 'yucky' protuberances of deconstructed bustles and swollen pinstripes (Plate 9). The evasive Kawakubo, herself, mumbled two words to the press, which were, 'inside decoration'. The oversized additions were stitched onto the shoulders, bust and arms with skirts equipped with panniers on each hip and were made primarily from menswear suiting fabrics such as charcoal worsted, grey pinstripe or red tartans, in two different check patterns. Hilary Alexander, from the UK's *Telegraph* newspaper (2010), added that, 'The clothes were beautifully made, but so curiously designed, "curiouser and curiouser" as Alice in Wonderland remarked, a girl who knows quite a bit about shrinking and enlarging.'

NEWNESS FOR NEWNESS'S SAKE

I don't want to be just another fashion brand. I wanted to make a new statement.

Kawakubo

The philosopher, Kiyokaz Washiba, argues that Kawakubo 'confronts the logic of fashion head on, by constantly renewing the "now"; in other words, by accelerating the change of fashion, or producing "now" before "now" is usurped. She moves faster than fashion . . . renewing herself so quickly that no one can keep up' (Yamamoto 2002: n. pag.).

In order to underline her philosophy towards designing, in the late 1990s, she purposely erected large billboards at the entrance to her main establishments which read:

NOT WHAT HAS BEEN SEEN BEFORE—NOT WHAT HAS BEEN REPEATED, INSTEAD NEW DISCOVERIES THAT LOOK TO THE FUTURE

As a young and idealistic designer, Kawakubo was determined to set the guidelines which became her hallmark and which inspired many of the other designers who were to follow:

From the beginning it was not just about making clothes . . . I wanted to design a company that expressed my inner values because I wanted to be independent and free of any money-men' (Kawakubo 1969).

Kawakubo's lifelong hatred of conservatism in all areas provoked what she sees as the evils of the 'multinational corporations, and the way that society moves and is motivated solely by money. (Mower 2006b: 660)

Kawakubo has a total commitment towards a holistic design process. She believes that shop interiors, advertising and graphic design are all part of a singular vision and are inextricably linked. She published her own bi-annual magazine, entitled Six (standing for the sixth sense), in 1988 as an alternative to her earlier catalogues, both of which featured images that she found inspiring from Japanese art and literature. Her cutting-edge magazine used its photographic essays as a vehicle for stream-of-consciousness, surrealistic and exotic images, and Zen influences, to imbue the work with an 'otherness'. In terms of presentation, she was the first designer to use non-professional models, art world personalities and film celebrities, both in photography for catalogues and on the catwalk. Interestingly, Anna Wintour of New York Vogue was the first editor to capitalize on this new marketing direction and quickly shifted the focus to images of celebrities rather than models, especially on the magazine's front cover designs. As Wintour is presently the most powerful person in fashion, all of the other fashion magazines followed suit.

Kawakubo became famous for her remark that she 'worked in three shades of black', an adage that had an international impact upon fashion everywhere. When black became the trademark colour of the decade and was copied by all other designers (see Yamamoto chapter), this led Kawakubo to announce in 1998 that 'Red was the new black', and she added, 'Black is no longer strong and has become harder to use' (Frankel 2001: 160). Made by any other designer, this comment would not have turned a single head, but coming from Kawakubo, it meant that the tide had turned and she ended, for herself at least, the ties that she shared with Yamamoto. Arguably, this statement was of great significance as it symbolized the next stage of evolution in Kawakubo's designs, moving away from the encompassing monochromatic vision first realized in her work.

Kawakubo's continuous collaboration with other visual arts practitioners and fashion corporations ensured that her clothing design would constantly evolve and champion new ideas and directions for future designs. 'Sometimes disturbing, sometimes provocative, always challenging' epitomized her philosophy towards design for thirty years. She designed a collection of thirty pieces, mainly in black and grey, for H&M which were released in November 2008, reinforcing the shift in consumer buying that heralded a new era in retailing (Figure 3.5). It forced luxury goods to be available all year round in stores like Zara and H&M, not just attached to the six-monthly collection showings. These stores emphasized newness, entertainment and the in-store experience. In December 2009, Kawakubo designed a *Jingle Flower* collection for Barbie Doll, part of a limited edition collection sold at the Dover Street Market, London, for

Figure 3.5 H&M building, exterior view with Comme billboards, Tokyo, 2008. Photograph: Ben Byrne.

£225. To celebrate forty years in the business (she started her own label in 1969), she brought out a guerrilla-style (see 'Guerrilla Shops' below) temporary brand called *Black*, to be sold in ten 'temporary' international shops around the world (first in Tokyo and then Paris). That epitomizes the style, inventiveness and originality of its owner. She also held an exhibition of her work, in collaboration with *Vogue* Nippon, at the Paris store, Colette.

In 2010, she collaborated with Speedo and produced a range of men's nylon and polyamide black trunks and shorts featuring the iconic heart logo. Always on the lookout for new talent, she teamed up with American conceptual artist, Stephen J. Shanabrook, to advertise her February 2010 collection. As Shanabrook's work deals with the subject of addictions, he has created a series of portrait images of women called 'Paper Surgeries', where the photographs are crumpled to create a psychological distortion as well as a physical distortion in the faces. Kawakubo is using these images to promote her Comme Shirts range in leading fashion magazines (see www. feelslikewhitelightening.blogspot.com). This work complements her own philosophy, which combines deconstructed design with a sense of humour.

THE BUSINESS OF ARCHITECTURE

> Everything that I do or that is seen as the result of Comme des Garçon's work is the same. They are all different ways of expressing the same shared values, from a collection to a museum, a shop or even a perfume.
>
> Kawakubo

Like Miyake, Kawakubo's design also draws on parallels with architecture. She believes that architecture has much in common with the structure of clothes. Her great respect for Le Corbusier and Tadao Ondo betray admiration for a certain degree of purism in construction techniques, which she used in both her garment construction and making. Her clothing is often architectural in concept, literally a construction in space, and decidedly abstract in terms of pattern-making. In the tradition of the kimono, it becomes a structure in which to live. Like the underlying simplicity of her clothing design, her stores are characterized by white and minimalist interiors, with the company's retail outlets being designed collaboratively by Kawakubo herself and interior designer, Takao Kawasaki. Arguably, not only did Kawakubo 'deconstruct' style, theme and technique, she also deconstructed accepted merchandising strategies by participating proactively in the design of her shop interiors and exteriors. This sparse, minimalist and eccentric theme characterized her boutiques, with their cracked concrete floors, fittings made up of industrial racks and shelves, warehouse tables for the display of folded goods and their use of old refrigerators for storage.

Future Systems

Working with an architectural firm called Future Systems, three architectural projects resulted. In 1998, Kawakubo opened a bold, space-age, futuristic shop in the Chelsea district of New York City. She chose a nineteenth-century building in the old meatpacking district and retained all of the existing signage and external industrial fire escapes. Through the central brickwork entrance arch, one finds an asymmetrical tubular entrance made entirely from aluminium, with a surface that is both mechanically- and hand-wrought. Finally one reaches the well-hidden doorway that allows the customer to 'discover' different aspects of the shop, personalizing the experience of shopping. The next year, Kawakubo worked with Future Systems again to design a unique architectural building, which was to become Comme des Garçon's landmark in Tokyo's fashionable Minami Aoyama district (Figure 3.6). Superbly designed, with a conical-curved thirty-metre expanse of street-level glass that is screen-printed with translucent blue dots, this sloping glass wall creates a pixilated effect from the outside, with the customers appearing to be moving across a huge television screen like actors on a set. Cleverly, this vision smacks of self-reflexivity, paralleling the notion that media advertising not only reinforces mass-market consumerism but becomes a reality in itself. The third stage of this collaboration to create new experimental spaces was realized in Paris in the form of a perfume shop. In this case, the historic, worn façade is covered by a sheer skin of pale pink glass sliding across the entrance, creating another visual metaphor for Kawakubo's 'what is in front and what is behind' concept.

Guerrilla Shops

The *New York Times* fashion journalist, Guy Trebay (2004), writes about Kawakubo's ultimate innovation in concept retailing by opening retail spaces (first in Germany) called 'guerrilla stores'. Based on transient distribution, they have a limited shelf-life—only meant to stay in business for a short time, perhaps one year, even if they are making a profit, and then they close and move to a different location. Her perfume ranges adhere to a similar philosophy, as they 'travel lightly and are not meant to last long' as they are issued in limited edition series. With the first store opening in Berlin in 2004 in a former bookshop (leaving the old name intact), and one in Helsinki in a 1950s pharmacy, they were to remain unsullied by architects and designers. Other locations in Barcelona, Singapore, Stockholm, Ljubljana and Warsaw emerged spontaneously in 'hip', but marginalised, areas of cities. Guy Trebay (2004) references Nicolas Bourriaud, 'the intellectual theorist and a director of the Palais de Tokyo, a contemporary art museum, who has made a career of flogging the idea of cultural production with a built-in expiration date'. Contextualizing this concept, in reference to the fashion

Figure 3.6 Comme des Garçons building with pixilated glass, Omantesando, Tokyo, 2010. Photograph: Troy Hansen www.troyhansen.com.au

design of both Kawakubo and Takahashi, Trebay states that the 'Japanese understanding of the concept is so ingrained that it is even incorporated in the language. This philosophy is, of course, endemic to the Japanese notion of wabi sabi—very loosely translated as the celebration of beauty in decay, which is a basic element in Japanese aesthetics'. In more general terms, Trebay comments on the 'fickleness of today's consumers' and 'how marketable obsolescence has become'.

The criteria for these inexpensive 'pop-up' stores, according to Kawakubo's husband Adrian Joffe, president of Comme des Garçons outside of Japan, is that the location must be historic, have character, and be set apart from any established commercial areas. The stores are to be 'Just like guerrillas who are always fighting for freedom, but change their tactics as they go along' (Vesilind 2008). While this paradigm of impermanency, in keeping with paper clothing in the 1960s, is novel, it is also a very lucrative marketing strategy at the same time. This 'provisional retailing' allows for companies to tap into new markets away from the central, high-concept flagship monoliths, pay cheap rents and have no advertising costs, with only 600 posters placed around the world and the information passed by word of mouth. It also provides an outlet to channel avant-garde clothes away from the runway and recycle old merchandise which, in itself, is a way to reduce inventory costs. Stores have become reclassified as

'spaces', and this underground approach is consistent with a trend towards more direct marketing. In a way, it defies the logic of Comme's original conceptual trademark,
where it was the idea behind the clothes and not the clothes themselves which was to
be the main priority. In terms of the guerrilla marketing, it is the 'act of shopping' and
the actual budget-priced merchandise that becomes the central focus.

Trying to find the hidden location is much the same as being on a treasure hunt for
consumers, making shopping an 'event', and this idea was quickly adopted by other
retailers, including Fila, Target and Hanes. For example, in September/October 2003,
Target opened a store for Isaac Mizrahi in New York's Rockefeller Centre for only six
weeks and, inspired by this success, sold goods from a boat moored at the city's piers.
According to Professor Nancy Koehn of the Harvard Business School, 'Accessibility
has really been redefined for consumers . . . this is the wave of the future. One of the
most cost-effective ways to reach a consumer is through their friends' (Horyn 2004).

It wasn't until 2008 that the first Comme des Garçons guerrilla store was opened
in the US. In a 100-year-old building in downtown LA, a one-room store with all four
walls covered in cracked white tiles looked like a cross between a New York City sub-
way bathroom and a padded cell. Industrial piping running through the beams horizon-
tally acted as racks for the clothing. In the same year, Kawakubo opened Comme des
Garçons II in Tokyo, a renovated boutique which was welcoming and focused on movement and interaction. Louis Vuitton and Comme des Garçons collaborated when they
opened this temporary space in trendy Aoyama, which had a three-month opening. In
the typically stark, minimalist interior, with grey concrete floors and an exposed metal
staircase, LV handbags were displayed on wall boxes, gold-flocked with the LV logo.
Kawakubo wanted to 'recreate the emotion she felt when LV came to Japan for the
first time thirty years ago and she witnessed the phenomenon as an up-and-coming
designer' (Kaiser 2008: 3).

Dover Street Market

In tandem with the guerrilla spaces, the Dover Street Market emerged in 2004 on the
sixth floor of an old office building off Bond Street in London's central Mayfair location.
Kawakubo invited Azzedine Alaia, Anne-Valerie Hache, LA's Decade's Vintage, Stoke
Newington discovery Universal Utility, Hedi Slimane furniture and the underground
label Undercover (Jun Takahashi) to set up shop selling their exclusive one-off collections, which were housed in mini boutiques in a chaotic market-style arrangement.
The designers were able to design their creative space in any way that they wished.
Kawakubo hired theatre and film designers to work on different parts of the building
and they created her vision of 'Picasso meets Shakespeare'. The Market established
a twice-yearly change of the concessions and spaces, so different retailers would

come and go every six months, adding to the vibrancy and spontaneity of the retail phenomenon. In July 2010, for example, the YSL label (head designer Stefano Pilati) and a shoe and bag company moved into spaces on the third floor. Deluxe shoes, such as Fendi, Maloles and Delvaux, are placed on charred wooden pianos and in distressed glass cabinets that stand on charred parquet floors in a space created by set designer Andy Hillman, whose theme was inspired by a burned-down ballroom. Kawakubo explains, 'It's a risky venture. But it's all part of that need to be doing something new' . . . I feel that if for one instant I'm totally satisfied . . . I worry that I won't be able to come up with the next creation. I always have to have that hunger. As long as I continue to do what I'm doing, I feel that I have to keep pushing on' (Sims 2004: 121).

Defiantly opposing the usual corporate approach, 'downtown meets uptown' shopping has become an influential lifestyle experience at Dover Street. Conceived partly as a revised version of London's famous, now-departed, Kensington Market in its 1970s heyday, the Market has since become the jewel in Kawakubo's retail crown and she comments, 'It's a store where the overall atmosphere of beautiful chaos is as important as the things that are in it' (Croft 2008). When she travels, Kawakubo loves to visit the local markets as she finds them to be infused with energy, an energy that breeds excitement. This was her vision for Dover Street.

PERFUME: ANOTHER EMPIRE

The idea was to express smells that nobody would recognize.

Kawakubo

Not only did Kawakubo introduce the concept of the guerrilla stores to the international fashion industry, but she also applied the same initiative, based on the ephemeral notion of transitory success, to the production of perfumes. The scent of her anti-perfume lines is not meant to last long, and these perfumes are issued in limited edition series. Quirky odours such as cellulose, mahogany and sherbet, not readily identified with traditional fragrances, identify the brand. Defying convention, Comme des Garçons fragrances have been developing steadily since 1993, when *Eau de Parfum* was launched around a swimming pool at the Ritz surrounded by bags of yellow liquid. Comme des Garçons brought out a new fragrance each year through the 1990s. In 1994, a range of unisex fragrances entitled *Series* was introduced and more masculine 'numbered' scents followed with notes of leather, dust on a hot light bulb and ink. The perfume creative director, Christian Astuguevieille, experiments with a wide range of offbeat fragrances and introduced the original anti-perfume, called *Odeur 53*, in 1998, which has notes of nail polish and burnt rubber and was composed of

53 non-traditional combinations of scents. Not only are the perfumes created with unusual smells, but they are also given poetically abstract names like *Leaves*, *Red*, *Incence* and *Cologne*. Each is packaged in an individual design which fits the image of the product.

Adrian Joffe's entrepreneurial skill in this field became apparent when he signed a deal in 2002 with Puig, one of Europe's most savvy perfume groups. He recognized that there was an increasing demand for niche marketing in this area. Throughout the 2000s, the fragrances continued to change and included *Harissa*, taken from a spicy ingredient in African cuisine, *Garage*, with leather, kerosene and plastic notes, and *Sticky Cake*, made from almonds, brown sugar and myrrh. *Series 6 Synthetic: Tar* was based on the urban smell of town gas, bitumen and grilled cigarettes; *Series 8: Going Back to Basics* had three citrus variations—grapefruit, lemon and lime; and fragrance 888, introduced in 2008, reflected the essence of gold with pepperwood, coriander, amber and geranium notes. Over the past few years, Joffe, who is developing a fragrance empire for Comme des Garçons, is collaborating with other designers, including milliner, Stephen Jones, to produce a range of scents under the Comme umbrella. Like the Dover Street Market, this project is an aberration in the era of exclusive branding and is set to break the existing *parfumerie* mould by managing individual designers and paying them a royalty.

In conclusion, Rei Kawakubo has been making clothes for over forty years, expressing herself radically and defiantly (Plate 10). She has received numerous design and business awards from Japan, Europe and the US, as well as academic honours: she has an Honorary Doctorate from the Royal College of Art, London, and was the third recipient of the Harvard Graduate School of Design's Annual Excellence in Design award. She has directly fostered the talents of Junya Watanabe, who has now become a world-renowned designer in his own right, Tao Kurihara, an emerging designer working under the 'Tao' label, and more recently, Fumito Ganryu, who is designing a youth-oriented label called 'Ganryu'. She has indirectly provided guidance for many others, including Jun Takahashi of Undercover fame. She has broken more rules, smashed more conventions and highlighted more issues than any other contemporary designer in the international fashion industry, leading the way forward in the twenty-first century. And she has never looked back.

–4–

The Next Wave of Designers

> In no other country in the world does innovation define culture as profoundly as in Japan.
>
> Bonnie English

Younger designers, who are apprenticed to leading fashion masters, take many years to develop their trade under the tutelage of their employers. In Japan, this is called *enryo*—a supreme void of ego that demonstrates a complete dedication to the group. For Westerners, it is difficult to comprehend and is seen as a kind of learned humility. Compared to Western cultures, the Japanese are highly collectivistic or group-oriented. Miyanaga argues that Japan is a highly distinctive society and that an important part of this distinctiveness is a great capacity for group loyalty and cooperation. While this tendency does seem to be changing in our modern world, these characteristics are acknowledged as an important part of the mentoring phenomenon. Miyanaga adds that

> Each group develops its own unique qualities whose values are incomprehensible to outsiders. Through submission to the culture of the group, its members become indispensable and homogeneous parts of the whole. Cohesion in the group is strong enough that members who leave are labelled not only disloyal but defectors. (1991: 15)

More recently, however, a greater mobility within the work structure has developed and this concept has been used to great advantage in terms of longevity of employment in corporations and, in particular, the Japanese fashion industry. According to the supreme master, Miyake estimates that it takes at least eight years of apprenticeship before a design protégé is ready to show his or her own collection to the world: 'Among the many works that I have endeavoured to bring you over the past 25 years, there are none which make me prouder than the young talents who have risen to independence from within my studio'. This often-quoted comment by Issey Miyake underlines the pride that Japanese fashion designers take in their role of mentoring new and innovative talents.

Japanese fashion designers work very closely with textile designers. Together, they consider new advancements in fibre and fabric development and the Japanese fashion designer uses the textile as the starting point for a new collection. Miyake, having set the standard for younger designers, 'always maintains a respect for the integral qualities' of the materials he uses (Brunhammer 1993: 90). As a perfectionist, he deals with each design stage, from the initial conception of the textiles through to the production, presentation and marketing of the garments (English 1997a). In the early 1980s, for example, a symbiotic collaboration began between Design House Kaze, fashion designers Hanae Mori and Issey Miyake and textile designer, Makiko Minagawa. Other legendary names include Reiko Sudo and Junichi Arai, who have created innovative textiles since the 1970s; they also founded the Nuno Corporation, so providing a framework upon which the Japanese fashion industry could flourish.

This chapter will discuss the contributions and innovations of a number of designers who have been apprenticed to the fashion houses of Miyake, Yamamoto and Kawakubo. They include Naoki Takizawa and Dai Fujiwara of the Miyake Design Studio, Junya Watanabe and Tao Kurihara of Comme des Garçons, and independent designer, Jun Takahashi.

NAOKI TAKIZAWA

In Paris in October 2006, Naoki Takizawa's last collection showing for Issey Miyake inspired a standing ovation from the audience. It signalled the launching of his own label, which was financed by the House of Issey Miyake. Since 1982, working together at the Miyake Design Studio, Miyake trained Takizawa in the art of fashion design and fashion showings. Takizawa has become renowned for combining a mixture of new and different materials in order to discover unexpected forms. Using a disciplined approach, he experiments with space-age materials, some developed by NASA scientists, and combines them with natural fibres. Making clothing that conforms to Miyake's functional philosophy towards design has allowed Takizawa to continue the evolution of the company's *Pleats, Please* collection. In 1993 he was given full responsibility for menswear and the label became 'Issey Miyake Men by Naoki Takizawa', and in 1999 he became head designer of the Issey Miyake label, leaving Miyake to concentrate on his *A-POC* line with Dai Fujiwara. When Issey Miyake retired as head designer, in 1997, Takizawa continued his mentor's legacy, designing for the international women's and menswear lines and receiving the Mainichi Fashion Grandprix award in recognition of being a leading fashion designer in Japan. Each year the Mainichi newspaper, one of Japan's leading dailies, confers this award on fashion professionals who have distinguished themselves in their field.

Takizawa's last collection for Miyake—for spring 2007—highlighted his central theme of transformation, where one garment is untied, unknotted, unwrapped and emerges as something entirely different. A mini apron dress becomes a floor-length lounging gown, brief spaghetti-strapped garments become swimsuit cover-ups and wrap skirts become asymmetrically-hemmed cocktail dresses. This collection was en-titled *A Rose in the Desert* and featured sleekly-tailored trousers and jackets which in-corporated jacquard-woven, rose-printed denim with lamé yarn and a chemical wash. The rose theme was laser-cut into, and embroidered onto, the fabrics, and bodices became floral shapes themselves. Similarly, his later 2007 collection featured lay-ered dresses edged with leaf-like, feathered points (Plate 11). In their entirety, the garments paid homage to fabric innovation, fabrication and treatment, in which areas Takizawa and the House of Miyake have been prominent.

Like Miyake, Takizawa's collections are cohesive, thoughtfully considered and well developed. In the 1990s he experimented with the notion of how inherent textile properties could create gender displacements. In his 1996 collection, he dressed men in unlined jackets of cotton which resembled fine calico and butter-coloured cro-cheted sweaters coupled with heat-pleated trousers cut like sweat pants—creating a Chinese-style worker suit that espoused a casual, feminine softness. In the same year, he experimented with fabrication methods, making clothes that were then shrunk to size, using a computer-controlled shrinkage method to create new shapes and surface texture. Seersucker fabrics clung to the body like a shapely jacket and neckties were shrunk to rope-like appendages. Members of the Frankfurt Ballet were employed to model chambray jackets and trousers made from two-way stretch fabric overlayed with monofilament twill. These dancers had a versatility not seen before on the runway, allowing them to show off the fabric's in-built flexibility and athletic prowess. Quilted jackets that shimmered and appeared to have metal encased under the collar, or were made from paisley prints that shone under a silver coating, rein-forced Takizawa's signature fabric innovation. The use of silver dominated many of Takizawa's collection showings, with models donning silver, insect-like antennae, sil-ver shoes and laced-up boots and silver-threaded fabrics, some with hologram sur-faces and set in a moonscape setting. His fascination with the universe of insects and a love of nature inspired his *Spirit of the Forest* show at the Fondation Cartier pour l'art contemporain in Paris, a visual spectacle which elevated fashion to a new level of global thinking.

In his spring/summer 2001 collection, Takizawa rejected the traditional circular hemlines and, instead, designed full-length dresses with square hemlines. He inserted square, inflatable tubes into the hems which gave them a structured square shape. In *The International Herald Tribune*, Suzy Menkes describes the outfits featured in the March 2002 womenswear collection:

> Some were extraordinary, like futuristic tribal outfits of tree bark patterned leather pantsuits; others proved his skill as a colourist, when mauve and green created a hologram effect. Cur-rent ideas interpreted his way included collages of fabric; dresses worn over pants whose zippered ankles revealed silver shoes; the tailcoat reversed, so that an apron front revealed a bared back; and a gilded tweed coat that ushered in a fine metallic finale. (2002a)

In his menswear collection of the same year, he developed an interesting conceptual comparison of three different tribes of men—one living in the icy north, one in a moderate climate and another in the blazing sun. Models interpreted the feel of the clothing through their body language and the show ascended to a crescendo that was packed with dynamism and energy. The visual display of clothes graduated from dull greys to brilliant patterns and bright sun hues and mutated from layering to undressing.

The intellectualizing of camouflage as a process of 'chameleon' transformation was central to his spring/summer 2003 collection, where he played with the viewers' perception of colour, shape and form. Suzanne Lee refers to the following effect: that 'his delicate floral patterns, when viewed from a distance confuse the eye, camouflaging garment details and accessories' (2005: 89). For this collection Takizawa used a technique called 'bluescreening', where a digitally-projected image on fabric creates the illusion of the model disappearing when he/she stands in front of similar imagery. This is similar to the effect seen in the Blue Butterfly fish, which has mirror-like scales and which disappears when the sun shines on its surface (Rivers 1999: 59). This concept inspired the European needleworkers who used fish scales as an early form of sequins. Veruschka, a well-known model of the late 1960s, became famous for photographs of her taken using this technique.

Working closely with Miyake for so many years indoctrinated Takizawa into appreciating the possible fusion of fashion and art. In 2007, his menswear collection featured variations of large graphic numbers printed on suit jackets, coats and trousers emphasizing vertical, horizontal and diagonal lines. The garments became a type of walking billboard and suggested how all-consuming numerical references were in modern society (Figure 4.1). Miyake, of course, has worked with photographers, artists and dancers, as well as film-makers and architects. Discussing the role of contemporary art within Issey Miyake International, Takizawa explained:

> Art serves as inspiration, allowing us to create new ways to touch people, enabling two different perspectives and ideas to come together as one new idea. The collaboration with Murakami had a very organic development. The encouragement came from our mutual understanding of each other's work as artists. Not looking back at the creation as a business idea, but as the nurturing of ideas. (In Kaplan 2004)

The pop artist Takashi Murakami expressed that he saw a connection between Takizawa's 'Pressed' collection (1999), in which flat, two-dimensional graphic designs became part of the 'pressed flat' concept, and his own 'Superflat' concept, finding many similarities in their work. They collaborated in 2000 in the *Kaikai Kiki* series and Takizawa explains why his menswear line became the basis of the collaboration:

> It was easier to express his artwork on the basic styles and shapes found in menswear . . . The Japanese feel beauty should be kept inside and not shown off, so I wanted to convey these ideas by having the art on the lining. (In Kaplan 2004)

Figure 4.1 Naoki Takizawa for Issey Miyake, menswear models wearing camel jackets and trousers featuring numbers 5/7/8, Paris menswear spring/summer 2007. Photograph: Catwalking/Getty Images.

This is in keeping with the ancient Japanese farmer who used a hand-painted paper lining for his kimono to keep him warm in the colder season. Menkes underlines this connection when she states that in Takizawa's 2006 collection he 'used Manga-inspired images on the inside, following a traditional Japanese aesthetic, as seen in kimono linings' (2006a). Takizawa often combines elements of the old and the new, seen clearly when he applied a series of creases to men's suits and coats resembling the folds in origami. 'To see this kind of innovative application is to observe a design intellect at work' (White 1999).

Like his mentor, Takizawa effectively collaborates with other renowned visual arts practitioners, and in his 2004 autumn/winter collection, entitled *Journey to the Moon*, he incorporated the popular cultural images of Japanese artist Aya Takano. In this collection, distinctively Japanese animé figures, set in pale blue and pink futuristic landscapes, embody eccentric street-style imagery. Takizawa also collaborated and premiered a limited-edition, pleated-silk T-shirt range with artist Tsuyoshi Hirano. Also, experimenting with multi-coloured thermoplastic mesh that moulded to the body's form, which was inspired by high-tech sports shoe styling and manufacturing technology, led him to design for the international Converse shoe moguls for their 2003 *All Star* collection. His sports shoe extended up the leg and was laced to look more like a boot. Other designers, including Yamamoto, as part of his *Y-3* sports collection (a collaboration with Adidas), has designed cool-looking, comfortable sneakers in techno fabrics, and John Varvatos has tinkered with Converse's classic gym shoes. Takizawa's design work carries on the tradition of sport, energy and graphic colour in the Miyake Design Studio and, while less experimental, looks towards the future with his moonwalk settings and lunar landings. With reflections of André Courrèges' 1960s space-age fashions, Takizawa has paraded grey sweat tops with tulle skirts as light as clouds, pleated skirts and white boots coupled with satellite-shaped baubles. Arguably, the second wave of Japanese designers, like Takizawa, not only look to the future for their inspiration but access their present as well, with references to Harajuku street-style garments, *kawaii*, and the youthquake that is imminent in Japan.

DAI FUJIWARA

Miyake and Fujiwara, another talent who emerged from the Miyake Design Studio, worked collaboratively towards finding a radical solution for a state of clothing that reflected its time and lifestyle, a clothing reformation that extended traditional methodologies and sartorial ideologies. Miyake's concept of clothing goes beyond the commercial whirl of the catwalk; instead, for this new radical project, he focussed on the creation of modern clothing for a future world (Plate 2). His idealistic vision relied on an unconventional method of tailoring that could be multi-functional, versatile, easily mass-produced and affordable. Miyake and Fujiwara called this project *A-POC*, which is an acronym for 'A Piece of Cloth', and presented it to the world in Miyake's Paris and Tokyo shops in 2000. As a conceptually-based ideal, the complex process of manufacture offered a creative solution to the challenge of design sustainability. 'A single thread enters a computerised machine and a finished, but customisable garment emerges at the other end (Lee 2005: 30). Miyake commented that 'the idea stemmed from my desire to make a contribution to environmental protection and the conservation of resources. The process not only cuts down on resources and labour, but is also a means to recycle thread' (Vitra Design Museum 2001: 68). Fujiwara adds that 'standardisation is required for the reduction of production costs, while a diversification of designs is necessary to meet the wide range of consumer demands' (Vitra Design Museum 2001: 72). The process itself heralded a futuristic development that mainstream fashion found difficult to embrace. The 'making' of the clothing became intrinsic to the end product and this, in itself, reflected the art process that is categorized as 'performance' art. The presentation of this new fashion concept was marketed widely in numerous gallery and museum spaces around the world. The prestigious Vitra Design Museum in Berlin was one of the first to exhibit *A-POC* in Europe, which was apt as the museum was conceived as the logical descendent of the Bauhaus School of Design, an institution which linked art to everyday living, focussing on industrial design and the integration of the visual arts with technology.

Photographic documentation of the process became inherent to the nature of the work, just as it did in the late 1960s with conceptual art, 'happenings' and performance art. In similar ways, the presentation was highly theatrical and dramatic and relied on the interactive involvement with the audience. The 'audience' in the commercial environment was, of course, the customer. The customer was forced to play a major role in the making and designing of the *A-POC* outfit. However, to a certain extent, the ensemble was pre-packaged. When the huge bolts of tubed fabric were unrolled, the outlines of the various pieces of the garments and accessories were revealed, all ready to be cut out. Through the use of computer technology, Miyake and Fujiwara have been able to use programmed machines to develop a multitude of three-dimensional models and variations, using textiles that conform to the shape of the human body through a strict matrix of warp and weft. This seamless continuum of knitted fabric and pattern does not require finishing features—no hems, rolled edges, darts or fitted pieces; one size fits all. Such rationalization of the manufacturing process is part of the logical evolution of the ready-to-wear production mode that emanated from the Industrial Revolution and that became intrinsic to the clothing industry from the late 1800s onwards.

In keeping with this utilitarian approach, Ronan and Erwan Bouroullec were commissioned to design a new interior space in the Miyake Paris store at 47, rue des Francs Bourgeois in 2000 to complement the unique needs of the *A-POC* range of clothing. According to Hanisch,

> [They] designed the elements to hang the clothes on, then the support system for the hangers. Rails running parallel along the walls cross at ceiling level. This establishes a system of coordinates that, in principle, means that every point in the space can be used to present clothes; display is no longer confined to the shop windows or walls. The system is structurally uniform and at the same time highly flexible. (2006: 2)

The nature of the sales outlet, the fixtures and the clothes collection have structural similarities and become integral to the holistic understanding of the creative process.

This revolutionary approach to clothing manufacture, through the embrace of technology, consolidates the link between the designer and the scientist, as it has in the textile research areas as well. This phenomenon led to the trend in recent years for the designer to see him/herself in this new role as 'inventor' and design studios became 'design laboratories'. This led to a worldwide trend for some designers to wear pseudo laboratory coats as a fashion statement.

During the 2000s, Fujiwara also turned his attention to athletic sportswear, created in collaboration with karate masters, and the results have been very impressive. He used the catwalk to test the durability and stretch of the fabrics by using the karate masters themselves instead of models, and this visual dynamic underlined Fujiwara's technical brilliance. This same sense of moveability was reflected in his concertina pleating (Miyake's signature), his filmy, triangular-pieced overlays, his printed textile designs, his diagonal seaming and his cut-and-paste patchwork leggings (Figure 4.2). His somewhat uninspiring October 2009 collection of the same year, entitled *NewsMix*, addressed the plurality of cultural eclecticism and the bipolarity of past and present. Regrettably, this collection did not sustain the level of continuity evident in his earlier lines.

JUNYA WATANABE

Watanabe began his career as a pattern-maker for Rei Kawakubo's Tokyo-based company, Comme des Garçons, in 1984. Kawakubo remarked that she was impressed by his decisiveness and his ability to act on an idea. Promoted to a designer, he worked on the Comme des Garçons *Tricot* line for a further seven years. By 1992, he was given his own label, and launched his first collection in Paris under the Comme umbrella with financial backing from Kawakubo. After twenty-five years, Kawakubo's compatriot has become one of Japan's leading fashion designers. His design work is aesthetically challenging and he, like Takizawa, has continued the traditional heritage of experimental textile development. Watanabe's work relies on complex construction techniques, tactile surfaces and a sculptural interplay of light and shade. While he extends Kawakubo's conceptual approach to fashion, his work responds to existing stylistic trends more directly (Plate 12).

Since the 1990s, Watanabe's work has consistently exhibited his innovative and energetic cutting, his interest in changing textural surfaces and his ingenuity of design. He has created jackets that plunge in the front and fit the body closely, yet can be pulled over the head without buttons, as well as trousers with seams that give at the thigh so that sitting down is a comfortable exercise. Developing an idea from one collection to the next is very much in keeping with his underlying Japanese heritage. Every few seasons, Watanabe returns his focus to the puffer jacket, a touchstone that

Figure 4.2 Dai Fujiwara for Issey Miyake, model wearing blue/black striped garment with black leggings and boots, autumn/winter 2009. Photograph: Francois Guillot/AFT/Getty Images.

links his conceptual designs to a common element of street fashion (Wilson 2009a). His fascination with garment construction has allowed for a reworking of seaming and darting to create new silhouettes and to reinterpret classic shapes in an attempt to re-define form. Like his mentor, Kawakubo, Watanabe consistently explores the endless possibilities of the draped fabric and the versatility it lends to a diverse age range.

By the late 1990s, his signature techniques began to evolve around elaborate pleating, seaming and piecing and, by 2001, he had established origami as his signa-ture style, with whole garments made from hundreds of layers of nylon organza resem-bling 3-D Japanese paper lanterns. He experimented with the manipulation of cloth to form folds and used wire to hold the parts together or keep them apart so that nothing fell symmetrically. Wire hoops or rings were used to secure pleats in place or to hold the material away from the body. His techniques surpassed the conventional methods of dressmaking and tailoring and he constructed shapes akin to architectural forms. Again, ten years later, parading his clothes in Jean Nouvel's Arab World Institute, 'his collection . . . looked as if it was designed just for the building . . . a wonderful mod-ernist rectangle that sits bluntly against the ancient skyline of the Seine. Its inscribed square windows were echoed on a graphic-print suit jacket that looked like a computer-generated landscape, giving the feel of multiple dimensions' (Wilson 2009b). His work is routinely included by curators around the world in international exhibitions that align fashion with other design disciplines, including architecture.

Watanabe, a graduate of the Bunka Fashion College, Tokyo, has always described Kawakubo as his mentor, whom he says he is eternally indebted to. In an interview with Susannah Frankel in *Visionaries* (2001: 86), he states 'that everything he knows was learned at Comme des Garçons'. Like Kawakubo, his work is concept-based and appeals to women who appreciate the meaning and ideas inherent in the clothing. José Teunissen, in his *The Ideal Woman*, refers to the Japanese designers as 'unique and exceptionally pure, owing to the fact that they never define the female image' (2003: 71). Watanabe, like Kawakubo, projects 'difference' in variations of femininity on the catwalk. In 1996, his models 'looked a little like escapees from a cult depro-gramming camp, a little like those gothic girl groupies for the Cure, with blanched faces and bright lips . . . [with] bushy black or close-cropped hair, tattoos painted down arms and dressed almost entirely in black leather and big boots, Mr Watanabe's toughs gave a new face to Japanese design' (Spindler 1996b). Jackets made with elbow joints hinged together fashioned the illusion of 'cruel clothing', a technique that he had used before for both elbows and knees, and often copied by other designers when technology allowed.

The dominance of this brutish black leather look was compromised seven months later with a collection of romantic prints and brocades made up in pieced green and purple vests and lacquer-red skirts with navy leaves blown across them. Coupled with Black Watch tartan jackets, the red-checked schoolgirl dresses provided a stark contrast to the earlier heavy-metal attire. In some Watanabe collections, femininity is defined as confection—something delicious to eat with models in dresses that are birthday cakes of tulle and carrying pictures of desserts. Yet in others, the feminist message is both blatant and sardonic. Fashion journalists comment that his collections are the most romantic and delicate in Paris, ingenious and beautiful, and make one fall in love again. This paradox inherent in his collections is often incorporated into individual designs as well. His October 2002 collection featured 'flower sprinkled dresses, ruched with tough canvas straps and parachute strings for a modern femininity. He said backstage that his inspiration was the backpack—a brilliant idea, because by using the universal and utilitarian accessory, the designer grounded his show in reality and then let his fantasy soar as high as the parasol he addresses' (Menkes 2002c). Watanabe explains, 'Sometimes while I'm working I stumble on a technical problem. That challenges me to make the next collection.' The design, the abstract idea, is what dominates, and woman is simply a signboard (Teunissen 2003: 71).

Unlike Kawakubo, who does not have formal technical training in fashion construction, Watanabe's concerns are embedded in technical prowess. Versatility in design is an outstanding feature of Watanabe's work, a premise that is underpinned by his ability to transcend time by extending, combining or replacing the old with the new. In his winter 2005/2006 collection, Watanabe, often described as a conceptualist who likes to reinvent the classics, acknowledged the old-school style, favoured by snowboarders—Moncler down vests in washed Donegal tweed worn under a blazer. He worked collaboratively with a number of conventional menswear companies like Moncler, Carhartt and Ben Sherman but added a touch of street-style to appeal to the younger generation. As a guest designer for Brooks Bros., an old American firm founded in 1818, he brought out his *Man Line* collection, which exaggerated the fit of the famous button-down shirt with a brightening of its conformist colours.

For many years, there has been an unequivocally conservative American tone in his menswear lines, with themes ranging from the military to the Wild West to biker chic, particularly in his extensive use of denim, and his work has been influenced by both the world of work and sports. His clothes, like those of other designers, took on a decidedly military focus in the post-September 11 period. His *Lovely Army* show, in July 2003, saw various treatments of military tailoring as battle jackets and cartridge belts fashioned from banker's broadcloth in colours of gloom and doom paraded the catwalk. Interestingly, when fashion and politics collide, designers are reluctant to admit that they are making an anti-war statement. Watanabe simply explained that he was 'fascinated by the construction of military uniforms' (Horyn 2003) and the Comme des Garçons studio responded similarly when Kawakubo's collection (2002) took on a decidedly political slant. Political reference appeared again in Watanabe's 2006 spring/summer collection, and again in autumn/winter 2010 (Figure 4.3). His references to militarism culminated in the latter show in cropped camouflage parkas and bondage trousers, topped with a duct-tape balaclava provocatively studded with steel spikes. Frankel described the approach more colourfully: where 'violent head coverings created out of ripped gaffer tape, tattered mohair, studs, pins and nails were the order of the day' (2006). While Watanabe is hardly seen as a political activist, this very direct political visual commentary was underlined in the 2006 show by his utterings of 'Anti-Anarchy Army' before he disappeared backstage.

While Watanabe's conceptual designs are not as provocative as Kawakubo's, nor as controversial, the element of anarchy does raise its head occasionally in his collection showings. Also in 2006, 'his models stormed onto a runway strewn with garbage, wearing patchwork coats made of army surplus fabrics with punkish black boots and belts studded with spikes . . . their heads were fiercely taped up with bits of latex, chains and protruding nails' (Wilson 2006). Whether it was intended to be threatening or not, the audience seemed to take it all in their stride. Perhaps this 'controlled' kamikaze approach was becoming overdone. This more aggressive stance was also reflected in his winter 2007 collection (Figure 3.4), when Watanabe (along with numerous other designers) deigned to celebrate motorcycle culture by reinterpreting the Hell's Angel look for the Paris runway.

Figure 4.3 Junya Watanabe, camouflage-coloured triangular coat with hood, autumn/winter 2010. Photograph: Chris Moore/Catwalking/Getty Images.

He built a collection around the classic zippered biker jacket, an iconic American garment that has been immortalized in Hollywood and enshrined in subcultural histories.

Despite such biker leanings, Watanabe, like Kawakubo, has embraced textile technologies throughout his career. He is known to describe his own design aesthetic as 'techno couture', as he fuses fluorescent fabrics with acid-coloured plastics and industrial fibres to create glow-in-the-dark textiles, uses glossy-coloured discs and rectangles in the construction of individual garments and incorporates the paper textile Tyvek into his collection. In his autumn/winter 1995–6 *Mutants* collection, he describes an experimental success,

> I created the image of cellophane by laminating polyuretþane onto a nylon tricot and then dyeing it, using a special technique. The process is delicate and time consuming, almost handicraft work. But it is washable and can be dry-cleaned. (In Mower 1996)

For this collection, Watanabe reinforced his use of laminated synthetics by producing tops that were made up from six layers of overdyed polyamide jersey and trousers fixed with a film over a thin fabric, which created a luminescent surface. The theme for the *Mutants* collection was

> 'Futurism', inspired by Fritz Lang's visions for the future in his 1927 film *Metropolis*. He [Watanabe] found it necessary to cut these high-tech fibres with cyber-like laser machines and employ contour seaming, fixed with flexible joints at the elbow, shoulder and knee to make the inflexible fabrics wearable. In this same collection he used knitted polyamide laminated with polyurethane, inspired by the cellophane gels used for theatre lighting. (Braddock and O'Mahony 1998: 126–7)

In other collections, materials used included computer film (a fine, anti-static material normally used on the inside of computers to protect the machinery), Neoprene and glass fibre (Braddock and O'Mahony 1998: 125). Watanabe's textile experimentation was endless. He produced shiny, industrial effects with lacquering and translucent coatings (Plate 13) and his delicate, sometimes sheer, fabrics could be spattered with stainless steel, a metal that provides protection from the heat. Stylistically, his futuristic design is in keeping with the experimental nature of the textiles that he uses. In *Techno Fashion*, Bradley Quinn points out that

> Watanabe's *Function and Practicality* collection (spring/summer 2000) was entirely waterproof—even the evening gowns. Watanabe's fabric 'performed' on stage for the benefit of the audience—he demonstrated his advances in waterproof-fabric technology by splashing models with water from above as they walked down the catwalk. (2002: 59)

Along with his masterful constructions and his limitless imagination, this cutting-edge approach is what has earned him the title of one of 'the most promising' avant-garde designers in the industry.

For over twenty years, Kawakubo has not interfered with Watanabe's design direction—neither to praise nor to admonish. High standards are simply taken for granted as Kawakubo's career sets the benchmarks for others to follow. Watanabe comments:

> Fundamentally, the idea is that we should make good things here. Because of what she's done, standards are high. So every season, doing a show is a totally horrible experience. It's like rock climbing. I've spoken to rock climbers. They say every time they climb the same peak, there's always a different way up. It's like that for me. (In Mower 2006b: 660–9)

TAO KURIHARA

A new generation of Japanese designers—many of them graduates of Central Saint Martins in London—have joined the ranks of existing design studios, or have ventured to create new businesses of their own. Tao Kurihara graduated from Central Saint Martins in 1997 and a year later became part of the Comme empire. Rei Kawakubo had an unerring eye for new talent. As a young apprentice, Tao Kurihara studied directly under Watanabe for eight years. Kawakubo entrusted her with designing *Tricot*, the company's biggest-selling brand, after just three years. With Watanabe's encouragement to use her imagination, Kawakubo invited her to design a modest collection for Paris in 2004 under the banner of Comme des Garçons. The next year, at the age of 31, she presented a solo collection of trenchcoats and T-shirts. These were very pragmatic garments, yet they were made of fine lawn and lace handkerchiefs which she collected from various Asian sources: some were Chinese, in hand-embroidered broderie anglaise with scalloped edges; some Japanese, cross-stitched with minute bunches of violets; some in Swiss voile with monograms in the corner, among others. The squares were pieced together to create a collage of delicate finery, a technique which initiated a trademark style, underpinning her collections for many years.

Her third showing, in the spring of 2006, was comprised of more poetic garments that spoke both of tender femininity and intellectual rigour. She presented stoles (a piece of clothing that she described as 'shapeless')—nothing more than a piece of cloth—and combined them with flowers. She believes that her quiet, non-aggressive clothing has powerful communicative implications. The international critics, when they initially viewed her work, used generic terms such as 'cute' and 'blissfully innocent', and saw her pieces as being made up of 'pretty', 'old-fashioned' crumpled tiers and ruffles. Despite this, her uniquely-focussed early collections, made in cotton, lace and tulle, and often resembling frilly bed coverings, highlighted her ability to address femininity in a romantic yet practical way. Her signature charm dominated other collections which followed (October 2006 and February 2007), with ruffle-front white shirts and tiered skirts with bows, reminiscent of wedding-cake confectionary. Her collection, inspired by lingerie, was described as a confection of wool and lace translated into coquettish corsets and shorts. While the party-pieces appealed to a younger generation, other garments, such as the silk-knit polo jersey tops, were deceptively simple, saleable commodities. Among the personalized, romantic collections of dresses with floppy ruffles and frills were more sporty, commercial lines featuring neon pink and black in running shorts and sweatpants coupled with fine-gauge knitted tops overlaid with cropped crochet tank tops. Like many other Japanese designers in the late 2000s, she acknowledged the strong consumerist leanings towards athletic lines. She now works with her own team of six designers.

In subtle ways the influence of Rei Kawakubo surfaces in Tao's work. In February 2008, her models' black lips were matched with girl-power scribbles 'Be Aware' and 'Be Powerful' below the models' eyes. Some garments took on a slightly sinister appearance but were camouflaged among the candy colours of the balloon shorts and sweater-dressing trends. In a later collection there was a hint of uniform references, exaggerated clown-like proportions and girlie associations. In the October 2009 collection, she broke away from conventional making processes by wrapping, binding and safety-pinning together strips of brocade, tulle, lace and other bits and pieces. Her sense of naivety and child-like abandonment has become part of the process as well as the styling. Individual saleable pieces/accessories become part of the bricolage that makes up the catwalk garment. Knowingly, she mirrored Kawakubo's sentiment that 'after all fashion is business'. Possibly, Kawakubo sees her own image in Kurihara's abilities: her focus, her commitment and her work ethic.

JUN TAKAHASHI

In contrast, Jun Takahashi launched his *Undercover* label (Figure 4.4) in Japan in 1994, having served no apprenticeship at all within the major design studios. He graduated from the Bunka fashion college in 1991, yet did not debut in Paris until over a decade later, in 2002. When he launched his collection on the catwalks of Paris, under the sponsorship of Rei Kawakubo, she referred to him as 'courageous' for showing in Paris. Almost twenty years later, he has opened over thirty stores in Japan alone and has others in Paris, Taiwan and Hong Kong, and his clothing is sold in fashion stores such as l'Eclaireur in Paris and London's Dover Street Market, owned by Comme des Garçons. He launched a childrenswear range in 2007 and in the same year signed with Comme to produce a perfume line.

His conceptual work attracted a cult following in Harajuku, a district of Tokyo renowned for its street-style fashions worn by the local teens. According to the Japanese edition of *Gap Press*, the well-known prêt-à-porter fashion magazine (2002–2003 autumn/winter collection), Takahashi's appeal emanated from his independent vision

Figure 4.4 Jun Takahashi for Undercover, woman's jacket made from black, white and grey feather shapes, autumn/winter 2007–8. Photograph: Francois Guillot/AFP/Getty Images.

and its 'twisted' aesthetic. His first shop, opened in Tokyo in 1992, featured stuffed animals and one-offs that had been taken apart and remade, and were displayed in the glass showcase. His collection theme that year was the 'Witch's Cell Division', where items were disassembled through fasteners and were all combined in different combinations, similar to robots with interchangeable parts. Black etchings, like tattoos, covered parts of the models' faces and moons, stars and witchy images decorated the garments—creating a unique and somewhat bizarre collection.

Takahashi, while Kawakubo's protégé, is uniquely different in his approach to design. More like an artist, he works in a loft-like studio called the 'Undercover lab', where the surreal dominates with the spreading branches of a tree dominating one corner. He surrounds himself with oddities collected from Paris flea markets—a wooden shrine filled with flowers, a case of butterflies, a kitsch big-breasted nude statue, a bust of Lenin—and his walls are covered in tiny, fairy-tale narratives which he painted with fellow Japanese artist, Madsaki. Seemingly obsessed with stuffed toys, which he initially made for his small daughter Lala, they have become a visual sign of his penchant for the bizarre. Decorating the interiors of his shops and studio, stuffed animal heads are mounted on the wall like hunting trophies, eerie and subversive at the same time. They are indicative of his leaning towards eccentric aesthetics. All handcrafted, they are a time-consuming past-time. This same sense of surreal paradox pervades his approach to fashion design: 'In my head, there is always something beautiful and something ugly, which are equal. Simple beauty does not interest me. But ugly does not interest me either' (in Limnander 2008).

Fashions described by journalists as 'disturbing romanticism', 'eerie poetry', 'covert' and 'sinister' explain the notoriety that some of his collections receive. Capitalizing on the name of his label, 'Undercover', his trademark drives the visual presentation of his collections. Models with bodies and faces sometimes entirely 'covered up' project a strange anonymity, a fracturing of the Western notion of beauty as perfection. When asked why he covers everything up, Takahashi replied that 'There was no reason, except to efface all feeling, like a destroyed doll. It was not about bird flu or some deep meaning. It was something aesthetic—I wanted to envelop them . . . It is not a question of appearances—it is more about a feeling' (Limnander 2008). The mummified masking of models' faces and the bandaging of bodies destroy any sense of individuality, of expression, and this sense of emptiness is echoed in the name of Takahashi's shop 'Nowhere', in Tokyo. This existentialist philosophy, if this is what it is, underpins Yohji Yamamoto's work as well, suggesting a greater influence, in that respect, upon Takahashi than the work of Rei Kawakubo.

His early work was influenced by Punk and street-style, and this influence is seen to reappear during the course of his career. Direct reference was made to animé, for example, in his September 2008 show, where signs were used to highlight themes common to the *Neon Genesis Evangelion* animé series where aliens inhabited the world.

Dehumanizing the show further, the clothes were shown on mannequins with little alien dolls perched on their shoulders. Deconstruction/reconstruction dominated his March 2003 collection, with clothing being rematerialized into something else. Paper doll tabs were used to fashion one garment into another and this visual metamorphosis served to crystallize Takahashi's child-like imagination. From the front, the garment looked complete but the back view revealed that the placard front did not have complete sleeves and only a partial back with tabs fastened to an under-dress. The concept of 'dress-up', of taking on a new persona, became the basis of the street-style fashions that dominated the streets of Harajuku in Tokyo. A whole generation of young Japanese people, influenced by fictional figures in manga and animé, were totally absorbed in cos play and Takahashi tapped into this (Plate 14). Later in 2003, at the showing of a spring collection, twin models were used to juxtapose a double entendre of textual messages. One model wore an oversized T-shirt printed with standard tourist souvenir 'New York City' lettering, while the other featured the lettering slipping down the front of the shirt. A surge of other paraded anti-war T-shirts closed the show.

Models wore stuffed bird-heads and roughly sutured, layered overcoats covered with buttons and felt military medals in Takahashi's March 2004 collection. Inspired by sock animal sculptures made by artist Anne-Valèrie Dupond, the collection constituted a form of fashion parody, similar to the work of Viktor & Rolf. These exaggerated garments were paraded in an android-like manner across the dance floor in a nightclub near the Place Pigalle in Paris. His March 2005 collection featured a signature use of shredded T-shirts made up into long white sheaths, jackets, skirts and windbreakers with appendages of short sleeves and banded neck holes peppering the garments. One particularly clever garment was a trenchcoat belted with the extra long sleeves of a T-shirt overlaid across the shoulders. In a March 2006 collection, his beautifully-tailored strapped trousers and fur coats—also with straps, which pinned the wearer's arms to her side—spoke of bondage and, again, the models' faces were wrapped inside eyeless cloth hoods with little chains to trace a nose or ear. However, by February 2007, Colin McDowell (2007) describes his 'knitted hot pants and sweaters, colours ranging from brown and beige to plum; bags and coats made from knit and cut fabric feathers, shoulders which rose to a curved point, looking like angel's wings from the back' as having now achieved a clarity of focus that was developing into a 'recognisable design creed' and indicative, as well, of an 'extremely competent knowledge of high tech fabric development'. It would seem that Takahashi had finally been given the nod from the French fashion court. Despite this, in an interview with Cathy Horyn (2007b), he intimated that 'he thought maybe his work was becoming recognizable' and that he found it difficult to 'satisfy his own desire to make interesting things' while at the same time being able to 'keep up with the six-month cycle of the fashion shows'. In fact, he 'sometimes thought about focussing on his stores . . . and skipping the Paris collections altogether'. Interestingly, these comments are in keeping with Kawakubo's ideas regarding marketable obsolescence and the fashion consumer.

In summary, the legacy of the great Japanese designers, Miyake, Yamamoto and Kawakubo has lasted over thirty years and has had an equally profound effect upon both Japanese and Western designers. Today, Japanese fashion seems to be heading in a new direction. The younger generation of Japanese designers, including Yohji Yamamoto's daughter Limi Feu, have come into the limelight over the past few years. Another graduate of the Bunka fashion school in Tokyo, Limi Feu presented her collection in Paris in 2008, eight years after she started to show her label at Tokyo Fashion Week. Undoubtedly, her decision to flag her collections in Paris could be attributed to her family background: 'It's impossible to gauge a Japanese audience because they never react. But in Paris, I get to see what the world thinks of what I do' (Holgate 2007: 230). Having developed her designing career under the mentorship of her father, similarities in styling such as baggy shirts and trousers and slouchy suits were evident. However, the trousers fashioned in a modern jodhpur shape had huge, hanging pockets and the tops were smudged with painted stripes or patterned with large polka dots and stripes. Limi's garments are younger, laid-back and more street-style focussed—possessing a casualness that compliments Yohji's sportswear line. Colours are lighter, with billowing blue chambray gathered dresses appearing on the catwalk or pretty cotton jersey dresses in sun-bleached pink and blue Tibetan-inspired prints.

The new designers have embraced colour, ruffles and sexuality. By 2005, it had become obvious that modern Japanese women simply wanted clothes that made them look beautiful. They have been seduced by Western celebrities. This new femininity has a rock star attitude and a street sensibility. Japanese conceptualism had taken on a lighter and less serious air. Most of the emerging designers want to establish a reputation in their home market before venturing overseas, which of course, is possible as Japanese consumers support a high-volume fashion industry. Despite the fact that many Western buyers attend Tokyo Fashion Week, acknowledgement from the West is no longer a priority for the younger Japanese designers and they have no desire to join the large fashion corporations. Their work challenges the existing intellectual profundity associated with the Japanese aesthetic of 'black, draped and asymmetric'. New labels, including Mint designs and the Yab-Yum collection, reflected the 'new look' of femininity in Japan with geisha-look-alike models, light voluminous dresses draped with lace or infusions of gothic-Lolita styling made up of shimmery culottes worn over layered leggings. Described as an aesthetic that is 'lacy and soft and lovely', its roots are embedded in *kawaii,* drawn from the streets of Harajuku (Figure 4.5).

Theatrical productions, akin to Galliano's productions, became the signature of designer Toshikazu Iwaya of the label Dress Camp and Takuya Nakanishi and Akira Takeuchi of Theatre Products. Another label, Toga, by Yasuko Furuta, combines different

Figure 4.5   Harajuku street-style, young 'kawaii' girl, Tokyo, 2006.
Photograph: Ben Byrne.

looks such as something masculine (rough wool sweaters), something feminine (slip
dresses), something athletic (sporty, sequinned skirts) and something vintage (Edwardian jackets). Her line has sold in the USA since 2006. The Sacai label by Chitose
Abe specializes in hand-knitted sweaters and lingerie.

As we move forward through the twenty-first century, the international fashion world
will undoubtedly look carefully at the trends emerging among Japan's youngest designers. In an obtuse way, these emerging designers disseminate ideas about authentic
street-style fashions in a purer, unadulterated way as they are not encumbered with
ties to fashion syndicates, and view society through an unclouded lens, uninhibited by
Western values and insecurities.

–5–

Techno Textiles

Tradition and innovation are the back and front of the same thing to me. What was innovation a hundred years ago becomes tradition in retrospect. I see no special reason to artificially preserve tradition.

Reiko Sudo, 2005 (in Harper 2005)

Yoshiko Iwamoto Wada is heralded as being the foremost authority on *shibori*, or shaped-resist dyeing—an ancient, complex way of embellishing cloth. As an educator, she is one of the key individuals who organized the World Shibori Network and the International Shibori Symposium, as well as writing, lecturing and arranging workshops and exchanges between scholars and textile artists. Her books have become the definitive authorities on the subject, outlining intricate techniques that have inspired a generation of fibre artists (Plate 15). She points out that *shibori* is a labour-intensive method for creating unique designs:

> To resist-dye, cloth is folded, tied, clamped, plaited or sewn, either alone or in combinations. During this process, the flat textile becomes temporarily three-dimensional. When released from its restraint it reveals not only the desired pattern but also the memory of the manipulation itself. (Weltge 2002/03: 41)

In her book, *Memory on Cloth, Shibori Now* (2002), Wada outlines the changing aesthetic and cultural context of *shibori* in Japan. Etymological evidence suggests that resist dyeing—or *yuhata* ('knotting cloth')—possibly existed in the third century AD but was used extensively in the sixth century AD. During the Heian period (794–1191), *shibori*-patterned cloth was worn by high-ranking women and by the end of the tenth century, a varied type was worn by soldiers and servants. Wada documents that 'Tax records included in the *Engi shiki* show that shibori-dyed silk was accepted as tax payment by the imperial court, as were thirty pieces of shibori-dyed leather from Dazai-fu on the island of Kyushu' (2002: 37).

According to Wada (2002: 38–40), during the fifteenth to eighteenth centuries a group of *shibori* textiles called *tsujigahana* became fashionable as banners placed around Buddhist temples during special religious ceremonies or boldly-coloured battle banners incorporating 'pictorial designs (*boshi* shibori process) delineated with fine stitching of hemp or ramie thread and then capped (a cover placed over them as a resist) to preserve the patterns as the cloth was dyed in various colours'. More complex *shibori* processes evolved, often combined with '*sumi* brush painting, gold and silver leaf stencilling, and embroidery'. Wada explains that 'these textiles embody extreme elegance and luxury and attest to the skilled craftsmanship cultivated in the imperial capital'. The fabrics were worn as an undergarment beneath the *kosode*—an antecedent of the kimono—by prominent shoguns and warlords. Arguably, dress was used for centuries as a means to identify one's social class standing within the society, whether in the East or the West.

The highly skilled artisans in Kyoto perfected numerous techniques to produce fabrics that were 'prohibitively expensive and reserved by law for the privileged classes and entertainers'. In the late Edo period, the wealthy actors of the Kabuki theatre worked directly with the kimono-makers and often set the fashions of the day. These developments led to a strict division of labour in *shibori*-making, with certain individuals who bound, stitched or pleated the cloth, others who dyed it and manufacturers who sold it. In terms of both production and dyeing, processes were labour- and cost-intensive. Wada points out that 'according to sumptuary laws, farmers, artisans and merchants were not allowed to wear fine *hitta kanoto*, gold embroidery, stencilling, silk material, or dyes of either red or purple'. Like indigo, known as the most effective and most colourfast dye from plant fibres, safflower red required the addition of copious amounts of *benibana* dye, extracted from a herb that had been known for centuries to be good for blood circulation and female reproductive health in addition to being the source of the dye for cosmetics and textiles. As many as twelve pounds of petals of '*beni*' were needed to dye a single *kosode*. Interestingly, the laws limiting the use of this dye were not only an attempt to keep the thriving merchant class in its place but were also aimed at regulating the economy by discouraging overspending; but, in fact, that made the dye all the more sought after.

By the middle of the nineteenth century (Wada 2002: 42–4), with the downfall of the feudal system and shogun rule, Japan was opened to the outside world. This necessitated changes in both economic positioning and technological development. Inflation, competition from *shibori* produced elsewhere, and the decline of traditional kimono items being used for everyday wear forced an old-fashioned cottage industry to develop into a modern industrial system. Textiles, as consumer goods in the areas of sericulture, filature and weaving, became Japan's dominant industry in the first half of the twentieth century. In the 1920s, Japan was the world's largest exporter of silk, often coloured by chemical dyes, trading with Korea, Taiwan, Singapore and Africa. Despite the development of *arashi shibori*, or pole-wrap resist, by Kanezo Suzuki in 1850, in which the fabric is stitched and pole-wrapped to produce an overall blue design, mainly diagonally oriented on a white ground, more contemporary methods of dyeing cloth emerged in the twentieth century. Modernization promoted the internationalization of taste and Japanese men, in particular, were quick to adopt Western-style garments. By the 1960s, the only remaining *arashi* artisans were Gintaro Yamaguchi and Reiichi Suzuki, and by the 1970s, *shibori* manufacturing houses like Takeda and Matsuoko shifted their *shibori* production to expensive luxury silk kimonos and men's neckties, as well as the traditional cotton *yukata*. By 2000, with a growing interest in techno textiles, *shibori* producers in Japan were limited to a few establishments in the Nagoya and Kyoto areas.

In global terms, there are three developments that helped to rekindle interest in the ancient art of *shibori*: its introduction to America in 1975; the documentation of its practices in an English-based publication in 1983; and the initiation of International Shibori Symposiums, which began in 1992. Contemporary Japanese artists and designers, including Miyake, Yamamoto, Kawakubo, Watanabe and Hishinuma, among others, continue these traditions in conjunction with experimentation involving high-tech processes. They not only work with textile designers internal to their own design studios but also in collaboration with others, such as Koichi Yoshimura, Eiji Miyamoto, Yoshihiro Kimura, Osamu Mita and Keiji Otani (Nuno), to name a few, to foster the indigenous fabric industry, an important part of Japan's heritage. Japanese designers' interest in the processes involved in creating clothes have influenced all kinds of designers worldwide (Figure 5.1). According to Braddock and O'Mahony, in terms of new hybrid fabrics, experimental chemical processes and sophisticated technology,

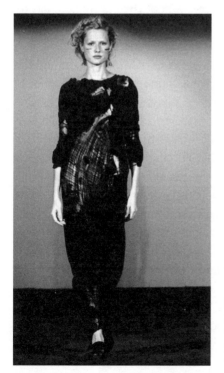

Figure 5.1 Rebecca Paterson SpppsssP, Deconstructivist/ Reconstructivist Rubens series, fabricated *shibori* dissolve wool dress, winter 1999. Collection: Powerhouse Museum, Sydney. Photograph: Leisa Hunt, www.leisahunt.com. Courtesy of Rebecca Paterson and Leisa Hunt.

Japanese fashion leads the field. In the East, fashion designers often work closely with textile designers and artists to create works exploring the potential of the fabric and the human body. Most of the leading fashion designers working with new materials and technologies are from Japan—the pre-eminence of Japanese research means that they have first access to the new developments. (Braddock and O'Mahony 1998: 116)

It was not surprising that a major exhibition held from November 1998 to January 1999 at MoMA in New York, entitled *Structure and Surface: Contemporary Japanese Textiles* and curated by Cara McCarty and Matilda McQuaid, assembled the work of the largest contingency of Japanese textile designers seen in America at one time. Significantly, 110 works by 29 artists, designers and manufacturers were installed according to six defining fabric characteristics: transparent, dyed, reflective, printed, sculpted and layered. In keeping with the Japanese aesthetic of coexisting complementary states, a single piece of fabric often combines a number of these qualities and so these classifications simply aided the organizational structuring of the exhibition.

First and foremost, this exhibition underlined that new processes and synthetic fabrics, developed after the Second World War, allowed for greater experimentation and manipulation of materials. Through continued research, it seemed that the possibilities were limitless. Advanced technologies now allow for thermoplastics to be moulded either by hand or machine to produce low-relief surfaces by embossing, pleating or refiguring the flat surface into distinctive three-dimensional forms by heat-treating in metal moulds. Crinkled surfaces can be created across a length of fabric by crunching the entire length into a tube and applying heat. Hybrid fabrics can be produced combining warps and wefts of natural and polyamide fibres which react differently to chemical processes, resulting in highly individualistic surfaces. Not surprisingly, these surfaces encouraged plausible analogies to skin and to the natural landscape to be made. Acids are used to stretch or shrink separate networks of threads, creating blistered textures. Synthetic textiles can be bonded with polyurethane to produce sculptural shapes in clothing. Aided by computer technology, a patterned photocopy can be translated into different weaving patterns, often incorporating windows or holes, and knitting machines can be programmed to produce sophisticated blendings of variable textures. Highly complex multi-layered cloths, with varying textures and surfaces, can also be achieved through high-tech lamination methodologies. Using new printing techniques, microfibres can be printed with newly-developed inks, including 'retroflective' ink, which throws light back to its source. Microscopic aluminium-coated glass spheres are suspended in the ink to achieve a highly reflective surface. Surface coatings of polyurethane will stop the oxidization of metal shavings embedded in some fabrics, while other coatings can produce holographic finishes. Chemicals such as a solution of silver nitrate can be used for stencil printing to highlight the silhouetted images of objects, scattered on the surface of the fabric, by altering (fading) the background surface. Highly reflective surfaces can be achieved using metallics and polyester slit films. This interface of science, technology, art and fashion can also consolidate 'fashion as function', especially when polyester garments can be spattered with a fine coating of stainless steel to provide a protective surface against heat exposure, ultra-violet rays and electromagnetic waves for the wearer.

This chapter will discuss the exploratory work of key textile designers Yoshiki Hishinuma, Junichi Arai, Reiko Sudo and the Nuno Corporation, Makiko Minagawa and Hiroshi Matsushita, and also textile companies, including Toray, Inoue Pleats, Asahi and Kanebo.

TEXTILE DESIGNERS

Yoshiki Hishinuma

While Hishinuma trained as a fashion designer, he turned to making his own textiles when he could not find suitable fabric for his fashion design work. He worked briefly as one of Issey Miyake's assistants, 'travelling extensively to research new, exotic fabrics and then returning to experiment with ideas on how to translate these materials into fashion items' (Lovegrove 2002: 95). As Hishinuma and Miyake held strong opposing views about textile development, they parted ways. At the age of twenty-nine, Hishinuma founded his own fabric design company, Hishinuma Associates Co. Ltd, in 1987. In 1992, he produced his own line of clothing and, in 1996, he was awarded the Mainichi Design Prize for Fashion for using technology to breathe new life into traditional Japanese tie-dye techniques. Working on his own, his design prowess evolved from the traditional Buddhist belief that the garment literally grows out of the fibre. Like many other art and design practitioners, including Miyake, he believed that it is the fabric that dictates the form. Hishinuma became famous in the 1980s for large pieces of clothing that were rather like kites and which were given their ultimate form by wind. Museums often used fans to simulate air currents to emphasize this aspect of his work, transforming the garments into sculptural pieces. Undoubtedly, in both visual and metaphoric terms, 'textile design meets fashion meets theatre' in his work. Miyake often used similar devices to activate movement in his 'hanging' creations, most evident in his work displayed at the Cartier Contemporary Museum of Art in Paris.

Moving away from natural materials to technology-driven synthetic fibres, both Miyake and Hishinuma recognized the versatility that synthetics offered as they could be effectively heat-treated, allowing for interesting textural aesthetic outcomes: 'Heat-setting can create a whole range of textures, not unlike the puckered effects possible with traditional Japanese shibori' (Braddock and O'Mahony 1998: 125). (Figure 5.2a) By using domestic items such as metal baking trays for moulds, Hishinuma could manipulate smaller sections of the fabric. Both concave and convex surface textures can be achieved by heat-moulding. Experimenting widely using traditional methods of tie-dying and smocking, Hiishinuma combined these with hi-tech materials and industrial processes, insisting that he only wanted to work with the most progressive Japanese manufacturers.

Working on a smaller scale is preferable to Hishinuma as he is able to sustain a sense of individuality and incorporate a craftsperson's touch in his work. Marie O'Mahony (2008) refers to this as 'Science fashion . . . when the worlds of science and fashion collide and give us a glimpse of what we could be wearing in the future'. She refers to Yoshiki Hishinuma as being, in her opinion, 'the most creative designer today . . . combining new technologies with traditional craft skills'. She argues that, 'craft is the answer', but only if it is 'introduced in a thoughtful way'. According to Gan and Browne (1999: n. pag.),

> Hishinuma wanted to make a three-dimensional dress without using a conservative process such as sewing. He created a large wooden frame and covered it with a piece of special fabric and placed the entire thing in a large oven. With the application of heat, the fabric shrunk

Figure 5.2a   Reiko Sudo/Nuno Corporation, *Melt-off* series/Contour Line textile, 1987. Photograph: Peter Page. Courtesy of Reiko Sudo and Nuno Corporation.

down into the form of a dress. He called this technique 'Propella Dress' which he has used in many collections.

By fusing materials together, Hishinuma makes new hybrids and specialty fabrics. For example, one fabric he worked with was a kind of polyester made from Lycra, synthetic suede thread and gloss enamel (Gan and Browne 1999: n. pag.), and he bound matt-coloured polyurethane paper by heat to woven polyester or knitted-cotton textiles. During the 1980s, in Japan, he created a series of garments made entirely from equilateral triangles. This process developed a single idea into a multitude of different possible design solutions and underlines the importance of design in the actual making process (Hishinuma 1986: 162–72). Bright, opaque, lacquered colours were placed over thin, supple art fibre and a metallic surface to decorate denim clothes. Quinn (2002: 142) argues that Hishinuma 'picked up Kenzo's fashion baton', as his work was reminiscent of a broad range of cultural nuances, by fusing 'colour with ethnic influences, often combining the organic with the synthetic'. He highlights Hishinuma's

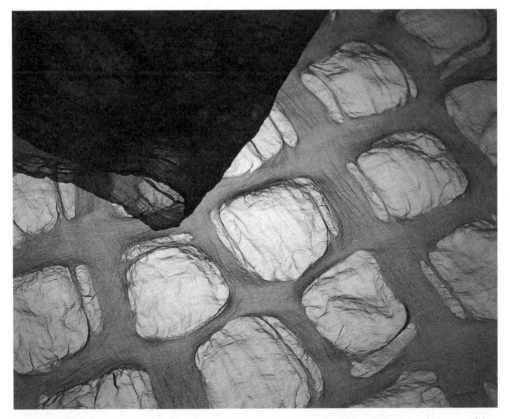

Figure 5.2b   Reiko Sudo/Nuno Corporation, *Salt Shrink* series textile, 1994. Collections: Museum of Art, Rhode Island School of Design, USA, The Israel Museum, Jerusalem, Los Angeles County Museum of Art, USA et al. Photograph: Sue McNab. Courtesy of Reiko Sudo and Nuno Corporation.

spring/summer 1997 *Tribal* collection, which 'epitomized his interest in using technological advances to turn synthetics into body-hugging pleats, which he covered in vibrant colours. Hishinuma used only black models, painting their faces with primitive tribal markings and giving them exaggerated, almost architectural, hairstyles'.

Hishinuma (Lovegrove 2002: 95) explains, 'I'm not interested in fashion trends. Concepts come from personal thought.' He added 'it's important for the first concept to grow and change freely'. His *Shrink* collections of the mid-1990s arose out of experimenting with the boiling of a sheepskin rug (Figure 5.2b). Applying the same principle to a range of materials he was able to produce a series of fabrics of varying surface textures. He also discovered that certain yarns, if heat-treated beforehand, did not shrink, leading him to partially boil parts of the natural yarn to create an uneven surface pattern. He found that he could make felt from repeatedly boiling and treading natural yarns. Experimenting with colour effects and working with an engineer for many years, Hishinuma developed a process allowing him to dye only the parts of the fabric he chose to colour by dabbing the colour on the surface. He has collaborated with numerous international designers throughout his career and is considered by many to be one of the most ingenious textile designers in the world today.

Junichi Arai

Junichi Arai has worked primarily as a freelance textile designer and has achieved notable recognition for his contribution to the evolution of Japanese textile design and process. In 1984, he won the prestigious Mainichi Design Prize for Fashion and in the same year co-founded the Nuno Corporation with Reiko Sudo. He has collaborated with many leading designers, including Issey Miyake (for the Miyake Design Studio [MDS]), producing textiles of great subtlety that appear rather like stone or clouds. While his work has been celebrated in numerous galleries and museums around the world, as an ambassador and motivator he has inspired a whole generation of devotees, who have attended the many textile workshops and forums that he has led.

The New York MoMA Japanese textile exhibition, *Structure and Surface: Contemporary Japanese Textiles*, paid homage to his work, among others, as it explored the theme of the compromise which exists between the natural and the man-made. Textile works in the exhibition translated the shiny, metallic finishes of the automobiles crowding the city streets, and discarded fragments such as nails and barbed wire, into a powerful visual metaphor describing a different type of Japanese landscape. According to curator Matilda McQuaid (1998: 3–4), 'in Japan, this coexistence is accepted, even revered, and its importance has more to do with time and continuity of life than with a stark presentation of extremes'. In fact, she argues, 'some of the most highly innovative and technically sophisticated textiles are portrayed in the most poetic terms'. Hi-tech fabrics made from industrial and synthetic fibres were often called 'birch bark', 'evening glow' or 'forest' to suggest the source of inspiration, to describe the surface texture, or to explain its origin. Junichi Arai, heralded as being one of the great technologically-innovative talents in texture design today, often used a polyester slit-film in which he sandwiched 'a layer of metal, such as titanium, chrome or gold', calling these materials 'contemporary natural fibres'.

He first became interested in the idea in the 1950s when, as the son of a weaving factory owner in the traditional textile town of Kiryu, synthetic gold yarns were introduced for weaving lamé and gold brocade. The town was famous for its silk and metallic brocade, used to make *obis*, the stiff, wide sashes worn around the waist over the kimono. He patented thirty-six designs related to metallic yarns which led him to Mexico to train workers and consult with textile manufacturers there. In the 1970s, Kiryu was one of the first traditional weaving centres to embrace computer technology integrated into jacquard looms and Arai quickly 'became absorbed in this new technology and found ways to incorporate it into traditional textile processes such as filature and finishing to create surprisingly unconventional textiles' (Wada 2002: 53).

The 1980s saw remarkable advancements in fibre engineering, with collaborative efforts between designers and scientists. Arai metallized sheer polyester fabrics with aluminium and then coated the surface with an ultra-thin film of polyamide resin that allowed the aluminium to be dyed any colour. Quinn adds that 'a vacuum sealer is used to ensure an extremely thin layer of metal' so as not to alter draping qualities (2002: 86). His abstract, marine blue-green textile entitled *Deep Sea* (1994) is comprised of a woven polyester and aluminium fabric which is melted, and through heat transfer the metallic areas are dissolved, exposing a transparent cloth and transferring the underlying colours to the surface of the fabric. Heat-transfer printing, a technique first introduced in the late 1950s, culminated in more sophisticated technological advances in the coming decades. Arai used this thermoplastic method on his microfibres to create his textural art pieces and to transform them into three-dimensional forms. He discovered that it could also be used to permanently pleat and wrinkle synthetic fabric while simultaneously adding colour. Working intuitively like a painter, he uses the process of sublimation dyeing with disperse dyes to produce a rich, dynamic surface, akin to an unpredictable explosion of colour. According to Wada (2002: 59–60), this is achieved by applying several layers of shaping and colouring to polyester metallic fabric on both sides in the heat-transfer machine, using a different colour each time, on each side. In one piece, this resulted in fabric where one side created an impression of the reds and oranges of molten lava being dispersed out of the mouth of a volcano, while the other side took on a pleasant and restful green, blue and yellow rainforest effect.

Arai became renowned for his limitless experimentation and exploration of new design possibilities and his long-term friend Reiko Sudo wrote in the exhibition catalogue for *Hand and Technology: Textiles by Junichi Arai*, 'He is truly the *enfant terrible* of the Japanese textiles, delighting in snubbing convention, a naughty boy playing with ultra-high-tech toys (in Arai *et al*. 1992: n. pag.). By combining the latest materials with time-honoured techniques such as tie-dyeing, *sashiko* and *shibori*, Arai was able to generate novel fabric finishes. These fabrications utilize resist dyeing, a technique that became the basis of many of the workshops that Arai held in the 1990s for international designers in locations including Hamburg and South America. Using metallic polyester fabric of his own design, Arai, instead of dyeing *shibori*-resisted cloth, used a mild lye solution to melt off the aluminium coating on the polyester film yarn, creating a silver pattern against a transparent ground.

Reviewing Arai's exhibition at the Kemper Museum of Contemporary Art in Kansas City, Missouri in 1997, curator Dana Self underlines Arai's insistence that 'fabrics must resemble human skin in their flexibility and combinations of earthy elements, while possessing an ability to reshape themselves and retain their original essence'. Self wrote that

> Arai merges traditional and non-traditional, simplicity and complexity and draws on centuries of Japanese textile tradition . . . Textiles and clothing reverberate with ideas about how we clothe ourselves, how certain fabrics make us feel physically and emotionally, and how fabrics and clothing function in our culture. (Self 2001)

Through his unconventional, innovative methods, Junichi Arai has inspired textile designers around the world for over fifty years and he leaves a legacy unmatched by any other.

Reiko Sudo and the Nuno Corporation

The Nuno Corporation was founded in 1984, when its flagship store was opened at the Axis Design Centre in Roppongi, Tokyo. While both Reiko Sudo[1] and Junichi Arai had established reputations as innovative textile designers since 1970, they joined to become the first directors of the company. Arai left after three years to work as a freelance designer, producing art textiles.

Under the directorship of Reiko Sudo, the Nuno Corporation continued to be a leading force in Japanese textile development. She encouraged her textile designers to work at the cutting edge of design, manipulating forms to suggest 'origami' folds, 'tsunami' swirls and 'jellyfish' puffs. She explains,

> I take fabrics that, in the past, could only be produced by hand and reinvent them in contemporary ways. I am always exploring industrial means to create things that are seen as traditional, in order to give them a new lease on life in the present. (In Wada 2002: 60)

Nuno developed a reputation for its use of computers, which were integral to the design and production of its innovative textiles and were often custom-designed for

Japan's leading designers, including Miyake, Kawakubo and Hishinuma. Macintosh-driven jacquard looms created airy textures induced by contrasting controlled shrink-age rates and multi-layered and tubular weaving that made seamless cloth of any length. Also, Nuno utilized the most advanced technologies to create unique designs during the 1980s. These included: *Bashofu*, based on Okinawan banana-fibre weaving (Figure 5.3a); the *Sashiko* series, based on traditional Japanese cross-stitching; the *Crepe* series, using ultra-spun yarns to create wavy surface textures; the *Burn-out* se-ries, where chemical etching corrodes to produce surface patterns on the textiles; the *Melt-off* series, using fibres that dissolve in baths leaving a gossamer opalescence; and the *Spattering* series, which borrowed spray-plating technologies from the auto-mobile industry to create a silky, stainless steel finish (Figure 5.3b). In the 1990s, all kinds of experiments—weaving fine threads of various metals; making patterns by stamping rusted iron on fabric; creating worn and torn fabrics through heat, chemicals, machines and by hand; using caustic burning to reveal multiple layers; and shaving high-pile, luxurious velvets—consolidated the company's trademark design approach of combining artisan work with industry.

In keeping with postmodern practice, Nuno melded tradition with contemporary practice, producing the *Salt Shrink* (*Enshuku*) series, where a traditional Japanese seawater-reactant treatment adapted to the modern textile mill was used and strings of persimmons in Japanese handmade paper (*washi*) were glued onto a velvet base with durable synthetic glue. They created one-of-a-kind woven fabrics that could only be made in Japan, and yet embraced sustainability through their new-millennium pur-suit of recycled fibres that were in keeping with traditional methods. The company takes responsibility for the waste management of remnants and off-cuts, an outcome of the actual production process, and reuses them to create collaged fabrics which they call *Nuno Tsugihagi*. Diverse materials are incorporated into the fabrics, such as phosphorescent pigments that store sunlight and shine in the dark with soft waves of light, seen in the *Baby Hair* textile (2007; Plate 16a), and wefts of copper wire coated with polyurethane used in their *Copper Cloth* fabric to prevent brittleness and discolouration. These specific materials are widely used for safety devices and fire prevention. Such fabrics not only underline Nuno's unique and innovative approach to new-age textile design but also suggest that subtle beauty, neutral colouring and textural surfaces can be intrinsic to both functional and non-functional textiles (see Nuno online).

Braddock and O'Mahony note (1998: 11) that Nuno makes many of their woven fabrics from rough, slub and highly-twisted yarns and that this, in itself, provides the 'decoration' for the fabric. The subtle changes in the fabric are integral to the structure and the woven structure lends itself to the creation of abstract patterns. The authors argue that,

Figure 5.3a   Reiko Sudo/Nuno Corporation, *Bashofu Avanos* textile, 1994. Photograph: Sue McNab. Courtesy of Reiko Sudo and Nuno Corporation.

Figure 5.3b   Reiko Sudo/Nuno Corporation, textile from *Spattering* series (*Stainless Steel Plates, Stainless Steel Emboss, Stainless Steel Gloss*), 1989. Collections: Museum of Modern Art, NY and The St Louis Art Museum, USA et al. Photograph: Takashi Sagisaka. Courtesy of Reiko Sudo and Nuno Corporation.

In Japan the essence of an artefact lies in its imperfection, individuality and an honest and true approach to the materials, features that are still highly regarded. Originally likened to the tea ceremony, this philosophy has become an important part of artistic expression—a work of art or design is enhanced by evidence of the hand that fashioned it. For Nuno this concept is fundamental.

Art in America's January 2002 article on Sudo's installation at the Kyoto Arts Center describes the six rooms as areas transformed 'into brilliant textile meditations on transparency, light and three-dimensional form' where the textiles were treated 'as sculptural form, weaving together visual wit with technical understanding and wild fearlessness' (Kushner 2002: n. pag.). In one room, multiple transparent fabrics became screens for video images of close-ups of Sudo's fabrics, creating an illusionary and spatially disorienting space.

In 2005–6, the exhibition entitled *21:21—The Textile Vision of Reiko Sudo and Nuno* toured Britain and Austria,[2] and this first retrospective show highlighted the pertinence of craft to industry by celebrating the twenty-one-year span of the work of Reiko Sudo. Thirty-two columns of fabric illustrated the breadth of experimental effect that Sudo was able to produce in her work. In the exhibition, *Feather Flurries* (around 1992; Figure 5.4), for example, relies on real feathers pocketed within a silk double-cloth to add another dimension to Sudo's work. *Bubble Pack* (1995) is an off-white silk which uses dye dots as a resist paste, and where exposed areas of the silk have been chemically shrunk to produce a relief surface not unlike the packaging material, Bubble Wrap. *Tanabata* (2004; Plate 16b) uses an origami method to cut the fabric. Mary Schoeser comments on old Asian techniques that have been revisited:

> using starch-resist and the use of alkaline pastes to alter or destroy fibres to create subtle patterns, a practice documented in the east as early as the mid eighth century. At the other end of the spectrum are such cloths as *Burner Dye* (since renamed *Karadaki*), made of an eight-micron stainless-steel fibre developed in 1997 by a Japanese tyre manufacturer. Three years of experimentation were necessary to discover that this extremely fine-steel thread could be made suitable for the loom by coating it with a water-soluble fibre, which is washed away after weaving. (2006: 33)

Interestingly, Schoeser points out that the tactile sensuality of the fabric increases the desire to touch the cloth and this is catered for in the exhibition by attaching sample fabrics to the labels as 'feelers'. Sudo's innate belief that the senses respond to textiles underlies the motivation for her design work.

In general terms, Nuno's design work and production 'responds to a desire to explore the very limits of structure, material and process in textile design' (Hemmings 2006: 362). Recognizing that fabrics with charcoal as a component can filter odour and pollution, in 2001 Nuno developed a blended fabric made of wool, silk, charcoal, polyamide and polyurethane. Charcoal was used for its health-giving properties

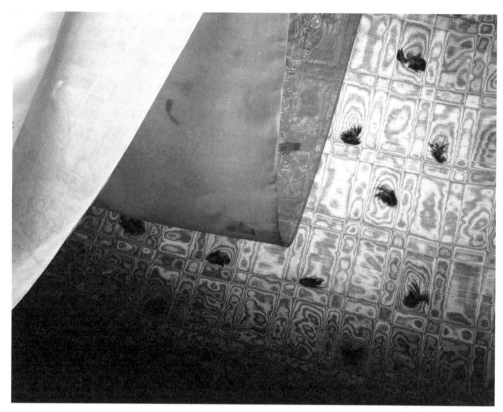

Figure 5.4 Reiko Sudo/Nuno Corporation, textile *Feather Flurries*, photo 1994. Collections: Philadelphia Museum of Art, Museum of Fine Arts Houston, USA, Montreal Museum of Fine Art, Canada, Hiroshima City University Museum of Art, Hiroshima et al. Photograph: Sue McNab. Courtesy of Reiko Sudo and Nuno Corporation.

as it has the ability to absorb chemical impurities in the air. In another combination, Nuno prepared a blended fabric in which bamboo fibres were combined with rayon, silk, polyamide and polyurethane. Bamboo has anti-bacterial and anti-odour properties. Undoubtedly, Japan is a leader in the design and production of highly innovative contemporary textiles that blend tradition and technology. Reiko Sudo has revolutionized the design of fabrics at Nuno by incorporating traditional Japanese crafts with new engineering techniques, new finishing processes and unlikely combinations of materials. The extraordinary visual impact of the work has led the Nuno Corporation to be viewed as one of the most prolific, pre-eminent textile producers in the world. Sudo's work is held in permanent collections worldwide, including MoMA, the Metropolitan Museum of Art and Cooper-Hewitt National Design Museum in New York; Boston Museum of Fine Arts; Victoria and Albert Museum, London; and the Tokyo National Museum of Modern Art.

Makiko Minagawa

Minagawa, a third-generation Kyoto kimono-maker who is esteemed for her exemplary expertise in the craft, was educated at the Kyoto City University of Art. Minagawa was an independent designer, known for her ability to combine a rural craft tradition with cutting-edge technological fabric science, before joining the Miyake Design Studio in 1971, where she has worked ever since as its textile director, a leading researcher and designer of woven fabrics. In 1989, *Texture*, a compilation of her work over a seventeen-year period, was published by Kodansha Press. The tactile subtlety of her surfaces and the minimalist simplicity of her fabrics gained her the 1990 Amiko Kujiraoka award of the Mainichi Design Prize. She has been distinguished in the last few years with many fashion and design awards and a solo exhibition in Japan.

According to Wada (2002: 77–81), when Minagawa collaborated with Miyake, communication took the form of a Zen dialogue with a few esoteric words spoken by Miyake regarding his ideas for future designs. Describing their working relationship, she relates that he would simply say, 'white in winter' and then she would ask herself, 'I wonder, the white of ice? The white of a salt field? The white celadon of the Korean Li dynasty? Or simply the white of snow' (Wada 2002: 77). Minagawa would then attempt to respond to these minimalist directions by producing new textiles that might take two to three years to produce. One of the most wondrous fabrics in the Miyake range was seen in the *Pleats and Twist* collection of 1993, where the rusty brown fabric emulated the bark of a tree and wrapped the arms as if they were branches. Many of the larger Japanese fashion houses, like Miyake, are investing considerable sums of money in textile research and development, and by incorporating textile development within the company, they control the entire process from beginning to end.

Minagawa also worked with leading specialist textile manufacturers to develop new fabrics. Like Arai, she was very experimental and bold in her designs, combining handicraft with new technologies. Braddock and O'Mahony point out that she was 'acutely aware of the physical and sensuous properties of textiles, particularly in the way in which a fabric absorbs and reflects light' (1998: 107). Combining natural and synthetic fibres, she explored their inherent properties and this led to a continuous experimentation with fabric constructions. She was able to create patterns in the fabric by folding, machine-stitching and dyeing layered cloth. In Japanese culture, the emphasis in textile design concentrates more on the process rather than the outcome. For example, in an attempt to counteract the tendency of synthetic fabrics to adhere to the body with static electricity, most of the MDS polyester fabrics are woven with a minute amount of metal in the fibre to protect against this static cling. McQuaid (1998) argues that 'No other fashion and textile design team in Japan has used layering more effectively to create an intriguing three-dimensional work than Issey Miyake and Makiko Minagawa.' She cites, in particular, the *Prism* series in 1998, where coats and dresses are made from layers of materials that combine hand-work with a traditional industrial method called 'needlepunching', originally used in carpetmaking. In these dresses, this method joined chiffon to batting to create a collage effect of layered colours. In keeping with Miyake's interests and references to ancient Japanese techniques in his work, this precedence for layering was established during the evolution of the kimono in the Heian period, when women of high rank wore ten or more layers of robes (visible at the neck, front and sleeve-openings) (Figure 0.1) which varied in colour and cut, carefully chosen to off-set one another.

Hiroshi Matsushita

Hiroshi Matsushita, a pioneer of printed textiles and a specialty weaver, collaborated with Rei Kawakubo over a long period of time, helping her to define the final look of Comme's collections. For example, Kawakubo commissioned Hiroshi Matsushita, designer at the Orimono Kenkyu Sha Fabric company, to produce the stretch gingham fabric that became famous in her *Bumps* collection of 1997.

Earlier, it had been Matsushita who, following Kawakubo's instructions, reformulated the actual fabric on the loom for the 1981 launch of her 'loom-distressed weaves'. She experimented with the actual looms in order to create the complexities, the imperfections and the novel textures of the final fabric. The following year, her 'lace' knit-wear was achieved when, as mentioned previously, she instructed the operators of the knitting machines to loosen a few screws so that holes could be knitted into the sweaters. These seemingly random holes inspired Deyan Sudjic to comment (1986) that Kawakubo could possibly be critiquing the redundancy of handicraft in an era of machine-made perfection.

Matsushita, producing other fabric that crumpled and wrapped, or draped coarsely as layers, was recognized for her highly original, innovative practice in modern textile manufacture. According to Sudjic's 1990 study of Comme des Garçons (which provided practical information regarding the manufacturing process):

It was Hiroshi Matsushita who devised the rayon criss-crossed with elastic that allowed Kawakubo to make the garments in the women's collection of 1984 bubble and boil as though they were melting. And it was Matsushita who formulated the bonded cotton rayon and polyurethane fabric Kawakubo used for her asymmetric dresses of 1986 . . . For Matsushita, the distinctive characteristic of a Comme des Garçons garment can be traced back to the thread that will be used to weave the fabric from which the collection will be made.

Kawakubo was renowned for her abstract instructions to her pattern-cutters, seamstresses and textile designers. She might tell Matsushita, for example, that she would like something using thin thread, rather than bulky thread, or something with a cold feel, something flat as opposed to something bumpy, something with depth and texture. Loyalty, respect and professionalism were at the core of these relationships, enabling and sustaining high levels of creativity for decades.

TEXTILE COMPANIES

While there are a number of monolithic factories in Japan, such as Toray, the largest textile company in the world, which are technically advanced and automated, the majority of operators are small and simple by comparison. Toray has expanded its base of synthetic fibres and textiles to include many other fields, such as plastics and chemicals, advanced composite materials, pharmaceutical and medical products, construction materials, housing, and engineering. Many of the smaller factories, including Kaneko Orimomo, Mitasho, Inoue Pleats and S. Yoshimura, formerly made kimonos and other garments and have operated for generations. Each company tended to specialize in a particular process, such as cutting, chemical etching, wave-red weaving, pleating or flocking. For example, in 1943 Inoue Pleats Inc. became the first company to process pleats in Japan. Since the emergence of acetate material in 1953, its pleating process has used thermoplasticity to allow the designers to develop highly complex, detailed, wave-like patterns through the application of heat and pressure. The Teijin Fibres Company is renowned for its colour-morphing satins, the Kyokuyo Sangyo Company for its thermal change fibres and, in the seventies, Toray Industries for introducing the world to ultra-suede, a waterproof fabric that pushes raindrops to the surface and is now its sculpture cloth.

In the Fukui prefecture, textile and paper industries were often housed under the same roof. Paper has been used traditionally with clothing because of its warmth and durability. A number of companies today combine synthetic threads with paper as a specialty and, when processed, the fabrics actually resemble *washi*, or Japanese handmade paper.

Two of the largest textile companies in Japan, Asahi and Kanebo design house 'Kaze' (which means 'wind' in Japanese) in Kyoto, specialize in heat-finished synthetics, using good-quality polyester fabric textiles that are printed and then finished with a chemical sealant. The process is labour-intensive and therefore expensive and more apt to be used in haute couture clothing. The Asahi textile design company supplies fabric for both haute couture and prêt-à-porter ranges, and now uses computers to change colourways quickly and efficiently, revolutionizing textile manufacturing. Kanebo manufactures the high-density polyester and polyamide woven fabric called

Belseta, made from the microfibre Belima-X, which is used in fashion and sportswear. Kanebo also introduced a microencapsulation technology to release perfume from its fibre. These types of 'scented fabrics' can be used to make lingerie and hosiery. The Japanese company Omikenshi has developed a type of viscose made from crab shells, which is claimed to have anti-bacterial properties. Another Japanese company, Kuraray, produces ultra-fine synthetic fibres as alternatives to leather. Their products are called Clarino and Sofrina, and they are used to produce fabrics used in sportswear, fashion and luggage. Presently, scientists and textile engineers are building microfibre fabrics which can be made windproof and breathable. These two qualities together imply that the fabrics prevent the smallest drops of water from entering while allowing the water vapour from perspiration to pass through. These properties allow the fabrics to maintain an even body temperature in all types of weather conditions and will, undoubtedly, revolutionize sportswear clothing.

In Kyoto, fourteen textile companies that produce textiles for women's fashion have amalgamated under the name Kyoto Scope. Twice a year they stage their textile shows at the Kyoto International Conference Hall to correspond with the spring/summer and autumn/winter fashion collections. One of Kyoto Scope's ranges, called *Zero*, is a result of the collaborative effort between all the companies and is known for its originality, uniqueness and quality. On a broader scale, an international textile trade fair called Première Vision has been held in Paris twice yearly (March and October) for almost thirty years.

Japanese textiles and art share common traits: they contain elegant imperfections and asymmetrical forms or patterns and respond both to the natural and urban landscapes. On the one hand, the surface of some textiles might reflect decay, weathering or elements of renewal or post-industrial practices, often recycling and reusing materials (MDS and Nuno); or on the other hand, they attempt to negotiate new surfaces inspired by industrial processes such as Bubble Wrap or incorporate marks into materials such as rusted nails or barbed wire (Reiko Sudo's *Scrapyard* series). One of the key issues of our time for all avant-garde designers, both Eastern and Western, is the reconciliation of craft and the look of the handmade with high-tech, mass-produced processes. In one instance, for example, 'computer-driven mechanized looms are routinely interrupted so that tiny elements, like feathers or paper, can be inserted by hand' (McCarty 1998). By doing this, designers embed the meaningful mark of the hand with the poetic in their work. In Japan, this practice of manipulating and imposing structure on cloth was undoubtedly inspired by traditional *shibori* techniques, and continues with contemporary textile designers, who take extraordinary measures to ensure that individuality and diversity, which has always been the hallmark of Japanese artistic practice, is sustained.

Plate 1 Issey Miyake, spring/summer collection, October 2001. This collection mirrored the freshness of a spring garden with ribboned fabric which intricately wrapped the body, creating a celebratory display of colour and technique. Photograph: Petre Buzoianu/Avantis/Time & Life Images/Getty Images.

Plate 2 Issey Miyake, *A-POC* display, *Radical Fashion* exhibition, V & A Museum, London, October 2001. Photograph: David Benett Collection/Hutton Archives/Getty Images.

Plate 3 Issey Miyake, multi-coloured 'Accordion' dress for spring/summer 1994, RTW, Paris. Photograph: Pierre Verdy/AFP/Getty Images.

Plate 4 Yohji Yamamoto, silver and black bustle-front dress with ruffles, Carreau du Temple, spring/summer 2008. Photograph: Eric Ryan/Catwalking/Getty Images.

Plate 5 Yohji Yamamoto, gathered red dress with black scarf and gloves, March 2009, RTW Paris. Historically, this gathered and draped garment, more reminiscent of European haute couture than Japanese design, is akin to the work of Vionnet or Balenciaga. Photograph: Chris Moore/Catwalking/Getty Images.

Plate 6 Yohji Yamamoto, long, white, panniered, full-skirted dress with white ropes draped around neck and shoulders, spring/summer 2006, RTW Paris. Photograph: Pierre Verdy/AFP/Getty Images.

Plate 7 Comme des Garçons, 'Abstract Excellence' patterned skirt and jacket, spring/summer 2004; on display at RMIT, Melbourne Collection: Peter Boyd 'S!X' designer. Photograph: author.

Plate 8 Junya Watanabe for Comme des Garçons, model on catwalk wearing black, fedora-styled hat with ribbons and black, multi-layered coat-dress, autumn/winter 2006–7 collection. Photograph: Francois Guillot/AFP/Getty Images.

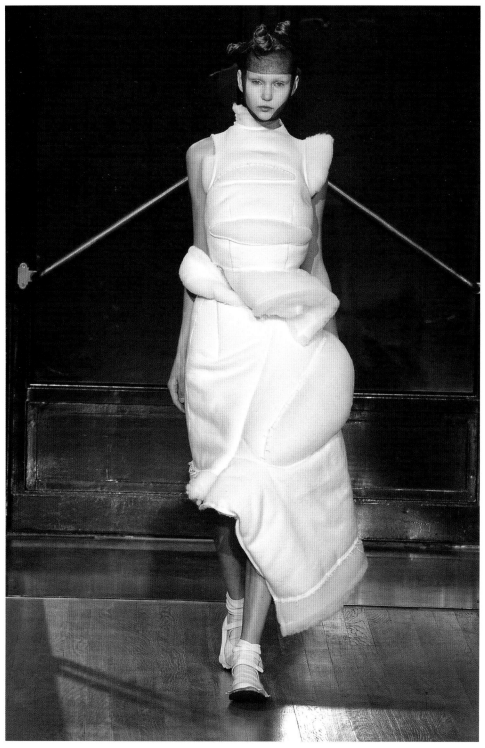

Plate 9 Comme des Garçons, white dress made from pillow-form outcrops of padding, *Inside Decoration* collection, autumn/winter 2010. Photograph: Chris moore/Catwalking/Getty Images.

Plate 10 Comme des Garçons, checked coat, model with face veiled, March 2009.
Photograph: Chris Moore/Catwalking/Getty Images.

Plate 11 Naoki Takizawa for Issey Miyake, green leaf motif (feathered) dress, autumn/winter 2007–8. Photograph: Francois Guillot/AFP/Getty Images.

Plate 12 Junya Watanabe Man, men's red-and-white checked jacket and knickerbocker pant-suit, spring/summer 2010. Photograph: Chris Moore/Catwalking/Getty Images.

Plate 13 Junya Watanabe, quilted black coat over bronze dress, autumn/winter 2009.
Photograph: Pierre Verdy/AFP/Getty Images.

Plate 14 Jun Takahashi for Undercover, 'but beautiful II homage to Jan Svankmajer', turquoise blue dress with large bow and hair swatches at waist and large, flowered hat, spring/summer 2004–5. Photograph: Pierre Verdy/AFP/Getty Images.

Plate 15 Indigo-dyed fabrics, shop in Yanaka, Tokyo, 2008. Photograph: author.

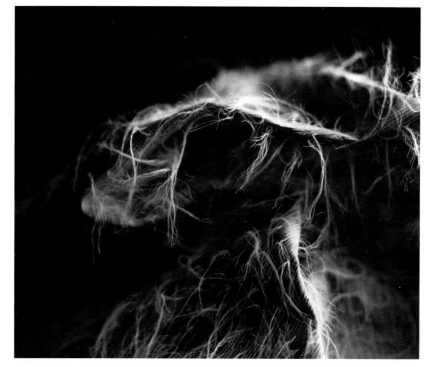

Plate 16a Reiko Sudo/Nuno Corporation, textile *Baby Hair*, 2007. Collection: The Museum of Modern Art, NY. Photograph: Sue McNab. Courtesy of Reiko Sudo and Nuno Corporation.

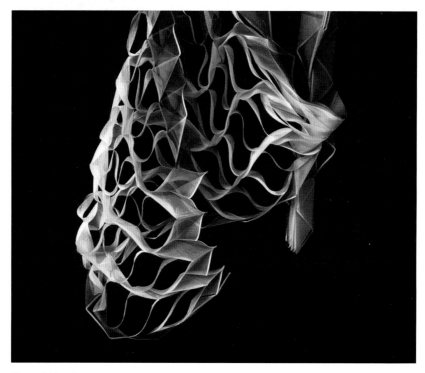

Plate 16b Reiko Sudo/Nuno Corporation, textile *Tanabata*, photo 2006. Collections: The Minneapolis institute of Art, USA and The Museum of Modern Art, NY et al. Photograph: Sue McNab. Courtesy of Reiko Sudo and Nuno Corporation.

Plate 17 Yohji Yamamoto, mannequin with constructed wooden bodice and Hussein Chalayan fibreglass mannequin with measuring tape. Photograph: Robyn Beck/AFP/Getty Images.

Plate 18 Ann Demeulemeester, long camel dress with black, deconstructivist coat with fur lining, 1999–2000. Courtesy of Ann Demeulemeester.

Plate 19 Ann Demeulemeester, black with red deconstructivist garment, 2005. Courtesy of Ann Demeulemeester.

Plate 20   Dries Van Noten, 2004, fiftieth collection parade, Paris: models walking on long banquet table. Photograph: Patrice Stable. Courtesy of Dries Van Noten.

Plate 21 Hussein Chalayan, copper spiral skirt, London Fashion Week, February 2000.
Photograph: Sinead Lynch/AFP/Getty Images.

Plate 22 Helmut Lang, white deconstructivist top, vest, trousers and jacket with hood, Mercedes-Benz Spring Fashion Week, NY, 2008. Photograph: Biasion Studio/WireImage.

Plate 23 Hussein Chalayan, remote-controlled dresses—closed version/open version, spring/summer 2007. Photograph: Pierre Verdy/AFP/Getty Images.

Plate 24 Viktor & Rolf *Couture Crunch* peach tulle evening gown with holes cut out, MTV Europe Music Awards, Berlin, November 2009. Photograph: Jeff Kravitz/Film Magic/Getty Images.

–6–

Global Influences: Challenging Western Traditions

The next wave of revolutionary designers after Kawakubo and Yamamoto came from Belgium.

Akiko Fukai, Kyoto Costume Institute[1]

The Japanese designers have had an unprecedented impact upon other leading fashion designers throughout Europe, Britain and America. According to fashion journalist Mark O'Flaherty (2009),

in the three decades since Y came on the scene, his once radical ideas have excited colleagues as diverse as Junya Watanabe, Jun Takahashi and Martin Margiela. His odd shapes and skewed proportions have informed an entire generation of Belgians and lately seem to be turning up everywhere, thematically threaded through collections as unalike as those of Marc Jacobs and Miuccia Prada and even highly praised newcomers like the American Jasmin Shokrian, who was not even a decade old when Y first showed in Paris.

Undoubtedly, deconstructionism in fashion began with the Japanese designers, Rei Kawakubo (Comme des Garçons) and Yohji Yamamoto, who established themselves as the leading avant-garde in Parisian fashion circles in the 1980s. Claire Wilcox, fashion curator at the V&A, explained, 'Western fashion at the time was surprisingly conventional . . . they had a huge impact, creating a disruption of construction' (in O'Flaherty 2009). German fashion writer, Vinken, remarked that their shows 'spectacularly marked the end of one era and the beginning of another. The creative impulses now came from prêt-à-porter and not from haute couture . . . fashion becomes a co-production between the createur and those who wear the clothes' (2005: 35). Author Ingrid Loschek (1999) underlined in 'The Deconstructionists' that 'In the 1990s, the Belgians, Ann Demeulemeester and Martin Margiela, emerged as its main representatives.' Demeulemeester recalls: 'I was just finishing my studies [when the Japanese designers had their European debut] and it was a brave new step in fashion—the beginning of a new freedom for me as a designer and as a woman' (in O'Flaherty 2009). According to O'Flaherty (ibid.), people who took the new Japanese designers' influence to London and New York included John Richmond and fellow London clubland prodigy Maria Cornejo, who started their 3D Richmond Cornejo label in 1984. Richmond says,

> When I was growing up you couldn't find black clothes. It was only with the Japanese that black really started. I love using black because I grew up in Manchester where the light always makes colour look grim. (ibid.)

Cornejo, whose label Zero was created in New York in the late 1990s, commented that for her the influence of the Japanese was in 'their cutting . . . and they also . . . broke new ground' (ibid.). Similarly, O'Flaherty feels that Rick Owens, then a 19-year-old Goth art student, shows an 'artful deconstruction . . . [that] shares the Japanese spirit' and that Owens found the Japanese designers' 'outsider status as much an inspiration as their cuts' (ibid.).

For the Japanese, 'deconstruction' meant that seams did not just hold two pieces of fabric together but, when exposed, gave energy and dynamism to the design, and asymmetrical points created movement and an interesting imbalance. One of Belgium's leading designers, Martin Margiela, who singlehandedly brought deconstruction to European shores, extended this concept one step further by combining things together that did not necessarily belong together. For example, he attempted to fragment the body by placing sleeves that were too wide into armholes that were too narrow. When Kawakubo and Yamamoto presented their first collection, in the early 1980s, of seemingly shabby, hole-ridden clothing, it was made from new materials. Margiela did not make the old out of new but used the old and the used as it was. This form of deconstruction was not meant to elicit a deeper sociological message about poverty or oppression, but to create a unique art piece that showed signs of the time, an aestheticism of its own.[2]

Deconstruction encompasses a wide range of possibilities, both tactile and conceptual. Notions of displacement, taking materials from one place and recontextualizing them in another, are juggled with the dissection of parts, where the process is underlined and the partial completion becomes the end product. In dressmaking terms, a *toile* is used to experiment with ideas, often stripped back and started again, but with the deconstructionists, the process becomes the final product. The dressmaking and tailoring techniques such as tailor's markings, basting, tying threads and attaching buttons, dress studs and zippers become forms of surface decoration in themselves. Self-reflexivity necessitates self-assessment and re-evaluation. Beauty is often found in the actual dressmaking process, and in order to preserve this state, the garment must be 'fixed in time', thereby deconstructing the illusion of perfection. To a certain extent, this process is underpinned by a kind of *naïveté*, as it entertains both serendipity and chance. The process necessitates the breaking of traditions, the rethinking of old ideas and reconfiguring of old forms. After all, why should the 'finished' product be finished at all? Do frayed edges, unravelling hems or underlining that is not hidden constitute a threat to the aesthetics of beauty? These avant-garde thinkers argue, through their work, that new lexicons of design must challenge existing norms and attitudes in order to create a new visual language of clothing.

Belgian fashion design has had an unprecedented following in Japan. Many young designers felt that they would never have been able to get a foothold in fashion if their work had not been embraced by Japanese youth who were looking for innovative clothing to express their personalities. Linda Loppa, appointed head of the Fashion department at the Antwerp Art Academy in 1982, and later instrumental in establishing the Flanders Fashion Institute, pointed out that,

> The success of Belgian designers in Japan is, to my mind, due to the fact that the Japanese and Belgians are kindred spirits to some extent. Added to which, there's the receptiveness to creativity among young Japanese buyers. (Derycke and Van de Veire 1999: 303)

Interestingly, the essence of the Japanese meaning of *wabi-sabi* applies equally to the work of the key Japanese designers, Miyake, Yamamoto and Kawakubo, and to the Belgian designers as well. According to Leonard Koren,

> *wabi-sabi* refers to the beauty of imperfect, transitory and unfinished things. It refers to the beauty of the unpretentious, simple and unconventional. It is anti-rationalistic and implies an intuitive world view; it aims at individual solutions that are specific to every object; uniqueness instead of mass production; organic forms; toleration of neglect and wear; corrosion and contamination used to intensify the expression; ambiguity and contradiction; suitability being less important. Beauty can be enticed out of ugliness. (In Schacknat 2003: 103)

MARTIN MARGIELA—THE RAG-PICKER

> The designers that we most admire are 'those with an authentic approach to their work.'
>
> The Maison Margiela team

Margiela, a member of the Antwerp School, is as reclusive as Rei Kawakubo. He shuns publicity, does not allow himself to be photographed, and will not make public appearances. This anonymity tends to make sense to individuals who do not want to become celebrities. He insisted that garments that came out of the Maison Martin

Margiela were the products of a collaborative team, not an individual person.[3] Like the Japanese designers, including Miyake, Yamamoto and Kawakubo, Margiela does not follow international trends, instead choosing to refine and recontextualize ideas formed in earlier designs and collections. In 2001, fashion writer and educator Rebecca Arnold (Polan and Tredre 2009: 230) argued that 'Margiela's approach undermined the notion of the designer as a unique, individual creator, by conceding that each design is the product of fashion's history' and that Margiela shared 'the same spirit as Japanese designer Rei Kawakubo, recognising imperfection as a route to authenticity . . . in contrast to fashion's traditional role as the purveyor of ephemeral, perfect fantasies' (Figure 6.1).

His clothing design is built on paradox—a combination of contrasts and juxtapositions. For instance, in one garment, one side may favour a hard, structured shape, while the other side may be soft and fluid. This interplay creates a performance: 'Margiela claims the fashion designer as puppeteer, suggesting a directional role in shaping the performance that is implicated by the clothes. The performance here is the act of making and unmaking, while the garment adorns a moving body' (Wilcox 2001: 39). He uses old forms, old mannequins and clothes hangers to show his collection. Garments, epitomizing a practised 'plainness', are of over-sized proportions, with long arms and with linings, seams and hems shown on the outside, and seams and darts torn open to reveal new textural effects. Devoid of ornament, except for loose dressmaking tapes that wrap around the sleeves, pick up skirts and mark high waistlines, they defied the glamour, excess and status of the 1980s. After four years at the prestigious Royal Academy of Fine Arts in Antwerp, studying cut, draping, anatomy, marketing and design, Margiela had become one of its most notorious graduates.

His anti-fashion tactics include empty labels sewn into clothes—an absence that marks his presence. Exposed on the outside of his early collection garments, his labels included a series of numbers printed on a white rectangle, attached with four white stitches. When circled, 1 = women's wear, 10 = menswear, 22 = shoes and 11 = accessories. This obsession with anonymity extended to collections that had no names and stores that had no signs. His collection showings took place in old, poor, often disused areas of Paris 'such as Barbès . . . inhabited mainly by Africans and Arabs, in empty Metro shafts, in deserted parking lots, in disused railway stations' (Vinken 2005: 139). Signs of wear and tear extend to his models, who are unrecognizable to the audience and are often non-professionals. They wear strips across their eyes, or their heads are swathed in veils to preserve their anonymity. These strategic devices, in themselves, obliterate the 'artist-as-genius' label, eliminate elitist glamour and status, often attributed to the model, the garment and the venue of the collection showing, and deny the cult of the supermodel. While seemingly mimicking the traits of the Japanese designers, challenging all existing fashion

Figure 6.1 Martin Margiela, five mannequins with jackets in twentieth anniversary exhibition, 2010. Photograph: Sylvain Deleu. Courtesy of Sylvain Deleu and Somerset House, London.

tropes and using the colour black extensively in his early work, Margiela is much more than just a clone of the Japanese avant-garde. In many ways, Margiela is more radical than Kawakubo, bordering on the subversive, challenging sartorial institutions as a form of defiance, not necessarily laced with humour as Kawakubo's work was purported to be.

When he showed his first collection under his own label in 1988, after having worked for Jean Paul Gaultier for two years (1985–7), Margiela was heralded as one of the new revolutionary avant-garde designers fashioned in a mode similar to Rei Kawakubo and Yohji Yamamoto. His inside-out bohemian design reacts to traditional notions of dressing and sexuality. It comments critically on the notion of glamour and the obsession with celebrity. It shouts at consumerist rituals by combining unconventional materials like jute and plastic with light, transparent weaves. His nonconformist fashion, often constructed and reconstructed several times, underlines a cult of the individual. However, while Lipovetsky in *The Empire of Fashion* (1994) initially argued that individualism was the prime focus of fashion in the twentieth century, evidence in recent times suggests that a shift has taken place. Andrew Hill, author of 'People Dress So Badly Nowadays' argues that, within a postmodernist framework, 'questions of individual identity and a reflexivity about these questions have come to be fore grounded in a way not seen in earlier eras' (2005: 67). Reinforced throughout Hill's text is the idea that anti-fashion, which initially challenged the conventions of fashion, has, in turn, been accepted as mainstream. In other words, non-conformity has become the norm.

With seams barely tacked together, Margiela's clothing bordered on the disposable and seems to become a metaphor for transience and superficiality in contemporary culture. His first show, held in a Paris parking garage, had models with blackened eyes and pale faces walking through red paint which left their footprints on long sheets of white paper. This paper was used to make his next collection. In subsequent shows, he wrapped bright blue garbage bags around recycled, throwaway clothing, made coats out of old synthetic wigs, used second-hand flea-market scarves for skirts, decon-structed tulle evening gowns to make jackets, and used partly unravelled knitted socks to make new sweaters using the knitted heel for the breasts or the elbows. He also made waistcoats out of broken crockery. Margiela's idea of transforming abject materi-als into designer fashion paralleled the work of a number of postmodernist conceptual and installation artists, including Britain's Tony Cragg, Russia's Ilya Kabakov, China's Yin Xuixhen and Mexican-born Gabriel Orozco, who also perceived the commodification of cultural detritus as a significant emblem of contemporary lifestyles. In 1991, an ex-hibition of Margiela's work was held at the Palais Galleria, Paris, where the decor and all its contents, originally painted white, was covered totally with graffiti for the duration of the show (Derycke and Van de Veire 1999: 285). This, by the way, was encouraged as part of the 'interactive experience' for the viewing audience. His work appeared to most as a satire of couture values. Yet, at the same time, his work inspired worldwide trends. His cutting technique became legendary and his deconstruction of a number of denim garments led to the popularity of shredded jeans as a fashion item. Com-mercially, it was indicative of the powerful influence that he exerted in design circles. By exploring the possibilities inherent in adopting vintage dress, by rethinking it and infusing it with poetic sentiment, it became a desirable entity—something to be cher-ished and admired.

Perhaps Margiela's greatest challenge to haute couture, underlying his mastery of deconstruction and reconstruction, was this use of second-hand clothing which was torn apart and reassembled or fashionably recycled for the consumer. In the seminal text entitled *Belgian Fashion Design*, Derycke and Van de Veire explain,

> He finds inspiration in the past, reusing old clothes, as well as doing couture work. Margiela is fascinated not only by the structure of the garments, but also their history. His extensive use of 'recovered' items . . . challenges the authenticity of the creation. His 'flea-market style' is, in fact, a sophisticated study of traditional tailoring . . . Margiela restructures the form of the piece with cut-outs or darts, and dyes them to change colours and patterns. He gives the old, rejected and condemned clothes a new life. Old clothes have an emotional meaning for him, they are witnesses of the past, of life itself. The fact that the 'new' old

clothes are not always finished (an unsewn hem or a frayed seam) is intentional, because what is unfinished can continue to evolve. (1999: 290)

As well as giving a second life to old and rejected garments, Margiela recreated vintage-store 'finds' into new garments that sometimes looked identical to the originals. He chooses carefully and replicates the exact proportions of the old, handmade, made-to-measure clothes. These used clothes, referred to as 'artisanal production' were reworked by hand and they retained traces of the past as if time had stood still. But, for Margiela, this did not equate to appropriating history:

I'm interested in the entire culture of fashion . . . but I'm not interested in taking one moment in history and copying it. Commercial stuff is always in the themes. This was one of the details no one could understand in the beginning. There was no theme. (In Spindler 1993)

Unlike Yamamoto's, Margiela's garments are quite literally infused with meaning, with reminiscence of past times or previous owners. It is this nostalgia that transforms the value of a garment from a superficial novelty to a vestige of historical resonance. Trying to avoid presenting different 'new-for-newness-sake' seasonal collections, he recycled some of his collections by re-dyeing them grey. This inspired younger designers to take the next step, which was to re-design other designers' work. Several years later, Margiela experimented with *trompe l'oeil* techniques by using photographs of garments and printing them on light and fluid fabrics that were made up into garments of very simple construction. This produced 'confusing images—like the heavy cardigan which, on closer inspection, turned out to be a simple silk blouse' (Derycke and Van de Veire 1999: 291). These garments, using modern photo-prints depicting paradoxical textures, including wrinkles or handwork, became an important part of his legacy to cutting-edge fashion design in the twenty-first century.

Both Evans and Vinken argue that, underlying Margiela's deconstructionist approach to fashion design, is his obsession with the mannequin, the dressmaker's dummy, or the doll. Significantly, this idea has dominated his collections for many years. In 1994, apparently as a joke, he produced an entire collection based on what Barbie's wardrobe would look like if it were blown up to life size. The clothes were enlarged 5.2 times and replicated identically. This corresponded to Comme's *Metamorphosis* collection of autumn/winter 1994–5 being photographed by Cindy Sherman for the Kawakubo's direct-mail campaign, in which the garments were placed on slumped, dysfunctional dolls. Other designers, including Chalayan and McQueen, 'substituted dummies for fashion models on the catwalk by playing on the robotic qualities of the model, stressing the inorganic at the expense of the organic' (Evans 2003: 165). In 1996, Margiela recreated the tailor's dummy as a linen waistcoat and pinned the front half of a silk chiffon draped dress over this, thereby virtually transforming the model into a mannequin. He christened this 'semi-couture' as it reflected the idea or concept, which was more important than the garment. In other examples, Margiela creates a garment made from individual pieces of cloth where hems and darts are externally visible and could quite literally be pinned to the cloth doll. Vinken, attempting to elucidate the fetishist nature of fashion, argues that,

> The irony is not the suggestion of woman as doll, but the doll as 'woman', as the woman that women are not. These 'unfinished' pieces expose the fascination with the inanimate, with the statue as doll, as the hidden nexus of fashion. In postfashion, this process is laid open and reversed, turned inside out. The lifeless model appears as a living person, and conversely, the living human body appears as a *mannequin*, as cloth doll. (2005: 141).

A number of other contemporary designers, including Yohji Yamamoto and Chalayan, have alluded to deconstruction relating both to the garment and the model by 'reconstructing' the body into separate body parts. In 1992, for a man's three-piece suit, Yamamoto used unpainted plywood panels to construct the front of a vest, made from twenty separate pieces (Plate 17). Chalayan incorporated a variety of moulded pieces, including materials used in aircraft construction to make garments that had moveable parts. This allowed for transformations to take place—from pieces of furniture to garments and from garments to video screens. Using remote control devices, he was able to transform models into mechanical robots or doll-like figures.

McQueen (Evans 2003: 188) more blatantly highlighted the 'uncanny equivalence between model and dummy' by using a model whose legs were amputated beneath the knees to model his clothing. The photographic prints, taken by Nick Knight, that appeared in the September 1998 London magazine, *Dazed & Confused* (edited by Mc-Queen himself) emphasized the wooden prosthetic lower limbs attached at the knees. The model and athlete, Aimee Mullins, was depicted as a 'fragile and pretty doll' with legs smudged with dirt, fingernails chipped and generally in a run-down 'mechanical' state. This message is obtuse, as other images in the magazine instead canonized her ability to rise up to the challenge of athletic contest—enabling her, and infusing her image with the heroic.

In 1999, McQueen used doll-like, red-headed twins in his autumn/winter snow-storm show, *The Overlook*; Viktor & Rolf placed a petite, doll-like model, Maggie Rizer, on a revolving pedestal and proceeded to overwhelm her slight frame with nine layers of clothing—the greater the bulk of the clothes, the more she resembled an inanimate, fragile doll; and Margiela substituted life-size wooden puppets for living models, who were operated, from above, by black-clad puppeteers who moved with them along the length of the catwalk. Clearly, this common theme, used in these presentations, inspired many designers and suggested a renewed interest in the mass-produced, mechanized human forms that were dominant in the early twentieth-century modernist art tradition. One remembers the Parisian photographer, Eugène Atget, who became obsessed with the inanimate mannequins in store windows that were dressed in corsets, men's suits and hats; or the German artist, Hans Belmer, with his 1930s sculptures made from parts of broken dolls; or of Fernand Léger's paintings of cylindrical figures embedded in the new industrial landscape.[4]

The notion of scale, as highlighted in the Viktor & Rolf collection and earlier in Margiela's *Barbie* collection, was resurrected in Margiela's 2000 *Dolly Mixture* show, where 'models dressed and made up to look like Victorian dolls were juxtaposed against images of real Victorian dolls dressed in similar clothes'. Both models and dolls were the same size and were 'made to appear dysfunctional with bald foreheads, hair askew and jerky poses' (Evans 2003: 166). In blatant terms, the comparison was unmistakable. At London's Victoria and Albert Museum, a 2001 exhibition called *Radical Fashion*, curated by Claire Wilcox, featured the work of eleven visionary designers who had in common 'a radical, uncompromising and highly influential approach to fashion' (Wilcox 2001: 1). The designers who were invited to exhibit their work included Chalayan, Comme des Garçons, Lang, McQueen, Margiela, Miyake, Watanabe and Yamamoto, among others. The exhibition included garments from Margiela's autumn/winter 2000–1 collection and consisted of clothes expanded from 100 per cent to 200 per cent of their original size. These colossal, over-sized garments, often five times the normal scale, offer different interpretations. Wilcox suggests that they 'question our place within the inherent dimensions of society' (2001: 4); some insist that they comment on the ideal 'Size 0' for women, projected by the fashion industry, as unrealistic and perverse; others argue that they are part of Margiela's fixation with scale, inspired by an original, 1930s customized tailor's dummy sized to provocatively replicate a very large women's figure.

On only one occasion, in 1997, did Rei Kawakubo and Martin Margiela show their collections together in a 'two-person' event. Amy Spindler, writing for *The New York Times* (1997), notes that it was significant that the two designers shared the same space and time, considering that Kawakubo 'was the woman who had influenced him the most'. Kawakubo relates that

> For me, the reason for presenting our collections one after the other is because I hope that our belief in the importance of creation will be more strongly felt due to the impact of the simultaneous expression of our similar values. (In Spindler 1997)

Spindler argued that, in reality, what the event underlined was how distant Ms Kawakubo's vision actually was from the man she once so obviously shaped. Spindler described Kawakubo's experimental garments as finding a balance between being pleasing and soothing on the one hand, and challenging and optimistic on the other.

In contrast, without any subtlety, Margiela's concept clothing was blatantly described in text on cards held out from the garments, presented by attendants wearing white laboratory coats. Justifiably, his more aggressive presentation marked the dramatic difference between the two. This followed in 1998–9 with the presence of models deleted completely and replaced by 'fashion technicians'. On the walls were projected:

> the written descriptions [of the clothes] were montaged with video shots of models wearing the clothes, to a soundtrack of thunderous applause. At the same time men in white coats (reminiscent of the white coats worn by master technicians of haute couture such as Hubert de Givenchy and Cristobal Balenciaga) 'demonstrated' the clothes by carrying them around on hangers and pointing out their features. The following year, for spring/summer 1999, Margiela sent out models wearing sandwich boards with pictures of each garment rather than showing the actual clothes on the model. (Evans 2003: 80–1)

Working with a microbiologist, Margiela[5] experiments with the notion of patina and ageing in textiles. In this he is like Kawakubo, who was renowned for her explorations into achieving a worn, tattered, threadbare effect, and subjected her fabrics to being scrubbed, ravaged by the elements, and treated with chemicals to achieve this end. Extending this concept, Margiela explores the Dadaist idea of relying on an accidental transformative process—in his case, of the effect of decay on the material structure of fabric. His 1997 exhibition entitled *9/4/1615*, held at the Museum Boijmans Van Beuningen in Rotterdam, featured clothes displayed on eighteen mannequins placed outside the Henket Pavilion; succumbing to yeast, mould and bacteria, the garments became a living commodity like flowers or fruit. By creating a scenario where the mannequins are viewed from inside, looking out through the floor-to-ceiling windows, Margiela, in his inimitable style, paradoxically reversed the concept of window shopping (Figures 6.2a–6.2c).

With time, such deteriorating surfaces begin to suggest another intention or meaning—that of decay, a theme that has been central to the work of many contemporary artists. The beauty created by the process of decay becomes an inherent component of the work. Heide Skowranek, in her essay entitled 'Should We Reproduce the Beauty of Decay?' (2007) notes that the German artist, Dieter Roth, is perhaps the best example of an artist whose interests have centred on decaying surfaces and 'its changing forms, colours, variations of putrefaction and mould, and their ornamental aspects, the natural mutation of things—and felt that chance, as a shaping element, should be part of the creation process'. Umberto Eco reminds us that 'a work of art is both a trace of that which it wanted to be and of what it actually is, if the two values do not correspond'.[6] Margiela's garments might suggest to the viewer that their mutability draws a parallel between the transient life of the work and of human existence. In other words, mortality is, in effect, paraded in front of us.

Figure 6.2a Martin Margiela, installation view of *9/4/1615* exhibition at Museum Boijmans Van Beuningen, Rotterdam, 1997. Photography: Caroline Evans. Courtesy of *Fashion at the Edge*, Caroline Evans.

Figure 6.2b Martin Margiela, pea jacket in external courtyard at *9/4/1615* exhibition. Photograph: Caroline Evans. Courtesy of *Fashion at the Edge*, Caroline Evans.

Figure 6.2c Martin Margiela, empire-waisted dress in external courtyard at *9/4/1615* exhibition. Photograph Caroline Evans. Courtesy of *Fashion at the Edge*, Caroline Evans.

Another interpretation, proposed by Ingrid Loschek, compared the ravishing of the clothing by mould and bacteria to the cyclical nature of fashion, and suggested that Margiela related 'the natural cycle of creation and decay to the consumer cycle of buying and discarding' (Loschek 1999: 146). However, Evans (2003: 36) reminds us that contemporary fashion has been framed symbolically between the extremes of 'élite fashion and ragpicking, luxury and poverty, excess and deprivation'. She also underlines the premise that 'although Margiela used the techniques of the avant-garde, his practice was rooted firmly in commerce'. Again, this ties his work with that of Rei Kawakubo, as her collection showings verge on the precipice of performance art, yet the underlying garments, however embellished, are still very saleable commodities. This is what has prompted Kawakubo to infer repeatedly that she is not an artist but a fashion business entrepreneur. To a certain extent, this notion of the nineteenth-century rag-picker is reliant on the melancholic associations that it conjures in the mind of the viewer. John Galliano's collections of the late 1990s—the age of 'cultural poetics'—also reflect these *fin de siècle* images of luxurious decadence.

It is not surprising that, by the mid 1990s, journalists were beginning to use the terms 'deconstruction' or '*le destroy*', at least in literal terms, to describe the physical signs of breaking away from the fine finishing techniques of traditional seaming, hemming and pattern construction. Garments that appeared to be partly finished or 'under construction' were often produced by designers working on small-scale production runs. The garments were, in essence, artisanal pieces, built on craft methodologies, and were extremely labour-intensive. These designers refused to be drawn into fashion syndicates and wanted to retain control of their own studios. For example, there were London designers such as Jessica Ogden, who came to prominence after participating in the Oxfam recycling project, and Robert Cary-Williams, who reused old garments or army surplus stock and took scissors to the finished product to reveal the armature of the original. In Melbourne, Denise Sprynskyj and Peter Boyd of the 'S!X label put Australian avant-garde fashion design on the map with their 'excavated' tailored vintage garments, especially other designers' clothing, which were cut up and re-stitched (Figure 6.3). Reflecting the strong aesthetic influence of both the Belgians and the Japanese, they became immersed in 'what might be called a "re-mix" mentality, where centuries-old traditional cottage industry materials were combined with contemporary forms and silhouettes' (English and Pomazan 2010: 226).

In 2002 the Maison Margiela, having achieved recognition for its contribution to environmental issues of sustainability and for lending fuel to the vintage boom, was incorporated into Italian Renzo Rosso's Diesel group, which was renowned for its innovative denim brand. Sales skyrocketed,[7] after the merger, driven by the designer's popularity in Japan, and Margiela launched a fragrance and jewellery line. A retrospective twentieth-year anniversary exhibition of his work was held in Antwerp in 2008, Munich in 2009 and Somerset house in London in 2010 (Figure 6.4). Soon afterwards he personally withdrew from Diesel as the head designer of his label. In 2009 alone, the Maison Margiela label had made $105 million for Diesel.

THE ANTWERP SIX

The original six members of this group consisted of Ann Demeulemeester, Dries Van Noten, Walter Van Beirendonck, Dirk Bikkembergs, Dirk Van Saene and Marina Yee. They studied at the Royal Academy at Antwerp in the Fashion department under the auspices of Mary Prijot. By the time they graduated, they were aware that the agenda of Parisian fashion had changed with the advent of one of Rei Kawakubo's early Paris fashion shows for Comme des Garçons. According to Derycke and Van de Veire,

> Her sudden introduction of a 'Hiroshima look'—with introvert white faces and torn pieces of clothing—rather referred to a memory, to an intense experience, than to a certain canon of taste, or of fashion. For the periphery this made it clear that fashion wasn't something that was dictated by some unknown universal entity, or by a 'hypothetical' body that frequented certain fashionable circles, but the work of human beings, influenced by factors such as time and place. (1999: 11)

Figure 6.3 S!X designers, Denise Sprynskyj and Peter Boyd, using an 'excavated' Hishinuma original deconstructed bodice and trousers. *Sculpted Packages* collection, March 2004. Photograph: Ryan Pierse/ Stringer/Getty Images.

Figure 6.4 Martin Margiela, glass display cases with accessories, Margiela's twentieth anniversary exhibition, Somerset House, London, 2010. Photograph: Sylvain Deleu. Courtesy of Sylvain Deleu and Somerset House, London.

While Belgium was undoubtedly seen as being on the periphery of fashion in the early 1980s, these young, emerging designers saw fashion as a mirror of the times—a way of expressing themselves and portraying their self-portraits. As they all had the same training, it was easy to mix and match different designers' clothes together. Dries Van Noten commented that 'there's a particular approach to clothing that certainly is Belgian. You also see that shops tend to stock several Belgian designers at the same time. What's typical is that they tend to design "item by item", rather than a total outfit. You sometimes see people combining a Bikkembergs shirt with a jacket by me and another piece by someone else again . . . there is a certain degree of neutrality of design' (in Derycke and Van de Veire 1999: 8). They saw catwalk shows as being authored by the designer so they could take place anywhere, at any time and by any means. Rather than a spectacle, a fashion show became an interactive performance where the audience was directly engaged with the clothing. Just as Margiela's models walked down city streets among the crowds, the parade could involve theatrical performance where entertainment or dancing was involved. Van Beirendonck's *Killer/Astral Traveller* show (summer 1996), held at the famous Lido nightclub in Paris, featured forty muscled black models with coloured space wigs, and his *A Fetish for Beauty* show for summer 1998 involved forty ballroom dancers and twenty girls in dazzling evening dresses, face masks and reptile gloves.

The Belgian Six attracted the world audience at the British Designer Show in London in the mid to late 1980s, where they paraded their garments together for several seasons before going their own ways. While Margiela, Demeulemeester and Van Noten became major figures in the international arena, others including Bikkembergs and Van Beirendonck were running closely behind.

Ann Demeulemeester

I'd like to cut an attitude into clothes.

Demeulemeester (in Todd 1997)

'Demeulemeester graduated from Antwerp's Royal Academy of Fine Arts in 1982, the same year that Rei Kawakubo showed her first Comme des Garçons collection in Paris. Kawakubo, with her almost brutal cutting techniques, proposed that women were strong and self-determined. Demeulemeester, born a generation later, just assumed that they were' (Horyn 2006a). (Plate 18)

Demeulemeester's aesthetic has continued to work in parallel with the promise of the Japanese revolution, shunning trend, embracing the avant-garde and focusing on monochrome, 'because like an architect, new structures are clearer in black and white' (O'Flaherty 2009). When she first showed her work in Paris in 1992, all eyes were on the stockings, which were laddered, askew and shabby, yet at the same time, when juxtaposed with her sophisticated designs, they created a visual tension—a kind of pleasurable paradox. Like Margiela and the Japanese designers, her clothing exhibits an unfinished and accidental quality. However, unlike Margiela, she highlights the woman wearing the clothes and does not attempt to hide her identity (Figure 6.5): 'I want the woman in the clothing, and not the designer who dresses her' (in Teunissen 2003: 63). Teunissen, in his essay, 'Knocking Woman off Her Pedestal', argues that Demeulemeester's designs are elegantly made and discreet and, like the Japanese, 'remain unique and exceptionally pure' as they 'never define the female image'. Arguably, these Belgians . . . 'regard the Japanese designers as role models' and this 'new perspective introduced by the Japanese—putting design on the pedestal—acquires a broad following' (Teunissen 2003: 71). In the 1990s, when romanticism, seen particularly in the work of Galliano, reigned supreme on the Paris catwalks, the spark of radicalism was re-ignited with the Antwerp-trained designers.

Figure 6.5 Ann Demeulemeester, black leather, double-belted, deconstructivist dress with zippered jacket, 2004. Courtesy of Ann Demeulemeester.

While Ann Demeulemeester's work is tempered, refined and sophisticated, as in the Belgian tradition, it is practical as well. When she is designing, it is as if she were designing the garment for herself. Perhaps, for this reason, her work is quieter, simpler and more sustainable than many of the others. It could be this sense of restraint which has evolved over the years to make her, by 2010, one of the leading Parisian designers. She infused her elegant work with a quiet confidence, a personal strength that she transfers to her clothing design, creating an authenticity that many saw as a plausible image of the modern woman. It translates as a new feminine Western ideal, an ideal that might not have been possible without Kawakubo's initial trailblazing. As seen in most postmodernist work, the designs are multi-layered with meaning, and different versions of modern womanhood are projected in the conceptual work of other designers including Hussein Chalayan, Helmut Lang, and Veronique Branquinho. In 1997, her bare-breasted models featured men's ties around their necks coupled with hipster pants, inspired by the problem 'How can I dress a woman with a tie?' According to Teunissen, Demeulemeester's clothes strike the right balance between male and female elements, between tough and sweet, how to be sensual without being drenched in sex. In Demeulemeester's work the erotic is accidental; it emerges in a sudden opening or a drooping shoulder. It's the studied refinement in this noncha-lant, almost ordinary, presentation that provides that spark of modern eroticism. (2003: 70)

Like Kawakubo and Balenciaga, Demeulemeester negates the influence of other de-signers and follows her own directions. Like the European master, she is preoccupied with volume and renowned for her masterful cutting—in her case, her legendary trou-sers. In the late 1980s, her designs seemed classical, especially with her use of a predominantly monochromatic palette, her attention to proportions and details and the strong lines of her signature long coats and dresses. By the early 1990s, however, a more complex deconstructed aesthetic evolves, coupled with the same austerity, and comes to dominate her work. 'Design-and-Not-Decoration' has always been her philosophy. Again, like Kawakubo, she became fascinated with twists and turns of fab-ric creating spiralling, draped garments, twisted tops and handkerchief-wrap dresses, asymmetrical lines, experimental fabrics, innovative surface treatments and feathers (Figure 6.6). Often a garment would be three times larger than necessary and drape in a very casual, off-hand way, or would include an unexpected detail at the back that takes the viewer by surprise. Like the Japanese, she works in a serial manner, with one idea evolving from the last. 'Every collection is one piece in a big chain. Each could not exist if the one before it was not there' (Demeulemeester in Blanchard 1998). Neither Margiela nor Demeulemeester work according to themes, as is the custom with other Parisian designers. According to Derycke and Van de Veire, 'her inspiration comes as she tries to answer the fundamental questions she has asked herself . . . how do you suggest movement? How do you un-balance a body? How do you "cut" a garment that challenges gravity?' (1999: 118). For Demeulemeester, design becomes a form of problem-solving to which her garments offer solutions.

While it may seem contradictory to the notion of 'fashion-as-business', Demeule-meester seems to be at odds with the concept of hyper-consumption. Kawakubo has also alluded to the sentiment echoed in Demeulemeester's words, 'I cannot stand to make another thing for the sake of consumption'. In an interview, Tamsin Blanchard of *The Independent* (1998) points out that

[Demeulemeester] is not interested in the idea of clothes as product. There has to be some-thing more. Designing a new collection, she sets herself a problem to be solved. Each item has to have a reason to exist. Each piece is only worked on by Ann. She does not have a team like other designers. She even makes her own lasts for her shoes, sculpting until she arrives at the perfect shape.

In her summer 1999 collection, she used a painter's canvas to produce an exclusively white collection which investigated the relationship of the material to the body, and

Figure 6.6 Ann Demeulemeester, beige gathered and roped deconstructivist pantsuit, 2005–6. Courtesy of Ann Demeulemeester.

questioned the idea of wearability. A difficult question needing a complicated solution. It is at this point that fashion garments become something more than superficial and attract women who seek more than 'styling' in their choice of clothing. Demeulemeester has been able to marry the avant-garde with enough commercial savvy to ensure a solid foundation for her business enterprise.

In financial terms, Ann Demeulemeester's business interests developed slowly and steadfastly. She worked as a freelance designer for international ready-to-wear men's and women's collections from 1981 to 1987. With her husband, her B.V.B.A. '32' company was founded in 1985 and opened a Paris showroom in 1992. She opened her first store in 1999, called 'Louis', selling both men's and women's wear, housed in an historic building in Antwerp close to her home. It is run by Gerrit Bruloot, who helped to organize the Antwerp Six to show their work at the London collection showings. Demeulemeester always worked from her home studio so she could be close to her son as he grew up. Her operation was self-funded and she did not license or subcontract her garment production, ensuring total control over design, manufacture and distribution. By the mid 1990s, with an expanding business, she hired Anne Chapelle to run and restructure her company.

During the first decade of the new millennium, Demeulemeester consolidated her singular direction in styling—her philosophy towards designing that was founded on integrity, strength and 'confident' beauty. By 2006, the rest of the world caught up with Demeulemeester's concept of the new, self-assured, self-contained twenty-first-century woman. Fashion journalist, Suzy Menkes, commented that 'this new decade's view of the strong woman is about nobility, rather than aggression' (2010). Conversely, Sarah Mower (2006a), writer for *The Guardian*, London, reports that, in the February 2006 Paris collection showings,

> so many designers have begun quoting ideas about warrior women, and getting excited about gothic northern layerings, kudos are due to Ann Demeulemeester. She, after all, invented—or rather inhabits—this style. For her, sending out a strong urban female with an elegant-barbaric wardrobe is no passing whim, but a way of life, thoroughly believed in for 20 years.

Interestingly, Demeulemeester contends that 'there are people who treat their clothes with honesty, while other people 'dress up'. And they're a different story altogether, but one that is easily unmasked' (Derycke and Van de Veire 1999: 47).

Due to the consistency of her styling, there are few surprises in her collection show-ings for journalists to write about. Her trademark black layering, long, asymmetrical skirts and narrow, sari-like tubed dresses, draped from one shoulder, have dominated her *oeuvre* for years. She adds subtle changes in keeping with general trends: in one collection (autumn 2006) she added wide trousers, metallic leather and a slim coat with a military air, plus multiple chains or straps made of plaited leather, twisted and draped over shoulders and chests or wrapped around the body over coats and jackets.

Demeulemeester's earlier collaboration with the artist Jim Dine in summer 2000 inspired a series of exquisite, asymmetrical dresses in which the fabric was covered in silvery grey photo-prints of birds of prey. In her summer 2009 collection, birds ap-peared again, but this time photo-prints of flocking seagulls covered cotton jackets coupled with barbed silver necklaces. Sometimes flashes of colour appear in her clothes: the most pronounced in her multi-coloured 2000 range, but later in a more subtle way with black juxtaposed with scarlet, a trope often seen in the work of Yohji Yamamoto (Plate 19). Her March 2010 showing featured her signature feathers and fur, which added an 'after-dark' lushness to this seductive autumn range. The *Women's Wear Daily* (2010) described the show:

> The Belgian's designer's idea of dressy clothes is rooted in tailoring, exemplified by the elbow-length leather gloves—clasped with ornate silver cuffs—that poked out of the jacket sleeves unbuttoned almost to the shoulder. A suite of terrific black pantsuits opened the show, with windblown lapels giving them a nonchalant chic.

After thirty years of designing, Demeulemeester has secured for herself a prominent position in international fashion. She has been able to communicate an image through her clothing, which epitomizes a look that appeals to women internationally. It is sleek, sophisticated and cool and it projects a self-assuredness, inherent in the designer's own persona. In a direct, straightforward manner, she achieves what Kawakubo only suggests in her more obtuse, cerebrally interpretative, creations.

Dries Van Noten

I love to make beautiful things and to translate art into garments by experimenting with textures and colours.

Van Noten (in Silva 2009)

Dries Van Noten won the C.F.D.A.—the International Designer of the Year—award in 2008 and the 2009 Award for Artistry of Fashion from the Couture Council Advisory Committee, New York. His label has a strong brand identity, but like Kawakubo and Margiela, he is somewhat cloistered and enigmatic. Descending from a Belgian textile family, he also studied at the Royal Academy of Antwerp and four years later launched his own label, in 1985. The following year, having presented his work in London, he received orders from the prestigious Barneys of New York, Whistles of London and Pauw of Amsterdam. In 1988, he opened his salon in Antwerp, called Het Modepaleis, and debuted in Paris with his men's collection in 1991 and his 1992 *Fame and Fortune* collection, which showed both men's and women's wear. During these early years, his design work found a developing market in Japan.

Like Margiela, his collection showings took place in unusual settings, whether a disco party at the Piazzale Michaelangelo, Florence in 1995 (womenswear collection for 1996), with a fireworks display following; an empty swimming pool in 1996 (summer womenswear) with the pervasive smell of chlorine, where only two of the seventy models were professionals; a Paris car park (women's winter wear 1996–7) with Egyptian belly-dancers performing in front of a gold backdrop lit with 100 coloured candles, and serving sweet tea and North African sweetmeats to the audience; or sitting around coal fires in the snow (menswear 1996), drinking soup and wrapped in brightly-striped blankets, like the homeless. The biggest event to mark his fiftieth collection (October 2004) was an elaborate sit-down banquet at a 450-foot table set with linen and lit by chandeliers in a factory on the outskirts of Paris. He said that he had always dreamed of this event, with models parading his clothes by walking on the linen between the main course and dessert (Plate 20). For Van Noten, it is important to create a complete mood and a strong image and therefore the garments that are on display must reflect a synthesis of the collection, an 'open picture'. According to Francine Pairon, 'Belgian fashion shows are always a happening, with Margiela having pushed this idea to an extreme . . . [bringing] us back to the philosophy of the creative process' (Pairon in Derycke and Van de Veire 1999: 18).

In the 1990s, his work bore traces of exotic cultures, primarily from India but other countries, including Egypt, Thailand, Morocco and China, feature either in his styling, his patterns or his colour combinations (Figure 6.7). He consistently combined wraparound skirts with white blouses and would swap his clothes around with jackets used as shirts to illustrate the flexibility of the garments to the prospective wearer. Exquisite scarves, either sequinned or embroidered and made in Indonesia, became his trademark. Recently, he has become intrigued with a 'digital' aesthetic as an alternative to screen-printing and has produced numerous multi-coloured, highly-detailed prints within the same garment. This new technology allows for a totally new kind of exclusivity, as shorter production runs are possible.[8] He has a lifetime affinity with textiles and, according to Derycke and Van de Veire,

> His fabrics are usually dyed and pre-washed specially for him. He uses natural materials like silk and wool; he prefers fabrics that don't look too new; it should feel soft and look as if it had been already worn, as if the garment has been 'broken in'. He experiments with textiles: obvious materials are replaced by something more transparent, heavier or lighter. Subtlety lies in the way the fabrics are used, one layer superimposed upon another, and the combination of different materials. (1999: 215)

His work shares an affinity with Demeulemeester's in that it is simple, yet sophisticated, as he incorporates classical elements, and superb tailoring, characteristic of the training that each of them received. His collection, often described as being 'beautiful or poetic', is what sets him apart from the others. His great sense of colouring is described in length by many fashion journalists. They speak of clothes full of colour and energy in aqua blue, orange, magenta and lime green, or more subtle combinations of pale green coupled with a flesh tone or brick and khaki. He presents a very personal view of contemporary glamour. He says, 'I prefer to make garments for people to wear in lots of different ways. It's important that they can make the clothes their own and wear them to express what they want to say about themselves' (in Silva 2009). His work counteracts the excessiveness of the eighties, work epitomized by Mugler, Versace and Montana. And it transcends the concept of deconstruction. In menswear, his 1996 collection reflected the leanings towards a return to the slightly dishevelled British classic look—a camel overcoat worn over an orange V-neck with cream jeans. Amy Spindler described it as 'a sort of angry-young-man elegance, like a rich youth in rebellion' (1996a).

However, Van Noten is not afraid to show warmth and sentimentality in his collections as well. *The New York Times*' Gina Bellafante describes his March 2004 collection as

Figure 6.7 Dries Van Noten, embroidered ethnic jacket with short skirt, 2004, fiftieth collection parade. Photograph: Patrice Stable. Courtesy of Dries Van Noten.

intended for women in the midst of defining themselves . . . [he] turned out pleated chiffon skirts in abstract floral prints that kept you staring at them. Sheared fur pullovers looked as if the patterns of trees and flowers had been engraved. Intricately embroidered copper tops lacked any sense of ostentation. (2004)

His summer 2005 collection was equally as romantic, with coats cut close to the body in faded prints in cocoa browns and silvery taupes highlighted with shots of red. The coat always features strongly in his work, sometimes slim, sometimes bulky, with one style dominating—oversized, wrapped, belted with big lapels—reminiscent of Balenciaga's 1950s work. In fact, it is only in his 2010 collection that Van Noten veers away from his signature style to display olive and camouflage garments, reminiscent of military uniforms like French combat fatigues. Perhaps he was following the direction of so many other designers that season, who felt it necessary to make some kind of comment, through their clothes, of the constant media coverage saturating all global reporting of military presence in Middle Eastern countries.

Shaping a silhouette, creating a sense of nonchalance, making references to the past all play an important role in Van Noten's sartorial repertoire. Like Demeulemeester, his collections can be viewed as a 'body of work' evolving gradually across the seasons rather than shifting directions radically or suddenly. While this is in keeping with the Japanese design philosophy, Van Noten insists that his work is instinctual, more than it is cerebral or strategic. Like both Kawakubo and Demeulemeester, he believes in economic independence, which informs and sustains creative independence—key to the success of his work. He does not advertise, nor collaborate on a collection with other designers. He enjoys the process of making clothes and does not see the necessity of expanding his business any further into accessorizing merchandise. He likes to be able to micro-manage his design and production processes. As yet, he has decided not to distribute his work through the commercial megastores like Uniqlos, Zara or H&M.

Walter Van Beirendonck

Kiss the Future.

Van Beirendonck's trademark slogan.

Fashion historian, Colin McDowell, argues that sex, whether unisex or not, was the driving force behind Van Beirendonck's popular collection called W&LT (Wild and Lethal Trash), which was backed by the German Mustang company. His first show, in 1982, was called Sado in homage to the British artist, Allen Jones, who created sculptural furniture made from fibreglass images of nude, life-sized women acting as hat-racks or on their knees with glass coffee tables resting on their backs. This early show, he says, was 'condemned as near pornography by many, and W&LT has a serious following among the young of Europe and all who are interested in S&M' (McDowell 2000: n. pag.). His July 1995 collection, made up of psychedelic patterns, cartoon colours, padded patches and Pop Art prints, was also a great success. Not surprisingly, his work and notoriety 'caught the eye of the members of U2, who later commissioned him to create costumes for their 1997 *PopMart* world tour. The Edge's cowboy look and Bono's 'Fly 2000' were inspired by cartoon superheroes and action-man dolls (Gan and Browne 1999: n. pag.). His spring/summer 1999 *Aesthetic Terrorist* collection combined a roughly-cut, graffiti-style T-shirt under an eighteenth-century dress with neon-graphic faces imprinted on the front. Strangely, the dress (which appears as the cover design for Caroline Evans' *Fashion at the Edge*) actually becomes an historical monument. In menswear, he has made his mark by departing even more radically from existing avant-garde styling. It wasn't until 1999 that he made his first runway show in Paris at the age of forty-two.

Van Beirendonck's collection showings are notorious for their flamboyance. The lavish spectacle of fashion as performance art is underlined in his presentations. For example, his Cologne summer 1995 *Over the Rainbow* collection featured a huge catwalk built to look like a white wedding cake, nine metres high, with fountains, built on the banks of the Rhine. His *Paradise Pleasure Productions* (autumn/winter 1995–6) collection had the audience seated in a black box around a transparent catwalk with slogans and images of nature projected on the walls. At the finale, one side of the black box collapsed and showed the 120 models, dozens of whom were wearing latex bodysuits, while others wore face masks, lined up on a tiered stage. According to Van Beirendonck, 'A show is, in the end, a very important occasion. For a brief moment, it gives you power over space and time . . . it is an opportunity to work out and realise my fantasies in greater detail' (Derycke and Van de Veire 1999: 28). Later he stated that 'the audience expects something more than the clothes, it wants a bit of spectacle. But if the theatrical side is used to make up for a lack of content, then I think things have gone wrong' (Derycke and Van de Veire 1999: 44). One of his most extravagant shows was the winter 1998–9 one, where an electric blue catwalk, lit by white light, meandered for one mile and members of the audience were led to their seats in the darkened hall by attendants with flashlights. At the close of the parade, the curtain opened to reveal a fairytale world with elves staring down on the audience from above. His 1999–2000 show, called *No References*, alludes to his plan not to follow any past references to fashion styling and consisted of assemblages with four different puzzles arranged in different ways. Symbolically, this was meant to anticipate the wearer's needs for the fashion of the future.

While fashion journalists were becoming somewhat dismayed by Van Beirendonck's collection show pranks (walking for miles in the freezing cold, sitting in unheated, near-zero-degree tents), they did admit that his work was original and not re-hashed from the street. Androgynous in nature, he argues that he does not design specifically for either men or women. According to Van Beirendonck, 'This has nothing to do with transvestism. It's just that I see the sexes as equivalent' (Derycke and Van de Veire 1999: 250). He makes his work affordable to young people, priced well below designer lines. He insists that 'one of the challenges for a fashion designer is to adjust his story to suit the economic situation, to make it communicable' (Derycke and Van de Veire 1999: 298).

Dirk Bikkembergs

> My clothes are never retro. I hate the idea of looking back. I don't have any idols from the past.
>
> Dirk Bikkembergs

Bikkembergs' career followed a similar path to that of Demeulemeester, but he came to fame as a designer with his first collection of shoes, not garments, which he took to the British Designer's Show in London, and later won the Golden Spindle award in 1985, two years after Demeulemeester. A pair of men's loafers he designed in 1995 seemingly combined the heaviness of a Belgian work boot with a traditional slip-on loafer and was included as part of an exhibition entitled *Remaking Fashion*, held at the National Gallery of Victoria, Melbourne, where they were described as being 'made by Flanders craftspeople and roughly overpainted in red; the grain of the wood and leather shows through the wedge heel, which has been stacked in order to expose the multiple layers used to form a strong sole' (National Gallery of Victoria 2008: 22). He presented his first men's line, sponsored by the Italian manufacturers Gibu, in September 1988 in Paris. His work extended to womenswear in 1993, and he developed a reputation for distinctive tailored silhouettes, minimalist lines with unadorned surfaces and clean-cut sportswear that appealed to the American market.

In keeping with the strong futuristic philosophy of Kawakubo, in the 1980s and 1990s Bikkembergs designed for the new generation of strong, confident individuals who were not swayed by passing fads or stylistic trends. He asserted that his clothing was designed for tomorrow and the distinctive macho image, that his menswear projects were based on traditional notions of masculinity. He echoed Yamamoto's words when he quipped, 'nothing so boring as a "nice and neat" look'. His clothing's image was described as being full of energy, masterful in cut and edgy. While his approach is more tempered than that of Margiela and Van Beirendonck, and there is little evidence of deconstruction in his clothing, he takes an uncompromising, intellectual view of fashion. The casual, yet seductive, quality of his clothes lies mainly in the personality of the designer. For Bikkembergs, this alludes to the use of rough, thick and textural materials, often incorporating leather, felt and heavy wool in his garments. Concentrating mainly on cut and fabric, his clothing often indirectly references sporting activities with a heavy-duty functionality. His early biker image, black boots and leather outfits heralded a look that dominated a number of collection showings in the late 2000s. In particular, his tight-fitting black leather men's trousers, with zips running up the back of both legs, paraded in his autumn/winter 1999–2000 collection, defined his own personal style of sexuality. For decades, his signature knitwear range of heavy-ribbed, V-necked pullovers became a staple item in every man's wardrobe.

Like many other designers, as Yohji Yamamoto did with his *Y-3* label, Bikkembergs turned to classic designer sportswear with his distinctively masculine edge during the financially volatile 2000s. Interestingly, Bikkembergs began to 'test' his collection garments on soccer players from the F.C. Fossombrone team, in which he later (2005) purchased a majority stake. From couture jackets to high-performance sports underwear, he promoted this classic, sporty look and his menswear became the epitome of urban cool. By 2007, his brand sales had tipped 120 million Euros, a profit driven by his marketing technique of using soccer players as models for poster campaigns, magazine articles and on the catwalk. The increased cult of the soccer celebrity became a fertile territory for the fashion industry. His 2010 Milan *Sport Couture* show featured form-fitting sweaters, body-hugging trousers, pullover knit vests, and laced-up, knee-high boots, which has become his modern signature look.

The Next Generation

The 'second generation' of Belgian designers, who graduated from the Antwerp School in the 1990s, carried on the tradition of quality tailoring that continued to distinguish Belgian students from their international counterparts. Among these newcomers were Josephus Thimister, Veronique Branquinho and her partner, Raf Simons, the label A. F. Vandevorst (made up of the design team An Vandevorst and Filip Arickx), and Olivier Theyskens, who dropped out of school in her third year. Interestingly, their main production and distribution centres remain in Belgium, rather than in France, thereby consolidating Antwerp as a key fashion city. Both Thimister and Branquinho display great strength in keeping with the Belgian tradition of robust practicality and sophisticated style. However, Branquinho, in particular, is known for her love of the dark side, her romantic version of clothing for the doom generation. The A.F. Vandevorst label, which has a great affinity with the work of Joseph Beuys, is known for its equally expressionistic designs, which explore the duality of women and the strong versus the vulnerable, highlighted particularly in their 1998–9 *Nightfall* collection, where the models' lingerie-sleepwear was evident under outer clothes, reinforcing sensuality and femininity. In 2003, they opened their collection with a trenchcoat made from brown paper with its sleeves belling stiffly over the model's thin arms, insisting that they were exploring shapes, structures and volumes. Alternatively, Theyskens, while still maintaining impeccably handcrafted garments, 'trashes up' his collections by combining plastics and fur, and has established a reputation for a 'raw brand of couture'. Not unlike Margiela, his first collection consisted of Edwardian-style dresses made out of old linen sheets. The element of darkness pervades Theyskens' work as well and his dramatic black satin coats, worn by Madonna at the Academy Awards, his 'Hitchcockian' dress covered with a frenzy of attacking birds, and his funereal dress smothered in black flowers all attest to this more serious aside of his design portfolio. By 2000, younger emerging designers, including Stephan Scneider and Anna Heylen, had also set up business within the designer precinct of the city centre of Antwerp.

When the new century began, it was the Japanese and Belgians who appeared to have laid the sturdiest foundations for the future, but it remains to be seen whether their radicalism will win out over the romantic heroicism promoted by many of the most powerful and influential designers currently working in Paris.

THE NEW CONCEPTUALISTS

The concept is more important than the dress itself.

Hussein Chalayan

Western fashion design in Paris has been slavishly tied to change. New ideas are picked up and then quickly discarded. Apparent from the 1960s onwards, Yves St Laurent once quipped that change was the only constant in the accelerated 1960s lifestyle and that fashion designers must look to the street for inspiration. During these postmodernist years, transforming styles reacted to popular art and music developments and hems raised and lowered in response to feminist ideologies, wars, economic recessions and social disenchantment.

When the Japanese arrived on the scene, things had already started to change. While a more confrontational punk fashion had emerged from London in 1978, the Japanese influence was more pervasive, seeping vicariously across time. Over a number of decades, their non-transitory, conceptual approach influenced Western designers into thinking more about concepts—different ways that ideas could be formulated to address the fashion system, the body and the notion of identity. From the 1990s onwards, many themed fashion collections adopted a serial approach, developed within the context of performance art. To counteract the realities of terrorism, global disputes and financial downturns, there was a growing trend towards the display of fantasy, towards an historical romanticism in collection showings that could sweep the audience away to a different time or a different place. The masters of these spectacles were

John Galliano, Jean-Paul Gaultier and Alexander McQueen. Others, including Viktor & Rolf, Helmut Lang and Hussein Chalayan (Plate 21), treated fashion design differently—primarily as a cerebral exercise, with the same intellectual rigour as if it were an artistic pursuit. Like the Japanese, their collections asked more questions that they answered. They did not make authoritative fashion statements as had been the conventional approach but, instead, attempted to foster a continuing dialogue. 'I really do think I'm an ideas person', said Chalayan, 'as ideas are very valuable. The concept is more important than the dress itself' (Frankel 2001: 68).

Parody, Pastiche and Performance: Viktor & Rolf

Viktor & Rolf, in particular, radically reassessed designer clothing and its relationship to the body. Graduating together in 1992 from the Arnhem Academy of Art, Viktor Horsting & Rolf Snoeren chose to concentrate on the 'constructs' of fashion rather than on fashion itself. In this respect, they were 'outsiders' or 'pretenders to the throne' who were ironically challenging the notion that sartorial status was defined not by the clothing but by association with the image of the designer. They became fashion's 'Duchamp-duo' by consistently reinforcing their standing not as designers, but as performers. Laced with humour, they chose to depict the body as an object with clothing being solely the 'packaging'. In their 1998 collection, their conceptual couture fashions featured distorted figures and exaggeration of forms as they piled one garment after another on the model, Maggie Rizer, until her slight form grew to enormous proportions, much like that of a Russian doll. Their pumped-up volumes created fashions that were larger than life. Not only did the work of Victor & Rolf illustrate and satirize the bankruptcy of ideas prevalent in early 1990s haute couture showings but it could also be argued that it was their response to Kawakubo's *Bump* collection (1997), shown the year earlier. Their provocative work inspired a number of other postmodernist 'readings'. As an art performance, it breaks away from the 'linear' progression of catwalk models to an 'accumulative' progression of garments which are collectively used to dress a single model. Like the Japanese clothing, it comments on the role of the body in contemporary fashion as a non-sexual and non-gendered object. Conceivably, it could also comment on the pomposity of couture fashion and its theatricality, which creates garments that are 'larger than life'.

Undoubtedly, their staged productions poked fun at traditional haute couture and turned the collection showings into pseudo-slapstick events. Informed by a sense of absurdity, they ridiculed the pretentiousness of elitist fashion, breaking traditions and conventions by riddling their clothes with intentional errors and contradictions. They were provocative, ironic and, in many ways, their frolics were a relief from the seriousness of the Japanese and Belgian fare. Their first collection, in 1993, for example, parodied Margiela's vintage clothing by featuring a ball gown made from old shirts and a dress revamped from an old jacket and trousers. In their 2001 collection (Figure 6.8), their models, dressed totally in black, wore, for example, ruffled leather blouses and black pearl jewellery and painted their faces entirely black as well, challenging the potent and pervasive Japanese aesthetic. Almost insolently satirizing the Japanese conceptual designers, they presented a collection that supposedly celebrated the introduction of black as a cult colour twenty years earlier. Conflating Americanism, consumerism and nationalism, their *Stars & Stripes* collection, in autumn/winter 2000–1, which made the cover of *The New York Times* magazine's fashion issue, not only satirized American capitalism, but became their best-selling collection. In retrospect, this was not difficult as they had sold next to nothing up until this point. Emphatic suggestions highlighting society's excessive consumption, evident in Viktor & Rolf's collection, have often been an underlying theme in the Comme des Garçons repertoire.

Viktor & Rolf's ultimate collection, which mirrored the sentiments of both Martin Margiela and Helmut Lang, capitalized on the facetious idea that the definitive

Figure 6.8 Viktor & Rolf, women's male-inspired black shirt, vest, tie and trousers with satin collar and cuffs, autumn/winter 2001–2. Photograph: Pierre Verdy/AFP/ Getty Images.

collection was one in which garments were not shown at all; instead they presented placards painted with the words, 'V & R are on Strike', as an art installation that only featured press clippings (about themselves). Their actions reiterated the growing reality that printed exposure, and the media-hype that surrounds the collection showings, is of greater value to the designer than the visual representation of the clothing design itself. Interestingly, this could be compared to the occasion when Helmut Lang sent CD-ROMS and videos of his collections to international editors in 1998 instead of holding runway shows. Significantly, it signalled a major change in the marketing of designer fashion. Again, after September 11, he stayed in New York and presented his spring 2001 collection on the Internet rather than flying to Paris. Not only did he not want to travel, he believed that this new method of e-fashion would make his show internationally accessible.

Viktor & Rolf, in keeping with their postmodernist art school backgrounds, deliberately appropriated the personas of two of the most famous 1960s performance artists. Adding another 'twist' in the presentation of their collection showings, they became entities in themselves by mimicking the Neo-Dadaists, Gilbert and George, as 'living sculptures'. They dressed in identical clothes and posed, like the earlier conceptual performance artists had in 1969, as a personification of art itself. Once again, by making themselves the centre of the performative event, they symbolized that the showmanship and status of the designer, not the clothes, was integral to the fashion system. From a marketing standpoint, their audience was so transfixed by the antics of the performers that no one was actually paying much attention to the clothes themselves. Despite this, they did, however, make a mark in the commercial marketplace with their shirts and blouses. They introduced multiple collars on shirts (2004), silk blouses that looked like upside-down shirts (2006) and a series of five white poplin shirts with satin and georgette detailing, which were inspired by classic men's dress shirts, festooned with a bib of blossoms and multiples of oversized bows (2010). Also, their perfume *Flowerbomb* became a top seller at Saks Fifth Avenue, NY and Selfridge's in London when it was first introduced in 2005, followed in 2007 with the men's fragrance, *Antidote*.

Clearly aware that the doll theme played a key role in many contemporary designers' collection showings, they began to build their own doll collection. Dressing each doll in a feature garment from each show, they turned the associated reference into a fetishistic game. In their book entitled *The House of Viktor & Rolf*, produced to commemorate their first solo exhibition at the Barbican Art Gallery in London in 2008, the images of the dolls dressed in exact copies of the garments are juxtaposed with the models on the catwalk. The publication draws attention to this very amusing visual paradox, intentionally exaggerated by the two Dutch designers, to reinforce the notion of anti-fashion for which they are internationally renowned.

Minimalism, Conceptualism and Technology:
Helmut Lang and Hussein Chalayan

In contrast, both the Austrian Helmut Lang and the Turkish-Cypriot Hussein Chalayan are very different designers. Taking a much more serious approach, it could be argued that these designers have more in common with Japanese and Belgian conceptualism in fashion than with their other European counterparts. While Chalayan is a graduate of Central St Martin's, Valerie Steele endorses that he has 'more in common with Rei Kawakubo than anyone else in London' (Wilcox 2001: 53). Like Chalayan, Lang's clothes are thought-provoking—perhaps excessively—and he often used slogans attached to his work. His collaboration with the artist Jenny Holzer, exhibited at the Venice Biennale, was projected with text such as 'I SMELL YOU IN MY CLOTHES', underlining that fashion can be read in obtuse ways. When Cindy Sherman collaborated with Kawakubo in her *Untitled Film Stills* (1977–80),

> Clothes [were] used as props, inserted into the composition to provoke a particular response about the women or femininity pictured. They reveal a tension within dress, setting and identity that creates an image that constructs its own narrative, a story that unfolds beyond the confines of the image. (O'Neill in Wilcox 2001: 41)

Communicating ideas, independent of a narrative theme, is central to the work of Kawakubo, Chalayan and Lang, who sought to re-think the formal logic of dress itself (Figure 6.9). Influenced by utilitarian street clothes, yet couched in luxurious, tactile materials, Lang's work, like Kawakubo's, comments on clothing as an unreadable surface, a mask of concealment, a tension between constraint and desire (Plate 22). In a more provocative way, Chalayan takes this idea one step further. One of his major themes deals with how religion can impact on human lives, and its subsequent oppression and isolation. His collection called *Between* (spring/summer 1998) portrayed women in Muslim body coverings. As the presentation progressed, the models discarded items of clothing revealing more and more of their naked bodies until only the faces were covered. While this would be viewed, particularly today, as very provocative and confrontational, Chalayan is a man who refuses to compromise his ideals or ethics and feels that 'clothing must be considered within the context of society, in a social and cultural context and not taken at face value' (Frankel 2001: 68). He is often described as living on the fault line between the Muslim and Christian worlds.

Lang, like Margiela and Chalayan, paid tribute to Kawakubo in terms of the notion of deconstructionism and experimentation with different materials. Wilcox argues that 'his uncompromising approach means that his collections are masterpieces balanced on the thin line between decadence and classicism.' (2001: 4). From the early 1990s, Lang's work was made up of multi-layered creations, often using minimal and

Figure 6.9 Hussein Chalayan, remote control dress in *Blog.mode Addressing Fashion* exhibition, Metropolitan Fashion Institute, NY, December 2007. Photograph: Amy Sussman/Getty Images

commonplace materials such as flesh-coloured net T-shirts covered by sheer blouses. By the turn of the millennium, his trademark became 'sleek and supremely flattering trousers, slim stretch tops and the best knee-length overcoats in the business' (Frankel 2001: 88). He was seen as the master of cool minimalism, a severe aesthetic which epitomised his devotion to creative purity. According to Frankel, because his presentation demonstrated a more modern and radical spirit at play, 'he is more closely aligned with the 'great avant-garde designers of our time—Rei Kawakubo of Comme des Garçons, Martin Margiela—as opposed to more mainstream brands' (2001: 88).

The evolution from deconstruction to reconstruction using both new and old materials, and second-hand and recycled vintage clothing, seemed like a natural progression and was evident in the work of numerous designers by the late 1990s:

> In London, Jessica Ogden used second-hand fabrics, saving their stains, darns and hand sewn seams to incorporate these vestiges of the past in her contemporary designs. The design company Fake London cut up and recycled cashmere jumpers in jokey pastiche themes; and Russell Sage revamped trademark fabrics like Burberry's in his *Sue Me* collection . . . In Paris in 1993, Watanabe showed ball gowns made out of old football shirts. Viktor & Rolf's tenth collection, shown in Paris in 1998, featured vintage 1960s Chanel and Pucci fabrics. In New York, Susan Cianciolo produced one-offs from vintage fabrics, and for his first collection

(autumn/winter 2000–1) the New York-based Spanish designer Miguel Adrover presented a 'garbage collection' that recycled, among other things [the expatriate British writer] Quentin Crisp's old mattress. (Evans 2003: 252)

One can only speculate on the influences of Chalayan's mother, a genealogist, upon his work. Evans (2003: 57) refers to 'historical layers, peeling one moment of history back to reveal another'. Chalayan recalls that 'the shredded black and grey garment [*Medea* collection S/S 2002] is a ghost of all the multiple lives it may have led. Nothing is shiny and new; everything has a history' (ibid.). He re-worked his older designs into new combinations, and then deconstructed them again. He might cut dresses from three past eras into fragments and almost poetically re-layer them together. He describes this process, based on historical traces, as archaeologically 'exhuming items from the past and giving them a new life in the future' (Evans 2003: 61). Like Yamamoto, he was preoccupied with the themes of memory and the ghosts of the past. For some, these garments spelled a sense of trauma and were misinterpreted as a response to September 11. Curator Jeff Kipnis[9] suggested that he confronted the fashion world with its own history. Unlike Kawakubo's often discordant finished garments, Chalayan, through simplicity, achieves poetic, beautiful clothes, clothes that are gentle on the wearer. In an interview with journalist Susannah Frankel (2001: 70), he states that he attempts to make clothes that women like to wear and for those 'who enjoy the intimate space between my clothes and their bodies. That, to me, is very important'. This view of architectural space is very much in keeping with the original concept of the Japanese kimono, and an underlying foundation in the work of Miyake, Yamamoto and Kawakubo. Echoing the sentiments of Miyake, in particular, Chalayan believes that 'by refining again and again, his clothes become minimal, and that functionality is the basis of modernism'. After all, he argued, 'It's harder to edit an idea than it is to add on' (ibid.).

When fashion draws upon the same sources as the avant-garde, it bridges the gap between art, theatre and life. Chalayan adopted new names for his various collections, indicative of his alternative approach to fashion. They include: *Temporary Interference* (1995), where he incorporated images taken from the air-traffic controller's screen, and *Scenes of Tempest* (1997), which used patterning based on meteorological charts in his textile prints. His *Airmail Collection* was made from non-rip paper; clothes that could be folded, placed in envelopes and sent through the mail. *Words* (2000) and *Afterwords* (2000–1) relied on transforming furniture covers into dresses while tables morphed into skirts. His themes have ranged from the inter-relationship between mankind, technology and nature to more socio-political orientations, including his 2003 *Manifest Dynasty* collection, which was inspired by the idea of America imposing its Western ideology on the rest of the world. His first ten years of design were exhibited in a retrospective show held at the Goninger Museum, Netherlands in 2005, where his fascination with flight and movement was evident in his *Aeroplane* dress, which featured plates that opened electronically to reveal part of the body. Also on show were garments with built-in neck-rests and chairs that were integrated with the garment. From 2006 onwards, there was a distinct focus on the possibilities of future fashions merged with technology (Plate 23). Chalayan, in collaboration with 2D:3D, a London-based design company, was able to mechanically program the outfits to alter the designs in some way. He inserted microchips in the corset or hat of each model, a power pack of batteries in a bumster also fitted to a controlling microprocessor, and tiny pulleys connected to cables that initiated specific actions. Lapels disappeared, hems changed length. In the December 2006 show, each of five dresses morphed through the iconic styles of three decades. *NYT* fashion journalist, Amanda Fortini, explains:

> The wedding cake tiers of a 1920s column dress folded into one another to form a basic '40s shift with a self-zipping neckline. The slats of a 40s A-line skirt opened outwards, umbrella-style, to become the full, New look silhouette of the '50s; the skirt then released and rose to mod mini-dress proportions while decorative metal plates dropped from hidden pockets in the bodice. As a final gesture, a gauzy sheath retracted into a model's wide-brimmed hat, leaving her naked. (2009)

These techno-fashions or 'smart-design' clothing referenced global warming and climate change in the 2007 collection, even though Chalayan insisted that, with his high-tech protection wear, he was not making a political statement. In collaboration with Swarovski, he also created crystal dresses with LEDs, powered by microchips, which displayed a video of changing seasons on the surface of the dress. Visually, this presentation was so breathtaking that the audience gave him a standing ovation.

London's Design Museum celebrated his success in a show called *Hussein Chalayan—From Fashion and Back* in 2009, his first exhibition in Britain. Menkes writes that 'the displays capture with quiet authority a style in which women are empowered but never exploited, the clothes gracefully embracing the body as the mannequins work at painting walls or clipping each other's dresses into a sculpted topiary' (2009a). Interestingly, these topiary dresses created by Chalayan in 1999 were investigated again—this time by Viktor & Rolf in their October 2009 collection. According to the duo, they were responding to the 'credit crunch' by bringing out a 'couture crunch' line of extravagant tulle evening dresses,[10] through which tunnels were burrowed and slices cut out (Plate 24).[11] 'The World is cutting back so we literally started cutting away chunks of the ballgowns—and with the remnants we created new clothes' (Menkes 2009b). According to Menkes, 'Chalayan [had] produced topiary tulle trimming with more grace, style and inventiveness'. Despite this, the collection was humorous and amazing at the same time and Viktor & Rolf appeared in the pages of *Women's Wear Daily* brandishing a chainsaw in front of a model wearing a froufrou tulle ballgown. Branded by many as another fashion 'recession' gimmick, fashion journalist Eric Wilson (2009b) attempted to contextualize the collection:

> Deconstruction, in less obvious forms, has had a revival in the spring collections, and it should be noted that its original heyday began during a deep recession two decades ago when Yohji Yamamoto in a decadent take, showed duster coats in black and buttercup peasant prints that looked as if the fabric had been eaten away by nasty mutant moths. The fabric was so worn it was barely there, hanging together by threads . . . the soundtrack alternated between Kiss and Doris Day.

How does one summarize the influence of genius? When you drop a pebble in a pond, concentric ripples spread from the centre—circles of energy that travel outward. *Japanese Fashion Designers: The Work and Influence of Issey Miyake, Yohji Yamamoto and Rei Kawakubo* has attempted to define the parameters of this energy. It has revealed the shifting paradigms in the design, manufacture, distribution and marketing of designer clothing over the past forty years and has indicated the breadth and depth of the influence of the Japanese fashion designers in both the twentieth and twenty-first centuries. It has shown how the intellectualizing of fashion has changed fashion's course, engaging curators, architects, academia and the intelligentsia. A new sensitivity has emerged, led by the Japanese designers, which underlines that women buy clothing for how it makes them feel, rather than the way it makes them look. This quantum leap has as much to do with meaning and memory as it has with culture and identity.

Minimalism and deconstruction in fashion, and in the other fine and applied arts, have become the two main stylistic characteristics of visual arts culture. For perhaps the first time in history, architects are looking towards fashion, and in particular Japanese fashion, for ideas about structure. All three designers—Miyake, Yamamoto and Kawakubo—have asked their audience to raise their consciousness regarding fashion as a sculptural form, fashion as an instrument of conceptual meaning and nostalgia, and fashion as a cerebral, and sometimes confrontational, force that can still be both beautiful and romantic.

Over the past ten years, fashion has questioned the modern aesthetic and a number of key designers say more about current global instabilities and uncertainties, and the rapid technological and social transitions, than they do about the aesthetics of fashion. Issues, for example, dealing with women and power, independence and the modern world underlie the collections of the Japanese, the Belgians and the other conceptual European designers. The new woman of the twenty-first century has emerged as being strong, steadfast and confident and this evocation is implied in the work of leading designers including Kawakubo and Demeulemeester. So compelling are Kawakubo's designs that many other designers look to her to take the lead in guiding new directions in fashion.

By fetishizing the new technological inventions, designers have articulated a new design language and by developing a socio-political aesthetic, designers become an important part of postmodernist discourse. By accepting alienation as part of the postmodern condition, designers such as Chalayan, Margiela and Lang pave the way for greater inter-media collaboration, allowing fashion to stretch beyond its conventional boundaries. Traditionalists might despair and, admittedly, all of these paradigms blur the boundaries between the time-honoured functions of clothing and dress. But perhaps this is not as important as it used to be, as fashion must move forward, exploring further new vistas during the course of the twenty-first century.

This book has relied on research material that has taken over twelve years to collect, and along with numerous trips to Japan to gain a better insight into the culture aesthetic, it has truly been a fascinating journey and I thank you for sharing it with me.

Notes

INTRODUCTION

1. By the eighteenth century, clothing became an index of economic rank and privilege and when this visual display was thwarted by the shoguns, many members of the merchant class chose instead to have parts of their bodies, usually those covered by cloth, tattooed with very extravagant patterns and colours. A number of renowned Japanese artists, such as the printmaker Utamaro, designed patterns to be used for this purpose. 'Dressing above one's station in life', thereby attempting to break down social class differences, has been a motivating factor of the merchant, or middle, classes across many cultures and time frames.

2. Change and 'modernity' have heralded progression and prosperity, often seen as the necessary foundation for a nation's economic stability. Between the 1820s and 1860s, 'beauty entered the lives of ordinary Japanese people as a wearable aesthetic in the form of kimono fashion trends and carried men as well as women into a new realm of aesthetic consciousness' (Ikegami 2005: 285). It also became apparent during this period that fashionable dress became an instrument that could denote cultural change and promote more 'modern' trends in cultural life. The growing popularity of more fashionable attire was fuelled by the kimono pattern books, first introduced in 1661 at the beginning of the Kanmon era. These textile pattern books, which appeared for dyed cloth called *hiinagata*, were used to place orders for kimonos (Ikegami 2005: 273). Also, a vast array of illustrations of high fashion modelled by courtesans and Kabuki actors, and an abundance of cotton fabrics produced for the extensive Osaka textile markets, supported the escalation of kimono production. By the 1860s, the population of Japan had reached 30 million and the growing textile industry was supported by the agricultural community, which grew cotton, cultivated silk worms and raised indigo plants needed for the coveted bluish purple indigo dyes.

CHAPTER 1 ISSEY MIYAKE

1. Fascinated by the concept of clothing in movement, Miyake first worked with dancers and created costumes for Maurice Bejart in 1980. These costumes presented a problem-solving challenge as they had to be lightweight, flexible for the dancers and visually impressive for the audience.

2. Taking a break from fashion, Miyake backpacked around Greece in 1991 to discover what people really needed in their lives. He had first experimented with pleating made from technologically made fibres in 1988 and realized that this method might be the answer for contemporary fashion.

3. As early as 1974, Miyake had coined the phrase 'a piece of cloth' when referring to using the basic element of a two-dimensional dress like the kimono as the foundation for his creations.

4. Author of *Art & Art Industries in Japan*, in which he compared arts and crafts in Europe with the differing aesthetic system of Japan.

5. Madame Marie Callot Gerber of the Callot Soeurs, Jeanne Paquin and Paul Poiret, among others, used kimono-inspired methodologies in their clothing design and construction.

6. The Shinto priest will shake a stick bristling with folded paper in the rite of purification; in traditional forms of exorcism, the sufferer's soul was represented by the piece of paper and as it was meant to absorb evil influences, it was burned or floated down the river. Origami pieces folded in the form of cranes and tied to long ropes were used as a memorial to the dead, as seen in Hiroshima, or as a heartfelt wish for luck or a prayer for recovery from an illness (1,000 cranes). Folded paper was also an important part of life for warriors and nobles as it was used to accompany gifts or written orders from subordinates. Ceremonial origami was used for the bride and groom's *sake* containers.

7. By the eighth century, paper-making became a native and secular art, rather than one based on Chinese practice and linked to Buddhism. *Washi* was invented, being made of pure bark fibre (often from the mulberry tree), and was found to be very strong. Subsequently it was used for woodblock printing and for making lanterns and folding screens (*byoubu*).

8. Before the days of microfibres, Miyake attempted to make a 'wind coat' and produced a design by Dai Fujiwara that used James Dyson's air vents to produce an ecologically friendly, carbon-neutral means of creating wind gusts which put movement into his garments.

9. Bunka Fashion College is Japan's first and oldest fashion college, and it opened in June 1923 under the name of the Bunka Sewing School for Women. In 1936, it was renamed the Bunka Fashion College and it began publication of the first in-house Japanese magazine devoted to the study of fashion, entitled *SO-EN*. By 1941, the number of enrolled students exceeded 3,000. French designer Christian Dior visited the College in 1953, followed by American Hollywood designer Howard Greer in 1954 and continuous visits by Pierre Cardin from 1961. The Fashion College became integrated with the Bunka (Gakuen) Women's University in 1964, with a mission to ensure the social and cultural development of fashion in Japan.

By 2000, the College had a teaching staff of 270 and enrolment of over 5,000 students, of which approximately 1,000 were male.

10. Chambre syndicale de la couture parisienne was established in 1868 and is composed of the haute couture houses and other firms which have made-to-measure dressmaking businesses in the Paris area. It was a professional body that determined policy governing the fashion industry (such as copyright protection), organized and coordinated major fashion collection showings on behalf of its members, and acted as a mediator between the press and the fashion industry. In 1873, it became part of the larger Fédération Française de la couture, du prêt-à-porter des couturiers et des créateurs de mode.

11. Miyake's first collection in 1970, presented to Diana Vreeland of *Vogue* (USA) consisted of 'a print design based on tattoos, which were closely associated with the downtown (Tokyo) *yakusa* gangsters' (Holborn 1995: 30).

12. Onitsuka designed the country's first marathon shoe with a slit that separated the big toe from the others, allowing for maximum comfort and ventilation. In turn this inspired many other fashion designers, including Margiela, to design a sports shoe range.

13. Universal Peace Day, held on 6 August every year, sees thousands of people from around the world walking across the Peace Bridge in Hiroshima, 'whose balustrades were designed by the Japanese-American sculptor Isamu Nogushi. Every step taken is another step closer to world peace' (Miyake 2009).

CHAPTER 2 YOHJI YAMAMOTO

1. Yohji Yamamoto graduated in Law from Keio University, Tokyo, in 1966, and studied at the prestigious Bunka College of Fashion, Tokyo, from 1966 to 1968. He then won a scholarship to study fashion in Paris from 1968 for two years, formed a ready-to-wear company in 1972, and showed his first collection in Tokyo in 1976 and in Paris in 1981. He launched his men's line in 1984 and the Yohji Yamamoto Design Studio was opened in Tokyo in 1988.

2. Their first show in Paris was held at the Intercontinental Hotel in April 1981, with only 100 people attending.

3. In Yamamoto's book *Talking to Myself* (2002) there are no page numbers—n. pag.

4. Carnegy's idea was reinforced in an interview in 2009 with Mark O'Flaherty for the *Financial Times* when Yamamoto spoke of his hatred for the Westernized youth of Japan, the mega-malls of Roppongi ('They all look like Disneyland') and the destruction of traditional Japanese culture at the hands of the West (O'Flaherty 2009).

5. Yamamoto was taught at Bunka under the direction of Chie Koike, who, in her youth, was a fellow student with YSL at the Chambre syndicale school in Paris.

CHAPTER 3 REI KAWAKUBO AND COMME DES GARÇONS

1. Parts of this chapter have been reproduced, with kind permission respectively from the Powerhouse Museum, Sydney, and Berg publishers, from two other works of mine: English (2005b) and English (2007: 117–35).
2. For a summary of the press releases documenting Rei Kawakubo's and Yohji Yamamoto's Paris debut, see P. Golbin, 'Constat d'état ou flashback sur le paysage de la mode parisienne', in M-P Foissy Aufrère (ed.), *XXIèmeCiel: Mode in Japan* (Nice: Musée des Arts Asiatiques), 2003: 29–35.
3. Notable feminist artists include Barbara Kruger, Cindy Sherman, Moriko Mori and the Guerilla Girls, among others.

CHAPTER 5 TECHNO TEXTILES

1. Reiko Sudo completed a postgraduate course at Musashino Art College, Japan, in Textile Design and worked as a research assistant there in the Department of Industrial, Interior and Craft Design.
2. The exhibition was held at the Foyer and James Hockey Galleries, University College for the Creative Arts, Farnham, Surrey, the HUB Gallery, Sleaford, Lincolnshire and Textile Kultur, Haslach, Austria.

CHAPTER 6 GLOBAL INFLUENCES: CHALLENGING WESTERN TRADITIONS

1. This was a comment made by one of the most influential curators in Japan today: Akiko Fukai, Kyoto Costume Institute, in a casual conversation in December 2005 (Mears 2008: 117).
2. The term itself, as applied to fashion, was coined by Bill Cunningham in *Details* magazine, in 1989.
3. Partner Jenny Meirens, who became the commercial director of La Maison Margiela, was the first to import and sell creations by Yohji Yamamoto and Comme des Garçons in her shop at the Graanmarkt in Brussels.
4. Evans also refers to the writings of Emile Zola, in particular his novel *The Ladies Paradise*, where he commented on nineteenth-century department stores and how women were viewed as 'spectacles of femininity', as both subjects and objects of consumer desire (Evans 2003: 165).

5. As students, both Margiela and Chalayan reportedly buried garments in the soil in 1993 to see how they would decompose.
6. *Das Offene Kuntswerk* (Frankfurt am Main, Germany: Suhrkamp Verlag, 1977), p. 11.
7. Sales had skyrocketed from 30 to 70 million Euros by 2009.
8. Normally, a 1,000-metre order for a particular textile is required by the mills.
9. At the Wexner Center for the Arts in Ohio, where an exhibition of Chalayan's work was held.
10. Each of these tulle dresses took 163 hours to make, being constructed from 149 yards of fine tulle for the skirt, 44 yards of stiffer tulle for the underskirt and 2.3 miles of very thin yarn. D.I.Y. instructions were made available by the designers describing the process: the skirt was built layer upon layer, hand-stitched together over a stiff inner crinoline-like structure, using camel-hair and boning in the shape of the final skirt with a cut-out strip below the hips. White sequins (547) were sewn to the front of the bodice (Limnander 2010).
11. It also provided an opportunity to launch their new perfume line, *Tulle, tulle much*.

References and Select Bibliography

Alexander, H. 2010. 'Comme des Garçons Autumn/Winter 2010/11 Collection', *The Telegraph* (UK), March 7.

Arai, J., *et al*. 1992. *Hand and Technology: Textiles by Junichi Arai* (exhibition catalogue). Asashi, Japan.

Barthes, R. 2006. *The Language of Fashion*. A. Stafford (trans.), A. Stafford and M. Carter (eds). Oxford, New York: Berg.

Baudot, F. 1997. *Yohji Yamamoto*. J. Brenton (trans.). London: Thames & Hudson.

Bellafante, G. 2001. 'Taking a Back Seat to Unfolding Events', *The New York Times*, 9 October.

Bellafante, G. 2004. 'The Frenchwoman, in All Her Moods', *NYT*, 5 March.

Bénaim, L. 1997. *Issey Miyake* (*Fashion Memoir* series). London: Thames & Hudson.

Betts, K. 2004. 'Rei Kawakubo: Comme des Garçons, Avatar of the Avant-Garde', *Time*, 16 February, p. 40.

Blanchard, T. 1998. 'Meet Your Dressmaker', *The Independent* (UK), 5 September.

Blanchard, T. 1999. 'Design For Living', from *Weekend Australian* in *The Independent Magazine* (UK).

Braddock, S. E., and O'Mahony, M. 1998. *Techno Textiles: Revolutionary Fabrics for Fashion and Design*. London: Thames & Hudson.

Brampton, S. 1983. 'Yohji', *Observer* (UK), 25 September, p. 29.

Brunhammer, Y. 1993. 'Les Vêtements Actifs D'Issey Miyake', *Connaissance des Arts*, en Mars, no. 493: 90–5.

Buxbaum, G. 2005. *Icons of Fashion: The 20th Century*. London: Prestel.

Carnegy, V. 1990. *Fashions of the Decades: The Eighties*. London: Batsford.

Chenoune, F. 1993. *History of Men's Fashion*. Paris: Flammarion Press.

Cocks, J. 1986. 'A Change of Clothes: Issey Miyake', *Time*, January, no. 4: 40–6.

Croft, C. 2008. 'Guerrilla Tactics', *The Sunday Times* (UK), 2 March.

Dalby, L. 1993. *Kimono: Fashioning Culture*. New Haven, CT: Yale University Press.

Dam, J. 1999. 'Issey Miyake', *Time* (Asia ed.), 23–30 August, 154(7/8).

Derycke, L., and Van de Veire, S. (eds). 1999. *Belgian Fashion Design*. Bruges, Belgium: Ludion Press.

Duka, J. 1983. 'Yohji Yamamoto Defines his Fashion Philosophy', *NYT*, 23 October.

English, B. 1997a. Interview, Miyake Design Studio, Tokyo, Japan, January.

English, B. 1997b. Interview, Bunka Fashion College, Tokyo, Japan, January.

English, B. 1997c. Interview, Akiko Fukai, Kyoto Fashion Institute, Kyoto, Japan, January.

English, B. 2005a. Interview, Laurence Delamare, YY, Paris, France, October.

English, B. 2005b. 'Fashion and Art: Postmodernist Japanese Fashion', in L. Mitchell (ed.), *The Cutting Edge: Fashion from Japan*. Sydney: Powerhouse Museum.

English, B. 2007. *A Cultural History of Fashion in the 20th Century: From the Sidewalk to the Catwalk*. Oxford: Berg.

English, B., and Pomazan, L. (eds). 2010. *Australian Fashion Unstitched*. Melbourne: Cambridge.

Evans, C. 2003. *Fashion at the Edge: Spectacle, Modernity and Deathliness*. New Haven, CT and London: Yale University Press.

Foley, B. 1997. 'Master Class', *WWD (Women's Wear Daily)*, 19 September.

Fortini, A. 2009. 'Techno Fashion', *NYT*, 10 December.

Foxe, D. 1999. 'Yohji Bared', *Weekend Financial Times* (UK), March, Issue 34.

Frankel, S. 2001. *Visionaries*. London: Victoria & Albert Museum Pubs.

Frankel, S. 2006. 'French Fashion Draws a Veil over Our Faces', *The Independent*, 9 March.

Fujimura-Fanselow, K. 1995. *Japanese Women: New Feminist Perspectives on the Past, Present and Future*. New York: The Feminist Press, The City University of NY.

Fukai, A. 1995. *Japanese Design*. Philadelphia Museum of Art (exhibition catalogue).

Fukai, A. 1996. *Japonisme in Fashion*. Kyoto: Kyoto Costume Institute.

Gan, S. and Browne, A. 1999. *Visionaire's Fashion 2001: Designers of the New Avant Garde*. London: Lawrence King.

Glasscock, J. 2003. 'Bridging the Art/Commerce Divide: Cindy Sherman and Rei Kawakubo of Comme des Garçons', at: www.nyu.edu/greyart/exhibits

Godoy, T. 2007. *Style Deficit Disorder: Harajuku Street Fashion—Tokyo*. San Francisco: Chronicle Books.

Golden, A. 1997. *Memoirs of a Geisha*. London: Vintage.

Graham, M. 2007. 'Issey Miyake's Populist Fashion', *Wired News*, 20 March.

Handley, S. 2000. *Nylon: The Story of a Fashion Revolution*. Baltimore: Johns Hopkins University Press.

Handley, S. 2008. 'The Globalization of Fabric', *NYT*, 29 February.

Hanisch, R. 2006. *Absolutely Fabulous: Architecture and Fashion*. Munich: Prestel Verlag.

Harper, C. 2005. 'Forest Tree: Reiko Sudo at the Surrey Institute', interview, *Selvedge* magazine, Sept/Oct 2007: 74–6.

Hasegawa, N. 1988. *The Japanese Character: A Cultural Profile*. J. Bester (trans.). New York: Greenwood Press.

Hemmings, J. 2005. 'Playtime: Maria Blaisse', *Selvedge* magazine online: www.concept-selvedge.org

Hemmings, J. 2006. 'Exhibition Review: The Textile Vision of Reiko Sudo and NUNO', *Textile*, 4(3): 362–7.

[The] Herald Sun. No author. 1998. 'Romance in the Modern World', 21 October.

Hildreth, J. C. 1983. *A New Wave in Fashion: Three Japanese Designers*. Phoenix: Arizona Costume Museum, Phoenix Art Museum, Phoenix.

Hill, A. 2005. 'People Dress So Badly Nowadays', in C. Breward and C. Evans, *Fashion in Modernity*. London: Berg.

Hirakawa, T. 1990. 'Comme des Garçons', *Gap* magazine (Japan): 21–45.

Hishinuma, Y. (ed.). 1986. *Clothes by Hishinuma*. Tokyo: Yobisha Co., 162–72.

Holborn, M. 1988. 'Image of a Second Skin', *Artforum*, 27 (November): 118–21.

Holborn, M. 1995. *Issey Miyake*. Cologne: Taschen.

Holgate, M. 2007. 'Youth of Japan; Cultural Exchange', *Vogue* (New York), October, 197(10): 230–4.

Horyn, C. 2002. 'Yamamoto Jumps the Haute-Couture Season', *NYT* (NY edition), 9 July, Section B, p. 8.

Horyn, C. 2003. 'Macho America Storms Europe's Runways', *NYT*, 3 July.

Horyn, C. 2004. 'A Store Made for Right Now: You Shop Until It's Dropped', *NYT*, 17 February.

Horyn, C. 2006a. 'Ann of Antwerp', *NYT*, 27 August.

Horyn, C. 2006b. 'Balenciaga, Weightless and Floating Free', *NYT*, 4 October.

Horyn, C. 2007a. 'John Galliano Kicks up His Heels', *NYT*, 28 February.

Horyn, C. 2007b. 'Here in Tokyo', *NYT*, 27 December.

Huckbody, J. 2002. 'Perfection is an Ugly Word', *i-D*, no. 219 (April).

i-D. 1999. *i-D* magazine, The Kinetic Issue, no. 184 (March) [no author].

Ikegami, E. 2005. *Bonds of Civility: Aesthetic Networks and the Political Origins of Japanese Culture*. New York: Cambridge University Press.

Imamura, A. E. 1996. *Re-imaging Japanese Women*. Los Angeles: University of California Press.

Irving, S. 2001. 'Yohji Wear', *The Sunday Telegraph Magazine* (UK), 16 September.

Jansen, M. B. 2000. *The Making of Modern Japan*. Cambridge, MA/London: Belknap Press of Harvard University Press.

Jones, T. 1992. *i-D* magazine, The Glamour Issue (May): 72–3.

Kaiser, A. 2008. 'Vuitton Opens Pop-up Shop in Tokyo', *WWD* (NY), 4 September, 196(48): 3.

Kaplan, C. 2004. 'Border Control', interview in *dbmag* online. At: www.db-artmag.com/archiv/2004/e/2/1/193.html

Kawamura, Y. 2004a. *The Japanese Revolution in Paris Fashion*. Oxford, New York: Berg.

Kawamura, Y. 2004b. 'The Japanese Revolution in Paris', *Through the Surface*. At: www.throughthesurface.com/synopsium/kawamura

Keene, D. 1981. *Appreciations of Japanese Culture*. Tokyo, New York and San Francisco: Kodansha Intern Ltd.

Kiss, E. 2004. 'The Art of the Fold', *International Herald Tribune*, 3 August.

Knafo, R. 1988. 'The New Japanese Standard: Issey Miyake', *Connoisseur*, March: 100–9.

Kondo, D. 1992. 'The Aesthetics and Politics of Japanese Identity in the Fashion Industry', in *Re-Made Japan: Everyday Life and Consumer Taste Society*, J. H. Tobin (ed.). New Haven, CT: Yale University Press, 176–203.

Koren, L. 1984. *New Fashion Japan*. Tokyo: Kodansha International.

Kurihara, N. 1993. *Ripples of Change*. Video. Women Make Movies, New York (57 minutes).

Kushner, R. 2002. 'Reiko Sudo at Kyoto Arts Center, Kyoto', *Art in America*, January.

Lee, S. 2005. *Fashioning the Future: Tomorrow's Wardrobe*. London: Thames & Hudson.

Leong, R. 2003. 'The Zen and the Zany: Contemporary Japanese Fashion', *Visasia*, 23 March. At: www.visasia.com.au

Limnander, A. 2008. 'Undercover: Strange, "but beautiful"', *NYT/Style*, 24 September.

Limnander, A. 2010. 'REMIX: Haute Economics', *NYT*, 28 February.

Lipovetsky, G. 1994. *The Empire of Fashion: Dress in Modern Democracy*. C. Porter (trans.). Princeton, NJ: Princeton University Press.

Lippard, L. (ed.). 1997. *Six Years: the Dematerialization of the Art Object*. Berkeley, CA: University of California Press.

Loschek, I. 1999. 'The Deconstructionists', in G. Buxbaum (ed.), *Icons of Fashion: The Twentieth Century*. Munich, London and New York: Prestel.

Lovegrove, R. (ed.). 2002. *The International Design Yearbook 2002*. London: Laurence King Publishing.

Lowthorpe, R. 2000. 'Watanabe Opens Paris with Technology Lesson', *The Independent*, 9 October.

Mackie, V. 2003. *Feminism in Modern Japan*. Cambridge: Cambridge University Press.

Martin. R. 1995. 'Our Kimono Mind: Reflections on Japanese Design: A Survey Since 1950', *Journal of Design History*, 8: 215–33.

Martin, R. and Koda, H. 1993. *Infra-Apparel*. Metropolitan Museum of Art, New York: Harry Abrams.

McCarty, M. 1998. 'Texturing Life', *Structure and Surface: Contemporary Japanese Textiles* (exhibition catalogue; Nov. 1998–Jan. 1999). New York: MoMA.

McDowell, C. 1987. *McDowell's Directory of Twentieth Century Fashion*. New York: Prentice-Hall.

McDowell, C. 2000. *Fashion Today*. London: Phaidon.

McDowell, C. 2007. 'Paris, Fashion City', *Timesonline*, 27 February.

McQuaid, M. 1998. 'Process and Technique in Contemporary Japanese Textiles', *Structure and Surface: Contemporary Japanese Textiles* (exhibition catalogue; Nov. 1998–Jan. 1999). New York: MoMA.

Mears, P. 2008. 'Exhibiting Asia: The Global Impact of Japanese Fashion in Museums and Galleries', *Fashion Theory*, 12(1), March: 95–120.

Mendes, V. 1999. *Black in Fashion*. London: V & A Pblrs.

Mendes, V., and de la Haye, A. 1999. *20th-Century Fashion*. London: Thames & Hudson.

Menkes, S. 1996. 'When the West Reflects the East', *NYT*, 23 April.

Menkes, S. 1998. 'Ode to the Abstract: When Designer Met Dance', *IHT*, 8 January, p. 11.

Menkes, S. 2000a. 'Fashion's Poet of Black: Yamamoto', *IHT*, 5 September.

Menkes, S. 2000b. 'Fashfile; Miyake Slice-your-Own', *IHT*, 12 September.

Menkes, S. 2002a. 'Miyake's Mysterious Language', *IHT*, 13 March.

Menkes, S. 2002b. '20 Years On, Yohji Gets a New Lease on Life', *IHT*, 2 July.

Menkes, S. 2002c. 'The Collections/Paris: From Galliano, Hard Core Dior', *IHT*, 4 October.

Menkes, S. 2006a. 'Hitting the High C's: Cool, Cute and Creative', *IHT*, 31 May.

Menkes, S. 2006b. 'Breaking the Fashion Mode', *IHT*, 27 November.

Menkes, S. 2007. 'YY and the Fashion Children of Comme . . .', *NYT*, 2 October.

Menkes, S. 2009a. 'A Life Story Told Through Folds, Tucks and Trims', *NYT*, 27 April.

Menkes, S. 2009b. 'When Creativity Goes Beyond Content', *IHT*, 4 October.

Menkes, S. 2010. 'Celine's Chic Severity', *NYT*, 7 March.

Mitchell. L. 1999. 'Issey Miyake', in B. English (ed.), *Tokyo Vogue: Japanese and Australian Fashion* (exhibition catalogue). Brisbane: Griffith University.

Miyake, I. 1978. *East Meets West*. Tokyo: Heibonsha.

Miyake, I. 1984. Speech delivered at *Japan Today* Conference in San Francisco, September.

Miyake, I. 2009. 'A Flash of Memory', *NYT*, 14 July.

Miyanaga, K. 1991. *The Creative Edge: Emerging Individualism in Japan*. London: Transaction.

Mower, S. 1996. 'A Bright Futurist', *NYT*, 28 January.

Mower, S. 2006a. Paris Fashion Weekend: Special Report, *The Guardian* (London), 28 February.

Mower, S. 2006b. 'We Are the Comme des Garçons Army', *Vogue* (NY), September, 196(9): 660–9.

Muschamp, H. 1999. 'Issey, The Genius That Is', *Sunday Morning Herald Review*, 2 January, p. 21.

National Film Board of Canada. 1984. *Japanese Woman*. Film. Distrib. EMA, Melbourne (52 minutes).

National Gallery of Victoria. 2008. *Remaking Fashion*. Melbourne: NGV.

Nuno online. At: www.nuno.com/Yarn/index.html (accessed 25/10/2008).

O'Flaherty, M. 2009. 'In the Black', *Financial Times Weekend*, 11 October.

Okakura, K. [1906] 1964. *The Book of Tea*. NY: Dover Pblrs.

O'Mahony, M. 2008. No article name, *Irish Times*, 25 April.

O'Neill, A. 2001. 'Imagining Fashion: Helmut Lang and Maison Martin Margiela', in Wilcox, *Radical Fashion*. London: V & A, 38–45.

Penn, I. 1988. *Issey Miyake: Photographs by Irving Penn*. Boston: New York Graphic Society. (Calloway, N., ed.)

Penn, I. 1999. *Irving Penn Regards the Work of Issey Miyake*. Boston, NY and London: Little, Brown & Co. and Bullfinch Press.

Polan, B. and Tredre, R. 2009. *The Great Fashion Designers*. Oxford and New York: Berg.

Quinn, B. 2002. *Techno Fashion*. Oxford and New York: Berg.

Reidel, C. 2004. 'The Fashion Spot', *IHT*, 24 January.

Rivers, V. 1999. *The Shining Cloth: Dress and Adornment That Glitters*. New York: Thames & Hudson.

Romano, A. 2008. 'What's in a Narrative? Interpreting Yohji Yamamoto in the Museum'. Conference paper—The First Global Conference on Fashion: Exploring Critical Issues, NY.

Saiki, M. K. 1992. 'Issey Miyake—Photographs by Irving Penn', *Graphis*, 48(280), July–August: 32–5.

Schacknat, K. 2003. *'Unbeschreiblich Weiblich!'*, in J. Teunissen (ed.), *The Ideal Woman*. ArtEZ Institute of the Arts, Utrecht: Centraal Museum.

Schoeser, M. 2006. 'Great Lengths', *Crafts* (London) 198, Jan/Feb: 32–7.

Self, D. 2001. 'Junichi Arai: Glistening Fabrics', at: www.Kemperart.org

Shackleton, H. 2009. 'You Can't Mistake My Biology', interview, Yohji Yamamoto. *i-D* magazine, The Manhood Issue, no. 296 (Feb): 162 (one-page article only).

Shoji, K. 2005. 'Turning out the Vanguard in Japan Design', *IHT*, 2 August.

Silva, H. 2009. 'Now Honouring Dries Van Noten', *NYT*, 8 September.

Simon, J. 1999. 'Miyake Modern', *Art in America* (NY), 2 February.

Sims, J. 2004. 'Comme Undone', *i-D* magazine, The Expressionist Issue (Nov): 117–23.

Sischy, I. 2001. 'Issey Miyake: Catching Up with the Man Who Pushes the Envelope of Fashion', interview. *Interview Magazine*. NY: Brandt Publications, November.

Skowranek, H. 2007. 'Should We Reproduce the Beauty of Decay?' 'A *Museumsleben* in the work of Dieter Roth'. In Tate Museum Papers online research journal. At: www.tate.org.uk/research/tateresearch/tatepapers/07autumn/skowranek.htm (accessed 16/5/10).

Sudjic, D. 1986. 'All the Way Back to Zero', *The Sunday Times* (London). 20 April.

Sudjic, D. 1990. *Rei Kawakubo and Comme des Garçons*. NY: Rizzoli Publ. See also Burt, J., 'The Factory of Comme des Garcons', Editions Ballard, at: http://editionsballard.files.wordpress.com

Sudo, R. 1992. In Arai, J. et al., *Hand and Technology: Textiles by Junichi Arai* (exhibition catalogue). Asashi, Japan: Yurakucho Asashi Gallery.

Spindler, A. 1993. 'Coming Apart . . .', *NYT*, 25 July.

Spindler, A. 1996a. 'In Paris, Men's Wear Fit for Parody', *NYT*, 30 January.

Spindler, A. 1996b. 'A Thundering Start for Paris Show', *NYT*, 13 March.

Spindler, A. 1997. 'A Mentor and Her Followers', *NYT*, 16 October.

Tajima, Y. (ed.). 1996. *Nijyu—Seiki No Nihon No Fasshon*. Tokyo: Genryusha.

Tanaka, K. 1995. 'The New Feminist Movement in Japan 1970–1990', in Fujimura-Fanselow, K. *Japanese Women: New Feminist Perspectives on the Past, Present and Future*. New York: The Feminist Press, The City University of NY.

Teunissen, J. (ed.). 2003. *The Ideal Woman*. ArtEZ Institute of the Arts, Utrecht: Centraal Museum.

The Story of Fashion: The Age of Dissent. 1985. Video. UK: RM Arts Production.

Tobin, J. J. (ed.). 1992. *Re-Made in Japan*. New Haven, CT and London: Yale University Press.

Todd, S. 1997. 'In the Court of Queen Ann', *The Guardian*, 8 February.

Trebay, G. 2004. 'Fashion Diary: Making a Surreal Trip onto a Nightclub Runway', *NYT*, 4 March.

Trebay, G. 2005. 'Mr Yamamoto's Blue Period', *NYT*, 13 March.

Undressed: Fashion in the Twentieth Century. 2001. Video. Little Bird/Tatlin Production. UK: Beckmann Visual Pubs.

Vesilind, E. 2008. 'A Hip Hideaway', *Los Angeles Times*, 17 February.

Vinken, B. 2005. *Fashion Zeitgeist: Trends and Cycles in the Fashion System.* M. Hewson (trans.). Oxford and New York: Berg.

Vitra Design Museum. 2001. *A-POC Making: Issey Miyake and Dai Fujiwara* (Berlin), Weil am Rhein, Germany.

Wada, Y. I. 2002. *Memory on Cloth: Shibori Now*. New York: Kodansha.

Warady, N. 2001. 'High Concepts, High Stakes', *Japan As The World Sees It* magazine, 157(17), 30 April.

Watson, L. 2004. *Independent Magazine*, 30 September.

Weltge, S.W. 2002/03. 'Memory on Cloth: Shibori Now', *American Craft*, 62(6), Dec/Jan: 40–3.

Wenders, W. 1989. *Notebooks on Cities and Clothes.* Video. Road movies Filmproduktion, Berlin.

White, C. 1999. 'Now Every Man a Sportsman', *NYT*, 12 January.

Wilcox, C. 2001. *Radical Fashion*. London: V & A Publishers.

Wilson, E. 2006. 'Anarchy is in the Eye of the Beholder', *NYT*, 6 March.

Wilson, E. 2008. 'Margiela Looks Back', *NYT*, 30 September.

Wilson, E. 2009a. 'Women in Black', *NYT*, 9 March.

Wilson, E. 2009b. 'Hot and Bothered in the City of Light', *IHT*, 4 October.

'Women Make Movies' [organization]. 1993 film: *Ripples of Change.* Video. New York, 57 minutes.

Women's Wear Daily. [No author.] 1996. 'Tradition with A Twist', 14 October.

Women's Wear Daily. 2010. 'Ann Demeulemeester RTW, Fall 2010', at: WWD.com, 6 March.

Yamamoto, Y. and Washida, K. 2002. *Talking to Myself* by Yohji Yamamoto. Gottingen: Steidl Publishing.

Yoshida, M., Earle, J. V., Katzumie, M., and Lehmann, J-P. 1980. *Japan Style*. Tokyo, NY, San Francisco: Kodansha Pblr.

Index

Note: references in **bold** refer to illustrations